Theory and Metatheory in International Relations

Theory and Metatheory in International Relations

Concepts and Contending Accounts

Fred Chernoff

THEORY AND METATHEORY IN INTERNATIONAL RELATIONS
Copyright © Fred Chernoff, 2007.

First published in 2007 by
PALGRAVE MACMILLAN™
175 Fifth Avenue, New York, NY 10010 and
Houndmills, Basingstoke, Hampshire, England RG21 6XS.
Companies and representatives throughout the world.

PALGRAVE MACMILLAN is the global academic imprint of the Palgrave Macmillan division of St. Martin's Press, LLC and of Palgrave Macmillan Ltd. Macmillan® is a registered trademark in the United States, United Kingdom and other countries. Palgrave is a registered trademark in the European Union and other countries.

Pbk
ISBN-10: 1-4039-7455-1
ISBN-13: 978-1-4039-7455-6

Hc
ISBN-10: 1-4039-7454-3
ISBN-13: 978-1-4039-7454-9

Library of Congress Cataloging-in-Publication Data

Chernoff, Fred.
Theory and metatheory in international relations : concepts and contending accounts /
    Fred Chernoff.
        p. cm.
Includes bibliographical references and index.
ISBN 1-4039-7454-3 (hardcover : alk. paper)—ISBN 1-4039-7455-1 (pbk. : alk. paper)
1. International relations—Philosophy. I. Title.
    JZ1305.C445 2007
    327.101—dc22

                            2007009642

A catalogue record of the book is available from the British Library.

Design by Scribe Inc.

First Edition: November 2007

10 9 8 7 6 5 4 3 2 1

Printed in the United States of America.

Contents

Preface and Acknowledgments

This book is an introduction to new debates in international relations. It attempts to show why anyone who wants to solve foreign policy problems must understand theories of international relations and the philosophical issues involved in determining how to choose the best theory. This book poses policy questions intended to motivate students to think critically about the assumptions and beliefs that underlay particular policy recommendations. It shows the specific links between policy decisions and principles of international relations theories and the further links to philosophical claims about how to choose the best theory. Thus this book shows why it is important to examine and contrast the competing scientific-style rationalist foundations of social science theory with constructivist and poststructuralist positions, since each offers a different way of understanding what constitutes a good theory of international relations.

This book also provides students with the tools necessary to analyze competing arguments by working its way from foreign policy problems to the contemporary debates about the nature and foundations of international relations theory. Chapter 1 discusses choices among policies toward Iraq, North Korea, and China. Chapter 2 discusses contending contemporary theories, which support different policy positions. Chapter 3 considers how the best theory is chosen in the natural sciences; it then draws an analogy to the social sciences in order to answer the question, how does one decide which theory of international relations is best? This, however, requires that we lay out the appropriate criteria for choosing a natural science theory. Chapter 4 raises some of the contemporary questions about applying the analogy with the natural sciences. The book concludes with a sketch in Chapter 5 of a possible solution to some of the problems of methodology and metatheory raised in the previous chapters.

This book began at the urging of David Pervin of Palgrave Macmillan and would not have been written without his vigorous encouragement. Toby Wahl seamlessly took over the project in the later phases. Patrick Jackson of the American University and Mai'a Davis Cross of Colgate University put much time and effort into reading the entire manuscript and making many insightful and important recommendations, which led to significant improvements in both content and structure. The treatment of a variety of issues was sharpened by conversations with colleagues at many institutions, especially with Dan Nexon of Georgetown University, Colin Wight of the University of Exeter, Doug Macdonald and Al Yee of Colgate University, and Doug Becker of the University of Southern California. Other colleagues in the Department of Political Science at Colgate University offered helpful suggestions. Luke Champlin, Ian Elliot, Lauren Fiola, Kelly Gabriel, Ben Jones, and Michael Sheflin provided excellent research assistance. The library of the Yale Club of New York City was also great help. Much excitement has been supplied by my partner in the ring, Monty, and his little cousin Gracie. There are some people whose contributions cannot be acknowledged too fully or too often, but one must try. I wish to thank Bruce Russett for his confidence in me, for decades of wise advice and for presenting me with the best possible model of scholarship and integrity; my senior IR colleagues at Colgate and predecessors in my current position, Bob Rothstein and John Vasquez, for having done the same over shorted periods; my wife Vida for her support and her foresight that made possible the timely completion of this book; my family—especially HDR, Myrna and Marshall Barth, and K. Nastassja Chernoff for their enduring encouragement—and my friends, without whom there is no point—especially Dick Heller, John Aguilar, Dusty Vinson, Lee Arnold, Jun Song, and Dana and Adele Levitt.

This book is dedicated to my students and their search for better answers.

New York City
July 15, 2007

Introduction

Central Questions of Theory and Policy

In the eighteen months after the terrorist attacks in the United States on September 11, 2001, some American and British policy makers advocated invading Iraq regardless of whether the broader international community supported such an act. Some advocated doing so only with approval of the United Nations (UN). Some advocated intense international pressure via the UN to make Saddam Hussein allow UN inspections of weapons arsenals and manufacturing plants. And some argued that no military-oriented action against Iraq was necessary. They argued that since Iraq was a minor irritant to Western security interests, attention should be focused on the real threats like Hezbollah, al-Qaeda, Iran, the Israeli-Palestinian conflict, and North Korea's nuclear program. How would someone in 2001 or 2002 know which policy is best for U.S. and Western security? Within a few years many of the predictions that poitical leaders made were shown to have been dazzlingly wrong. Secretary Rumsfeld said in April 2003 that American troops would be reduced by 75 percent within six months; President Bush said that the United States would uncover caches of illegal weapons and facilities producing them. Leaders are often wrong.

In fact, the right answers to security problems are often hard to find. Japan attacked the United States in 1941 with the idea that it would benefit the Japanese Empire. Alcibiades advocated the Athenian invasion of Sicily in 422 BCE. Napoleon decided to invade Russia in 1812. In June of 1941 Hitler launched an invasion of that same country. Six months later the Empire of Japan attacked Pearl Harbor. All of these interventions were overseen by experienced leaders in response to a perceived security problem. These decisions, and scores more that are easily found, led to disaster and often to the demise of the leaders who made the decision.

There are always distinct and competing policy options to any foreign policy problem. Moreover, we frequently find that influential figures within the same nation advocate different options. Superficial answers to the question of which policy is best are hopeless and not much better than choosing by flipping a coin. Deeper questions must be addressed by anyone who wants to provide a well-reasoned and rationally grounded solution to the policy dilemma. This book shows how this process must be handled by looking at three U.S. foreign policy problems: the Iraq war, North Korea's nuclear weapons program, and the growth of Chinese economic and military power. These cases show how a rational course of action must be grounded in evidence about what is likely to work. This, in turn, requires a clear theory of international relations—that is, a set of principles that tell us "how the world works" by stating what sorts of actions lead to what sorts of consequences. Since there are competing theories of this sort, a complete answer requires that we find a way to choose the best among them.

This book thus seeks to show that policy makers, whether they like it or not, must face the question of which theory of international relations (IR) is best.[1] The book will also argue that choosing the best theory will require that we think about how to make such a choice, which is a problem that unavoidably brings up issues of "metatheory." These issues include the new debates in IR over the "reflectivist" rivals to rationalism, such as constructivism, poststructuralism, and critical theory.

Through the twentieth century a dominant scientific-style view emerged, particularly among American scholars about how IR should be studied. There were, to be sure, vigorous debates among scholars. But most of the participants in the debates accepted a great deal in common—such as that there are objective facts; that theories should be rejected if new observations are inconsistent with the expectations generated by the theories; and that for any given problem-domain, there is one best adequate theory. In these three respects, IR is similar to the natural sciences. But relectivist critics challenge all three claims.

Three Levels of Debate

This book considers three different levels of debate. First is the level of policy decision-making; second is the level of theory; and third is the level of metatheory, which is also referred to as the "methodological" or "philosophical" level. The question policy makers faced in 2002–2003 over what, if anything, to do about Iraq is an example of a first-level or policy debate. Other recent examples include whether Norway should join the European Union, whether the United States should ratify the Kyoto protocol on global warming, whether the United Kingdom (UK) should replace sterling with the euro. Every year governments face scores of choices like these, some momentous and some mundane.

The second level of debate is over theory. Over the past centuries the authors writing about IR have proposed many different theories. The two broad theoretical traditions in IR are realism and liberalism/idealism. There are many specific theories within these traditions. The former includes theories of Thucydides, Niccolo Machiavelli, Hans Morgenthau, and Kenneth Waltz. The latter include theories of Immanuel Kant, John Stuart Mill, John Hobson, and Robert Keohane. At various times there have been alternatives to both realism and liberalism. Marxism, as advanced by Marx, Engels, and later Lenin, was prominent from the late nineteenth century until the late twentieth century. More recently some scholars contend that constructivism, as developed by Immanuel Adler, Freidrich Kratochwil, Nicholas Onuf, and Alex Wendt is another alternative.

A third level of debate is over the principles that govern how we should choose the best theory. Philosophers and philosophically inclined social scientists engage in this debate. In order to determine what makes one theory better than rival theories, we need to know what characteristics a "good theory" should have. A cogent answer will depend in part on what sort of study IR is. If one conceives of it as a science much like physics or chemistry, although it is obviously different in some ways, one set of features will be sought. If one conceives of IR as a puzzle of how to interpret actions, similar to the way one puzzles over how best to interpret a novel or a poem, then the features a good theory should have will be very different. Whether IR is more like physics and chemistry or more like literary criticism is one of the major philosophical questions that must be answered.

This book will attempt to show how a policy choice of the first level (Chapter 1) is linked with the choice of the best theory (Chapter 2) and how the choice of the best theory is linked with questions of metatheory (Chapter 3). It will also discuss the attack on traditional notions of IR theory and theory choice as well as how the attack alters someone's choice of a course of policy action (Chapter 4). Finally, the concluding chapter (Chapter 5) evaluates the strengths and weaknesses of the alternative approaches and briefly sketches a modified scientific or naturalist approach as a foundation for making policy choices. The introduction will also discuss different theoretical goals, especially those of describing relationships and behavior versus prescribing a course of action. It will be shown that prescription, unlike description, requires specified goals of action, which involve the choice of values. Prescription requires the choice of a set of values for the state, while description and explanation could proceed in a more objective way that parallels the description and explanation found in the natural sciences.[2]

Description and Prescription

Many scholars in the field of IR offer theories that help systematize what we observe, help identify persistent patterns, and help explain those observations and patterns. Such theories are descriptive and explanatory. Some scholars also give recommendations on what policies should be pursued, which involve "prescriptive theory." The latter are fundamentally different from the former. Someone who devises a scientific description or explanation is not thereby, without additional qualifications, entitled to offer a recommendation about what should be done.

Consider the parallel with natural sciences like physics, chemistry, and biology. Physicists might discover a theory of physical bodies and then carefully measure the causal interactions. However, just because physicists have devised a theory that has gained acceptance, they are not thereby entitled or able to say which policy actions are best. In policy analysis one must state what the particular goals or aims are before applying knowledge of physics to decide upon the most effective course of action.

Science and Interpretation: Inside/Outside

Many scholars, as just noted, make a fundamental distinction between "inside" and "outside" approaches to the study of IR. The "outside" refers to the "scientific" approach, which emphasizes causal reasoning and identifying regularities in the behavior of nation-states or other social actors. The "inside" approach rejects the notion that human behavior, as individuals or in any sort of groupings—governments, banks, political parties—can be studied scientifically. These scholars generally focus on getting "inside" the mind of the actors, trying to understand the world the way they understand it, and trying to find meaning in the actions we observe. The inside approach is often viewed as "interpretive:" it views the study of the social world more like the process of decoding meanings of literature than like the hypothesizing of causal relationships that natural scientists do. The outside approach has been dominant in the study of IR in the United States over the past half-century. But in the past twenty years it has run into a lot of opposition. This book will begin by taking the outside approach as standard as we look at the most important theories of IR that we find in the English-speaking world. However, Chapter 4 will be devoted to the inside theories that challenge this dominance. Chapter 5 will consider the claim that there is a compatibility between some inside and outside approaches.

CHAPTER 1

Three Policy Dilemmas

Three of the most important policy decisions that the United States confronted in the first years of the twenty-first century were the decision to invade Iraq, the challenges of North Korea's nuclear program and the rise of China as a world power. While there were other important questions for the United States—promoting peace between Palestinians and Israelis, relations with Iran, and managing globalization, to name a few—this chapter focuses on the former three by looking at the history of each case, the policy options that the United States had available, and the rationales for each of the main options. The rationales are necessary for an understanding of how theory and metatheory play a role in choosing a policy. The discussion of policy options in this chapter is intended to show how a reasonable policy maker who has a clear set of goals would select a policy. This is not intended to be a description of the actual policy-making process. The policy options and rationales are offered for illustration and do not exhaust all of the possibilities.

The Decision to Invade Iraq

Origins of the Iraq Problem

The United States had a complex history of security and trade relations with many Middle Eastern states throughout the twentieth century. On September 11, 2001, the United States was, of course, attacked by agents of al-Qaeda, all of whom were citizens of Middle Eastern states. Afghanistan, ruled by the Taliban, hosted al-Qaeda's leader, Osama bin Laden, and training camps for the terrorist organization. After the attacks the United States demanded that the Taliban surrender Osama bin Laden to U.S. custody. The Taliban leader Mullah Omar refused and two months later the United States invaded Afghanistan and removed him from power. The Taliban remains active as an insurgent force but controls relatively little territory.

As 2002 arrived, the United States began pressuring Iraq to open its territory to UN weapons inspectors. Iraq's President, Saddam Hussein, had ordered invasions of both Iran in 1980 and Kuwait in 1990. After a UN-authorized coalition led by the United States ousted Iraqi forces from Kuwait, the UN demanded that Iraq disarm in certain specified areas of weaponry under the supervision of UN inspectors. Inspections were suspended in December 1998, but in 2002 the UN began to demand that inspections be resumed.

The United States insisted that President Saddam Hussein allow UN weapons inspectors full access to suspected Iraqi weapons production and storage sites. Iraq complied with some but not all of the UN demands. President George W. Bush favored an invasion if demands were not met. However, the fact that Iraq did meet some of the demands, including allowing the return of UN weapons inspectors, complicated matters by making it harder for President Bush to persuade states that were reluctant to authorize force to go along with the United States.

While many governments around the world spoke in support of the U.S. goal of disarming Iraq, British Prime Minister Tony Blair was one of the few willing to participate in a U.S.-led invasion. Blair desired formal UN authorization for an invasion. In the autumn of 2002 the UN Security Council passed a resolution demanding that Iraq comply with prior disarmament resolutions. But the text did not specifically authorize the use of force. Most Security Council members said that they would take up the question again if Iraq did not cooperate. President Bush repeatedly argued that Iraq was not fully cooperating and repeatedly threatened to invade. Thus during the second half of 2002 and the first twelve weeks of 2003, there was an intense debate inside the United States and the UK over whether they should go to war against Iraq.

Competing Policy Options

Various political actors in the United States, the UK, and other key states endorsed several different broad lines of policy toward Iraq. The discussion that follows looks at the U.S. debate, where different people and groups argued for different courses of action. This sort of disagreement is typical in almost every state when important and potentially costly decisions are at issue. All of the parties in the U.S. debate concurred on the chief goals, which were to maximize the security of the American people and to prevent, as far as possible, more acts of terrorism against innocent civilians in the United States and around the world. But there were widely differing views about which course of action would most effectively achieve these goals. The policy proposals considered were suggested by members of the U.S. administration in Washington, DC, members of Congress, various scholars, and other prominent figures.

One option considered was for the United States and any supporting allies to launch an invasion of Iraq, irrespective of what the UN, fellow NATO member states, or other allies said. The objectives were to depose Saddam Hussein and replace him with an American-sponsored democratic government. This action required at least 150,000 troops of which over 90 percent would be American. The plan was to secure the approval of several key allies who could provide logistics, basing, and specialized troops. The United States would move troops to the region as quickly as possible in the coming months, offer Saddam Hussein the opportunity to surrender himself peacefully and then, if he did not surrender, strike with as much force as possible. This policy option was expensive for the United States, as it involved a large number of troops fighting far from their home ports and bases, while the enemy would be fighting on its home territory. There was also likely to be a post-invasion insurgency against the United States and allies. The advantages to the United States and allies were that the morale of the Iraqi troops was estimated to be low, in part, because Iraq's military had been suffering from eleven years of deterioration due to UN-imposed trade and military sanctions and, in part, because Saddam Hussein was hated by many Iraqis. The policy required many months or years of U.S. involvement to guide Iraq into a democracy of the sort that American leaders had in mind.

A second option was to push for a multilateral attack on Iraq with the authorization of a recognized international body. This option required UN support in the form of a Security Council resolution or, at the very least, a NATO decision. NATO approval had sufficed as a form of international approval in another recent intervention: the U.S.-led campaign against Yugoslavia. A resolution of this sort would be approved only if Iraq continued to resist UN inspections and continued to violate UN resolutions. This second option had two principal advantages. One was to spread out the potentially enormous financial and human costs over a broad global alliance of states. In the 1991 Gulf War, President George H. W. Bush garnered the support of the UN and a large coalition, and the United States ended up paying only about 12 percent of the financial costs. The other advantages of this option was that it created an international perception of legality and legitimacy for the use of force. Otherwise, the U.S. invasion might not appear any more legitimate than Saddam Hussein's invasions of Iraq or Kuwait.

A third option was to have the UN Security Council authorize a massive expansion of the UN inspections of suspected Iraqi weapons facilities—some even suggested a tenfold increase in the hundreds of inspectors. This course of action would raise the chances of finding any banned weapons in Iraq's arsenal, while at the same time avoiding the immense financial costs and the many deaths of soldiers and civilians that would result from an invasion of Iraq. This option left open a decision to attack if Iraq did not inadequately cooperate with inspectors' demands.

A fourth option was to do nothing in the way of military action. Terrorism is a continuing danger to the United States and the West. The safety of Americans could be improved more by using the money that an invasion required to implement an array of new homeland security measures involving improved intelligence collection and analysis, improved monitoring of U.S. ports and borders, et cetera.

Rationales for the Four Policies

Why would someone choose one option over the others? Let us consider the reasons offered for each of the proposed policies. There was, as is typical, more than one rationale for each of the available policies. Sometimes rationales for the different options overlapped, and sometimes they were mutually exclusive.

First Option

Those who advocated invasion irrespective of allied or international support used several arguments. The primary argument was that Saddam Hussein possessed weapons banned by UN Security Council resolutions, which might be transferred to terrorist groups who could use them or threaten to use them against the United States and European states. President Bush said that we must act before "the smoking gun" is "a mushroom cloud" (Bush 2002). It is thus imperative to remove Saddam Hussein from power, because **(R1) Saddam Hussein supports terrorists who are hostile to the United States by providing them with funding and weaponry**. Second, this is especially important, because **(R2) Saddam Hussein has an extensive arsenal of chemical and biological weapons and the nuclear weapons program is near completion**.

A third rationale was that replacing Saddam Hussein's Ba'athist government with a democracy would lead to a more peaceful relationship between the West and Iraq. Proponents offered a "democratic domino theory," according to which a democracy in Iraq would show other Arab states that they too deserve the benefits of democracy, which would lead to the overthrow of other autocracies in the region. **(R3) A democracy would lead to a more peaceful relationship between the West and Iraq**.

A further rationale was that Saddam Hussein must be removed from power regardless of what the other UN Security Council members decided because he is a dictator who cannot be deterred; it is impossible to reason or negotiate with him. He will continue to attack other states either through state invasions or through his support of nonstate actors, especially as terrorist groups. The only effective way to deal with dictators is to remove them by means of military force. **(R4) Saddam Hussein is a dictator who cannot be deterred from aggressive behavior and must be removed**.

Finally, some preferred a non-UN operation in order to avoid problems with the chain of command weakness under the UN that proved to be dangerous to troops on the ground in Bosnia. Commanders and UN officials who do not have a sound understanding of the specific dangers of combat would have to give orders to use force in particular situations, and some would be reluctant to do so, which would endanger soldiers' lives and the success of some of their operations. Thus, **(R5) there is a chain of command weakness under the UN**. There were many other rationales offered but they were not advanced as primary or presented as able to justify a U.S.-led invasion by themselves.

Second Option

The second option was also supported by those who insisted that Saddam Hussein illegally held chemical and biological weapons and was a danger to peace, in view of the fact that he had recently invaded Iran and Kuwait. Removing Saddam Hussein and replacing him with a democratic regime would improve Western and regional security as well as human rights. Advocates of this policy accepted at least two of the rationales for the first policy, particularly R1 and R3. They held that war-prone Iraq would be more peaceful if it were democratic. However, they generally did not see these as solely benefiting the security of the United States. Advocates of the second option held that it was more appropriate than the first option because they emphasized the importance of financial efficiency, national interest, legitimacy, and legality. These two lines of argument are distinct but compatible.

With regard to U.S. or Middle Eastern national interests, some believed that the cost of the war should be spread among many nation-states. On this view, Iraq posed no more of a threat to the United States than to any Western country. Thus, if there should be an action to remove the threat, it was the responsibility of the world community. If there was no common view of the Iraqi threat, it would be unwise for the United States to carry out the action unilaterally. **(R6) U.S. interests would benefit from having the costs of a war against Iraq spread among many states**.

On the question of legitimacy, some argued that no state has the right to cross borders to launch an attack on another state unless the latter is within hours or days of attacking, which was clearly not the case with Iraq. Scholars have long drawn a distinction between *preemptive* war and *preventive* war. A preemptive war occurs when one side knows it is going to be attacked within a matter of hours or perhaps days and chooses to fire the first shot rather than await the opponent's attack. This has been generally regarded as legitimate, given that the war would have begun whether it did so or not. This contrasts with a preventive war where one side attacks the other because it fears that at some point in the future, possibly the distant future, the opponent is likely to develop capabilities that could pose a serious threat. The legitimacy of the latter has been much more controversial among scholars. A U.S.-led attack on Iraq would be preventive and an infringement on the rights of another sovereign state. Hence, **(R7) an invasion of Iraq would be legitimate and legal only if sanctioned by the UN**.

A final rationale is that cooperation on inspections, diplomacy, and military force in Iraq would build deeper trust in states fighting terrorism and would thus produce further cooperation among them, thus rendering the war on terrorism more successful. **(R8) Cooperation in restraining Iraq will aid cooperation in the war on terrorism**.

Third Option

The third option was to increase the scope of sanctions dramatically. Many agreed with rationale R7 in which UN authorization is necessary to legitimate military action and with R8 in which cooperation on one issue breeds further cooperation among the same states. Most who advocated this option argued that war would be possible at a later date if it turned out that Saddam Hussein was guilty of significant violations of UN Security Council resolutions and possessed chemical or biological weapons. Proponents of this option believed that Iraq almost certainly possessed banned weapons. With more extensive inspections the UN member states could learn with greater precision whether Saddam Hussein had committed significant violations of the UNSC resolutions. **(R9) Improved information about Saddam Hussein's arsenal would make the policy option selected more effective**.

Some political leaders and scholars held that war is legitimate only when a state is attacked or an attack is imminent. Though they freely acknowledged that Saddam Hussein's rule was extremely repressive and violent, they held that the competing factions in Iraq were so hostile toward one another that Western-style democracy would not come about without a long period of Western military occupation and a long fight against insurgents opposed to Western involvement and creation of a democracy in Iraq. Thus invasion was, in their view, a bad idea because of the massive financial costs of war and occupation. They argued that there would be further costs to U.S. security from a premature invasion of Iraq, because a huge portion of the available fighting forces of the United States would be tied down in Iraq for years. This would effectively be a signal to other adversaries that they would have a much easier time if they should choose to challenge the United States. Increased weapons inspections in Iraq and more effective trade sanctions is the most the United States should demand without much more knowledge of Saddam Hussein's inventory of banned weapons. **(R10) U.S. security would be decreased as fighting forces would be tied down indefinitely in Iraq**.

War brings much suffering, has high costs, and should always be a last resort. A war in Iraq should be launched only if it is clearly a last resort; and increased inspections would obviously be a prior step. **(R11) A war against Iraq may be launched only as a last resort after inspections and other options have been tried**.

Others made the further argument that military action should be avoided because it would be immoral, on the grounds that one state does not have the right to impose its will or vision of good governance on any other state. An invasion would be a return to Western imperialism of the Middle East. Hegemons in the international system can be a danger to peace; any use of force by hegemons must be taken with extreme care and deliberation and legitimized by international bodies that represent the world community. **(R12) All steps must be taken to avoid hegemonic domination of former colonial areas and to avoid a return to Western imperialism**.

Fourth Option
There were several rationales for the fourth option—which was to take no military action. Some who opposed military action cited R12, but there were other rationales as well. For example, some argued that Saddam Hussein was not a

Table 1.1 Iraq rationales and policies

Rationale*	Policy 1: Invade	Policy 2: Invade only with UN support	Policy 3: Increase Inspections	Policy 4: No Action
R1 *Saddam Hussein supports terrorists through money and weapons.*	X	X		
R2 *Saddam Hussein is close to having nuclear weapons.*	X			
R3 A democratic Iraq will be more peaceful to the West.	X	X		
R4 Saddam Hussein is a dictator who cannot be deterred.	X			
R5 The UN chain of command has flaws and weaknesses.	X			
R6 *Spreading the cost of war to many states helps the United States.*		X		
R7 Invading Iraq is only legal if sanctioned by the UN.		X	X	X
R8 Cooperation in restraining Iraq helps to aid cooperation in the war on terror.		X	X	
R9 Information on Iraq's arsenal increases the effectiveness of policy.			X	
R10 *War in Iraq requires a large portion of U.S. combat forces.*			X	
R11 War against Iraq is only a last resort.				X
R12 A return to Western imperialism should be avoided.			X	
R13 *Iraq lacked the capability to threaten the United States or the West.*				X
R14 *Iraq does not aid anti-U.S. terrorist groups.*				X
R15 Killing Iraqi civilians is immoral and unjustifiable.				X
R16 Invasion reinforces war as a legitimate norm.			X	X

* Italics indicate factual or lower-level theoretical rationales

threat to the United States or the West. Although the attacks of September 11 showed that the United States is vulnerable to terrorists, Iraq was not connected with any attacks against Americans. Other states supported terrorists and various rogue states were developing nuclear weapons. Some advocates of this policy argued that the use of resources to overthrow the government of Saddam Hussein was wasteful, since Iraq was not poised to attack the United States directly; Iraq was not seriously moving close to gaining nuclear weapons capabilities; Iraq was not a fundamentalist Islamist state; and Iraq did not support terrorist groups involved in attacks on the United States or Western states. It would thus be a mistake to divert attention from the real and dangerous threats posed by states that held anti-American ideologies and were developing nuclear weapons, like Communist North Korea and Fundamentalist-led Iran, and by states that support anti-U.S. terrorist groups, like Syria. War would not enhance Western security because **(R13) Iraq lacked capabilities to threaten the United States or the West** and **(R14) did not have intentions of aiding anti-U.S. terrorist groups**.

Others who opposed a military strike against Iraq argued that military force is only justified when a state is directly attacked or when an attack is imminent. **(R15) The killing of Iraqi civilians is immoral and unjustifiable**. Pacifists would also support this option and would argue that the killing of Iraqis cannot be morally justified, even with UN approval. There were, however, no prominent political figures in the United States who advocated the pacifist position. We should add one final rationale **(R16)**, which is that **invasion or any use of force not directly used in self-defense reinforces the idea that war is legitimate, and thus supports war as a norm of behavior in the international system**. Whether or not the theoretical and moral assumptions are correct will depend upon the larger theories of IR and moral philosophy of which they are a part. Those theories will be examined in the next chapter.

North Korea

Origins of the Problem

In the aftermath of World War II, much of Europe and Asia were divided between the non-communist and the communist worlds. As soon as the Japanese were expelled from Korea, the peninsula was divided at the thirty-eighth parallel between the communist North and the non-communist South. From that point on, the United States was concerned about the actions of North Korea. Kim Il-sung took power and led the North for four decades.

In 1950 some of the West's worst fears were confirmed when North Korea launched an invasion and rapidly advanced deep into the territory of the South. The UN Security Council passed a resolution supporting an international response, which was led by the United States. UN forces pushed the Northern forces back and nearly defeated them until the Soviets and Chinese became involved. A military stalemate resulted. Dwight Eisenhower campaigned for president in 1952 promising to end the war. He signed an armistice in his first year in office. However, no peace treaty was ever negotiated to replace the armistice (or cease fire). The United States is thus still officially at war with North Korea.

Political Background

With the support of China and economic help from the Soviet Union, North Korea maintained a large, powerful army and an economy that was comparable to that of the more populous South. Per capita GDP in the North was greater than that in the South, and by 1960 the overall economic output of the North reached 75 percent of the South. Park Chung-hee led a military coup d'etat in 1961 and ruled South Korea for the next sixteen years. In the late 1960s there were several threatening actions by the North, including the January 1968 seizure of the *USS Pueblo*. The United States did not react forcefully to these actions. North Korea engaged in various further acts of terrorism against the South but not against the United States. Some argue that the North sought to foment revolution in the South by targeting the authoritarian leadership—for example, the presidential mansion was attacked in 1968, and there was an attempt to assassinate President Park in 1974. The North hoped that the citizens of the South would rise up and overthrow the government of the South and either join the North or establish a friendly socialist government. Recently disclosed documents show that the Soviet Union had to plead with Kim Il-sung to restrain hostile actions in order to not bring Moscow into another war in Korea (Cha and Kang 2003, 74).

Economics and Domestic Politics
For twenty years after the Korean War, the two Koreas were more or less on a par in economic and military terms. Both had growing economies and reliable, powerful allies. The North had military superiority over the South, very stable leadership, and the Soviet Union and China as allies, both of which were close at hand. In the 1960s and early to mid-1970s, the position of South Korea deteriorated. The United States seemed to back off on some commitments under Presidents Johnson, Nixon, and Ford, culminating in President Carter's decision to bring some U.S. troops out of South Korea. Leaders in the North were confident that their vision of the future of Korea would dominate and that the South would join the North in communism.

As the East and West détente developed in the early 1970s, there was some progress in Korea, especially the July 1972 Joint Communiqué, which set up the North-South Panmunjom Coordinating Committee to monitor the truce. But as always, there were setbacks and hostile actions, such as North Korea's fatal attack on the UN Command in March 1973.

In the mid-1970s, the South's economy overtook the North in per capita income for the first time. In 1979 President Park Chung-hee was assassinated, not by the North, but by his security forces. Political instability continued in the South as Chun Do-hwan led a military coup in 1980. But by the late 1980s democracy began to take root. Pro-democracy demonstrations in 1987 paved the way for a transition to democracy. The North committed a major terrorist act by shooting down a Korea Air Line flight in 1987. In the few years that followed, the United States began to hold low-level talks with North Korea.

The economy of the South boomed in the 1980s as a result of a strategy that emphasized chemical and heavy industry and exports. The end of the cold war was devastating for the North, which lost military, economic, and especially energy aid from the Soviet Union in 1990. The North also lost diplomatic and

There was no public discussion by the Bush administration about North Korea for ten days after the meetings. The U.S. administration at this time was working very hard to gain Senate approval for the use of force in Iraq and perhaps for that reason was insisting that there was no "crisis" with North Korea. After the Senate vote, the administration released information about North Korea's statements during the meeting, and the world learned of North Korea's nuclear claims.

In December 2002 the United States intercepted a North Korean shipment of missiles destined for Yemen, and in January 2003 North Korea announced that it would withdraw from the NPT—making it the first country ever to do so. North Korea evicted the three International Atomic Energy Agency (IAEA) inspectors from its territory, disabled the IAEA monitoring cameras, unsealed its experimental plutonium reactor at Yongbyon, and ended its moratorium on ballistic missile tests. In February the United States suspended heavy fuel oil deliveries to North Korea, and the IAEA referred the North Korea case to the Security Council, which is a serious move that occurs when experts in the IAEA determine that a country is grossly violating its international obligations under the NPT.

Just at the time when North Korea was looking most threatening because of these nuclear activities and missile exports, South Koreans began protests against the U.S. military bases; the protests were set off by the accidental deaths of two South Korean girls, which was caused by Americans. A number of commentators found it odd that at the height of the crisis with North Korea over its treaty violations and impending nuclear weapons capability, and as the North appeared to be proceeding both with plutonium and with highly enriched uranium nuclear weapons programs, South Koreans had taken to the streets to protest against the U.S. troops, who were in South Korea to protect them from the threat of North Korea. Polls showed that many South Koreans feared George W. Bush more than North Korean leader Kim Jong-il.

In recent years negotiations with North Korea have been conducted in the multi-lateral framework known as the "Six-Party Talks," which include the United States, North Korea, South Korea, Japan, China, and the UN. While talks were at a complete stalemate, the United States insisted that it would not give in to North Korean demands for direct U.S.-North Korea negotiations. The United States argued that such a move would be rewarding North Korea for bad behavior and would undermine the united front of America's allies involved in the talks. In the presidential campaign of 2004 the Democratic candidate, Senator John Kerry, criticized the United States' refusal to talk to the North Koreans. However, in July 2005, just before a short-lived agreement was reached, the United States reversed itself and conducted a series of direct bilateral talks with North Korean officials (Kessler 2005). The United States again met with North Koreans directly at the end of 2006. This case considers the issues the United States faced from 2002 through 2006 as North Korea was threatening to become a nuclear-weapons state. In October of 2006, the U.S. policy aimed at preventing a North Korean nuclear test failed: North Korea began a series of tests. After those tests the Bush administration reversed many of its negotiating principles (for example, about not rewarding bad behavior) and reached a deal with North Korea much like Clinton's 1994 Agreed Framework.[3] How that agreement succeeds will be seen over the coming years.

Competing Policy Options

Most American officials view North Korea as a clear threat to the United States and as a challenge to U.S. interests in Asia. Over the past fifteen years many proposals for dealing with North Korea have been suggested by scholars, U.S. policy makers, and allies. In the early 1990s the Clinton administration seriously entertained the possibility of using military force but ultimately reached the 1994 Agreed Framework. Subsequent dealings were regulated by the terms of that agreement. In 2001 the George W. Bush administration came into office determined to end the détente by using harsh anti-North Korea rhetoric. Both the Clinton and the George W. Bush administrations have negotiated with North Korea in multi-lateral frameworks and in one-on-one meetings. Both administrations have formally opposed North Korea's pursuit of nuclear weapons, though some American academics advocate allowing nuclear proliferation as a way of deterring all sides in future crises.

There are various options for the United States in dealing with North Korea. Some options involve the threat or use of force. For example, one might advocate the United States launching a war against North Korea similar to that against Iraq—air and ground—or a war similar to the one the United States launched against Serbia—air only. One might advocate extensive threats of the use of force, like the threats made against the Soviet Union early in the cold war. Another option would be to downplay any possible use of force, such as with the Soviet Union in the period of détente. Diplomatic and economic engagement might be avoided in favor of isolating North Korea, or it might be pursued only incrementally and conditionally as a reward for specific concessions on the part of North Korea. Alternatively, extensive engagement might be pursued in the hope that more integration into the world economy would create North Korean dependence on the outside world, which would moderate its behavior.

Although there are many combinations and permutations of the use of force, negotiating frameworks, and economic incentives, for simplicity's sake we will identify five alternative policies that various parties have recommended. First is the use of military strikes—the "military option"—to coerce regime change in Pyongyang while isolating North Korea and cutting it off from the benefits of good relations with others; these would support demands that North Korea cease its illegal nuclear programs and possibly eliminate some of the extensive human rights abuses.

The second policy option is to pursue limited engagement—"isolation and starvation." According to this approach, the United States should isolate North Korea to contain and deter hostile actions, in the near term, by denying it the means of carrying out problematic actions. If North Korea is cut off from the supplies it needs for its military programs and if the economy is weakened enough so as to be unable to support more military procurement, then North Korea would not be able to cause more trouble for its neighbors or the United States. And in the long-term North Korea's economy will collapse which will lead to reunification under a democratic government.

A policy of limited and conditional concessions (sometimes called "hawk engagement") is a third possibility. On this approach, engagement replaces the isolation of North Korea, at least as long as North Korea reacts properly. Any concessions offered to North Korea should be conditional upon its good behavior. Instead of isolation, the United States and allies should offer concessions. As North Korea responds with its own concessions, the United States might go further, thus creating a step-by-step process of burgeoning détente. If North Korea continues to cheat on agreements, then no new concessions would be offered and benefits that were contingent on promises that are broken would be revoked. This policy advocates deterrence and containment through engagement rather than isolation.

A fourth option is to follow the line taken by South Korean President Kim Dae-jung, which is to develop better relations with North Korea, even if North Korea gains disproportional benefits (the so-called "sunshine policy"). South Korea, Japan, and the United States, and the erstwhile rivals and enemies, would be more secure if North Korea sees itself as having the chance to gain more from continuing the path of good relations with others. This policy aims at eventual normalization of relations with North Korea. It is motivated by the belief that if North Korea is treated as a state like others, then perhaps it will behave more like others.

Rationales for the Four Policy Options

Proponents of the first policy see it as justified, due to North Korea's development of ballistic missiles and nuclear weapons, to force Kim Jong-il out of power by military action. **(RK1) North Korea will soon have the ability to attack the United States**, which is why the United States should act preventively to safeguard American security.

Some stress the lack of other good options. **(RK2) Military action is the only means the United States can be confident will succeed in removing him from power.** The Communist government of North Korea has no desire to conform to internationally recognized standards and norms. **(RK3) States that disregard international norms of behavior cannot be reformed.** In order to eliminate the problems that North Korea causes, the leadership has to be removed from power.

Negotiations with Kim Jong-il will not succeed because of his dictatorial nature, his irrationality, and his immoral character. That is, reform is possible where the leaders are interested enough in gaining concessions from the other side; in those cases they will live up to their commitments in such negotiations. Some would argue that because of the heinous crimes, human rights abuses, and wanton misery they inflict on millions of people, **(RK4) negotiating with**

reprehensible leaders is immoral, as it confers a legitimacy on them that must be avoided.

The second policy, which is to isolate North Korea from the rest of the world, is justified by the claim that **(RK5) without aid and trade from the West, North Korea's economy will collapse**. Proponents of this policy might also accept any combination of R3–R5—that North Korea cannot be reformed and that negotiations are to be avoided—because North Korea will not abide by any agreements reached since its leader will not behave rationally and because the regime is evil and thus should not be legitimized by such recognition. Some also advocate isolation because efforts to prevent North Korea from gaining the means and the opportunity to cause harm have a good track record of success. **(RK6) There has been no major war in Korea since the armistice was signed in 1953**, which shows that **(RK7) pressure can successfully contain and deter North Korean aggression**. In the short term, the prospects for deterrence are good. The long-term goal is the collapse of North Korea's economy and regime change.

Another common rationale for refusing to negotiate concessions with states like North Korea is connected to their bad behavior and violations of international norms. Thus some argue that **(RK8) bad behavior should not be rewarded**. While the negotiations might produce some small benefits, they send a powerful message that leaders of such states would do better by continuing their bad behavior.

The third policy—reforming the North Korean regime though engagement—is justified by the argument that offering North Korea concessions, especially economic benefits, will make the North dependent upon those benefits. **(RK9) As North Korea becomes dependent upon concessions, its behavior can be further moderated and influenced by the threat to take those benefits away, which increases the leverage of the United States and the West**. Thus today's carrots become tomorrow's sticks. Some also believe that this is a better strategy than trying to force regime change by an economic collapse of North Korea because **(RK10) the economy has already collapsed by any reasonable definition, and it has not produced any reduction of Kim Jong-il's power**. There is no reasonable mechanism to explain how economic hardship would lead to Kim's resignation or overthrow.

The observation that none of the negotiating partners in the Six-Party Talks support the military or isolation options might also support the policy of engagement. Effective pressure on North Korea can only be generated by all five parties working together, as North Korea is skilled in driving wedges between them. So **(RK11) a policy of engagement is most likely to produce change in North Korea, because it allows all five partners to take a consistent line**.

The fourth policy option adds to the third policy of engagement an emphasis on quickly moving to reverse, through incremental steps, the many years of enmity between North and South Korea; this might, unfortunately, require having to live with North Korea's extraordinarily repressive system. This approach recognizes that North Korea's fears of attack are legitimate and well-founded.

Table 1.2 North Korea rationales and policies

Rationale*	Policy 1: Use of Force	Policy 2: Isolate & Starve	Policy 3: Moderate engagement	Policy 4: Sunshine policy
RK1 *North Korea will soon have the means to attack the United States.*	X			
RK2 There is no other way to get Kim Jong-il out of power.	X			
RK3 North Korea rejects global norms and will not reform.	X	X		
RK4 It is immoral to negotiate with human rights abusers.	X	X		
RK5 The communist economy will collapse without aid.		X		
RK6 *There has not been a war in North Korea for fifty years.*		X	X	
RK7 Deterrence has worked for fifty years.		X	X	
RK8 Bad behavior should not be rewarded.		X	X	
RK9 Give North Korea the goods to lose; carrots will become sticks.			X	X
RK10 *North Korea's economy has already collapsed, yet Kim Jong-il remains.*			X	X
RK11 Unilateral U.S. punishment undercuts the coalition.			X	X
RK12 An insecurity spiral develops when increased North Korean fear leads o further military steps.				X
RK13 Incremental concessions and confidence-building measures produce cooperation.				X
RK14 If ordinary North Koreans learn more, they will demand reform.				X
RK15 North Korea will be more restrained if it develops nuclear weapons.				X

*Italics indicate factual rather than theoretical rationale.

These fears are largely what drive North Korea to its extreme emphasis on security and its heavy spending on conventional and nuclear weapons. On this view other states should seek to calm Pyongyang's fears, which can only be accomplished by a policy engagement and détente. So **(RK12) only a reduction in tension with North Korea will lead it to reduce its determination to maintain very large military forces**.

Improving the level of trust will be difficult, but it requires persistence and small confidence-building measures, such as exchanges of information, exchanges of observers to military exercises, and continued negotiations to air differences and concerns. This method will have positive effects on North Korea's behavior because **(RK13) as trust increases, so does cooperative behavior**. Increasing contacts, travel, and person-to-person access increases information, which will be beneficial because **(RK14) as North Koreans see what life is like outside of North Korea, they will demand reforms of their impoverished and repressive society**. Some authors add that even if arms reductions take considerable amount of time, this is not a problem, since the acquisition of nuclear weapons by North Korea is not a danger; it is, rather, a positive development. On this view, **(RK15) nuclear weapons in the hands of North Korea will strengthen deterrence on the peninsula and increase the chances for peaceful cooperation**.

The rationales for these policies all make use of one or more factual justifications and one or more theoretical—that is, causal, interpretive, or moral—justifications. Table 1.2 summarizes the rationales and policies they support.

China Policy

Origins of the Current Relationship

Relations between the United States and China today are not friendly but are at least cordial, especially in comparison to decades of bitter enmity after Mao Zedong came to power in 1949. Many argue that the United States and China are on course to become the two major world powers over the next several decades. At present the United States has a larger economy, more advanced technology, and a more powerful military. This is especially true in terms of nuclear forces and power projection capability. (The latter is the ability to move forces anywhere in the world for combat.) China, however, has a population four times that of the United States and its economy has shown much greater growth over the past decade than almost any other country, including the United States. China is a communist state with a centrally controlled political system, which does not recognize the importance of human rights in any way comparable to Western nations. The difference in the two states' internal political systems has been one of the sources of tension between them and creates a framework of suspicion that could lead to greater challenges in the next decade as China reduces the gap between its power capabilities and those of the United States.

The United States has consistently and vigorously criticized China's lack of democratic political institutions and its abuses of human rights. China has consistently attacked the Unites States' decisions to go to war against other countries, American bullying of others to conform to its will rather than negotiate in a fair and constructive way, as well as the United States' search for "hegemony" over global affairs for its own selfish purposes. But above all, China's anger toward U.S. leaders results from their support for Taiwan.

The People's Republic of China regards Taiwan as an historical and legitimate part of China and the Nationalist government as a rebellion against the legitimate government of China. The legitimate government in Beijing claims to have the right to put down a rebellion by whatever means it deems appropriate. Chinese officials are always quick to point out that during the American Civil War President Lincoln used force to bring the rebellious Confederacy back into the Union and would never have recognized any other state's right to threaten the United States for using force against the rebellion. In a parallel way, since Beijing does not recognize Taiwan as an independent nation-state, it rejects the right of the United States or any other outside power to dictate what China may or may not do to bring Taiwan under its control.

The United States and China were on the same side during World War II, and they were friendly when it ended. The United States, the UK, and other Western countries fought to defeat the Japanese, who had brutally occupied part of China. The Chinese especially appreciated this effort because of the enormous scale of Japanese wartime atrocities. However, after World War II came the midst of a twenty-year civil war between the government of Chaing Kai-shek and the Communist rebels led by Mao Zedong. In 1949, four years after World War II ended, the rebel forces took control of Beijing and mainland China. The Communists established the People's Republic of China (PRC) and forced Chaing-kai Shek's Nationalists to retreat to the island of Formosa, now called Taiwan.

During World War II the Soviet Union under Josef Stalin had been an ally of the United States and Britain: all shared the urgent goal of defeating Nazi Germany. But soon after the end of the war, the United States, Britain, and other Western Europeans viewed the Soviet Union in a threatening way because, for example, it maintained high Soviet troop levels and broke its promises to hold free elections in Eastern Europe. Throughout the Chinese Civil War, Stalin supported Mao's rebellion and after 1949 became the PRC's most important ally.

Although the Communists defeated the Nationalists on the mainland and established the PRC, the United States refused to recognize the new government. The United States insisted that the Nationalists, now on Formosa, continued to be the legitimate government of China. At that time, China was one of the poorest countries in the world and no real threat to the West. The military danger China posed arose from its alliance with the Soviet Union and the consequent expansion of Soviet influence. The moral danger was that six hundred million people in China had lost hope of political and economic freedom. Even though China had not been a democracy prior to 1949, some Western leaders believed that the Chinese Nationalists held out the hope of political and economic freedom in the future, while the Communist Party offered no such prospects.

While Sino-American relations took a brief turn for the better with an armistice in Korea, they worsened in 1954 as the United States offered the exiled government on Formosa a mutual defense treaty obligating the United States to defend Taiwan from invasion. In 1954 the United States also began its gradual involvement in the defense of South Vietnam when France withdrew its forces after significant battlefield defeats. The communist-controlled North, again with

China and the Soviet Union as allies, was attacking targets in the South in an effort to unite the country. That began the efforts of President Eisenhower and his three successors to support the South. For the 1950s and 1960s, the Vietnam War entrenched U.S. hostility toward the Soviet Union and China. On the Chinese side, U.S. involvement in Vietnam was a major obstacle to better relations. But for the PRC the paramount issue remained American support for Taiwan.

Although, as noted, China and the Soviet Union were allies, but the Chinese always felt that they were treated with less respect than they deserved. Tensions stemmed also from the fact that both states believed, for different reasons, that they should be recognized as the leader of the international communist movement. There were increasing strains between the two countries throughout the 1960s, which culminated in one a violent dispute. There was an unsettled border along the Ussuri River, and at one point in 1969 shots were fired.

The United States continued to worry about Soviet power. By 1970 the Soviet navy had expanded greatly and its nuclear arsenal approached that of the United States. To reduce the Soviet Union's power, which was still much greater than China's, President Nixon tried to take advantage of the Sino-Soviet split. President Nixon was planning to withdraw U.S. forces from South Vietnam, which would be controversial because the United States would be leaving without defeating the North Vietnamese despite having suffered considerable losses, including fifty-eight thousand service personnel. Nixon's decision to "play the China card" could help to not only contain the power of the Soviet Union but also lessen the domestic American discontent that would likely result from Nixon's announcement about the U.S. withdrawal from Vietnam.

An opportunity for easing relations came in 1971 when American and Chinese table tennis players met in Japan. China promptly invited the U.S. team to visit China, which began what came to be called "ping pong diplomacy." This was followed by visits to China by Henry Kissinger and President Nixon. By the end of the year both the United States and the UN recognized the government of the PRC. The United States had considered recognizing Communist regime as the legitimate government of mainland China while continuing to recognize the Nationalists as the legitimate government of the independent state of Taiwan. Nixon, however, chose to recognize the PRC as the sole legitimate government of all of China.

Throughout the 1970s U.S. relations with China gradually improved. Presidents Ford and Carter followed the outline of President Nixon's approach and took concrete steps to bring the United States and China closer together. The improvement allowed President Carter to establish formal diplomatic relations with the PRC. This required severing twenty-four years of formal relations with Taiwan, which Carter did unilaterally. The U.S. Congress then passed the Taiwan Relations Act, which established quasi-formal relations with Taiwan, that is, less than fall short of full recognition. Nixon and Mao, and later President Carter and Deng Xiaoping, agreed to proceed with the many areas that appeared to be mutually beneficial while agreeing that there could, at that time, be no complete and satisfactory solution to China's biggest concern—the status of Taiwan. Cooperation on strategic matters, especially containing the Soviet Union, and on economic matters, especially Most Favored Nation (MFN) trade status for China, could proceed with the Taiwan issue held to the side.

In order to initiate cooperation of this sort, the United States had to adopt a rather subtle position. The United States recognized that there is one legitimate government of all of China, but at the same time the United States did not abandon Taiwan altogether, insisting that China has no right to use force to unify with Taiwan or to dictate terms unilaterally. The United States and China did not become close friends or allies but ceased to see each other as outright enemies. Throughout the rest of the cold war the United States and China remained on cordial but not friendly terms.

As the cold war was coming to a close, United States relations with China took a major turn for the worse when Chinese students staged massive protests in Beijing's Tiananmen Square demanding greater democracy. After initially tolerating the demonstrations, the government put an end to them by sending tanks into Tiananmen Square. The result was a massacre of students. It was then politically impossible for President George H. W. Bush to offer China incentives or to move closer to China on any important issues.

Sino-American relations improved in the 1990s, as China was integrated into the Western trade system and the world economy. But there were several periods of tension. The first major post–cold war strain began in 1995 when President Lee of Taiwan requested a visa for travel to the United States in order to visit his alma mater, Cornell University. China remained adamant about its claim to Taiwan. By 1995 China was able to focus squarely on regaining Taiwan, as it recently settled terms for regaining the colonies of Macau, from Portugal, and Hong Kong, from the UK, for the first time in over a century. Because of its extreme sensitivity over any legitimacy that might be accorded to Taiwan, China vigorously opposed the United States' granting of a visa to President Lee. The State Department initially denied the visa, but U.S. Congress soon got involved and demanded a reversal of the decision. Members of Congress chose to pressure the White House to grant the visa by proposing and passing a resolution that the United States allow Lee's visit. Only one legislator voted against the resolution. The vote was 396 to 0 in the House and 96 to 1 in the Senate. The presidential election in Taiwan was approaching, and in an attempt to intimidate Taiwanese voters not to support the pro-independence incumbent, President Lee, China carried out military exercises in the Taiwan Strait. Lee, however, was reelected. Tensions mounted as the United States then sent naval forces to the area.

The second post–cold war strain developed, while Western nations were trying to stop Yugoslav President Slobodan Milosevic's policy of ethnic cleansing in Kosovo, a province of Serbia. The United States and Western countries wanted a UN resolution demanding an end to the ethnic cleansing and authorizing the use of force if Milosevic did not comply. China has a veto in the Security Council and made it clear that it would not pass a resolution authorizing the use of force—possibly fearing that such a precedent might make it more difficult for China to move against Taiwan if it should feel inclined to do so.

Western states began a bombing campaign after NATO's North Atlantic Council authorized the use of force to stop the ethnic cleansing. Many states questioned whether NATO, an alliance of which Yugoslavia is not a member, had any standing to authorize the use of force. In the course of the NATO bombing campaign, a U.S. aircraft bombed the Chinese embassy in Belgrade. The Chinese believed that this was a deliberate act of retaliation for China's refusal to support the UN action. The United States vigorously denied it, apologized, and offered an explanation for how the mistake was made. The Chinese remained dubious.

Tension arose again soon after President George W. Bush took office. A U.S. reconnaissance aircraft patrolling off the southern coast of China collided with a Chinese fighter jet and was forced to make an emergency landing on Hainan Island. The government of the PRC held the crew as spies who had violated Chinese airspace and negotiated terms for their return. The United States angrily denied that the incident was anything other than a minor matter of an aircraft straying slightly off course and a collision, probably caused by the Chinese pilot (Yee 2004). China eventually returned the crew but did not agree to return the intelligence-gathering aircraft immediately, which gave Chinese experts time to study its sensitive technology.

In the 2000 presidential campaign the Republican candidate, George W. Bush, agreed with most of the foreign policy views of the Democratic candidate, Al Gore. One of the few major disagreements was over policy toward China. Governor Bush criticized Vice President Gore and President Clinton for being too friendly with China and for bringing China into the world economy despite China's anti-democratic values and poor human rights record. While Gore argued that the United States and China could have a mutually productive, cooperative relationship as "strategic partners," Bush insisted that such an approach endangers U.S. national security and that China should only be viewed as a "strategic rival." However, less than a year after these debates, the terrorist attacks of September 11 occurred, and President Bush softened his rhetoric about China in an effort to focus on al-Qaeda as the most threatening enemy and to gain China's cooperation in areas, such as the sharing of intelligence.

Relations between the United States and China have gradually improved over the past forty years despite setbacks. The biggest step forward by the United States was recognition of the PRC as the sole legitimate government of China. Since then the United States has had to walk a fine line between honoring its pledge to protect Taiwan against any possible PRC use of force against it and avoiding any actions that could provoke the PRC to attack Taiwan. As a growing power, China is competing with the United States as well as with Japan and, to some extent, Russia for influence within East and Southeast Asia. This competition can be clearly seen by looking at the variety of regional institutions that have been proposed or put into place in the past few years, such as the Association of Southeast Asian Nations (ASEAN) free trade area and the ASEAN Regional Forum. The Shanghai Cooperation Organization (SCO) has been viewed by the

United States as an effort by Russia and China to blunt American influence in the energy-rich region of Central Asia. The SCO includes China, Russia, and the former Soviet republics of Kazakhstan, Kyrgyzstan, Tajikistan, and Uzbekistan.

Competing Policy Options

The rise of China's power is widely seen as one of the most important strategic issues confronting U.S. foreign policy over the coming decades. Future policy toward China will have to deal with one or more of the three main issues that concern the United States: whether to alter or maintain support for Taiwan; whether to advance or halt the integration of China into the world economy; and whether to pressure, negotiate over, or ignore China's military build up before it reaches the point where China is able to challenge U.S. force capabilities in Asia. Various rationales for different policies appear in scholarly debate and the popular press.

One policy that has been suggested, though not at present by government figures, is to consider an *attack* on China. This would involve preparations for a war to defend Taiwan and prevent potential Chinese hegemony in East Asia. China is developing the potential to challenge the United States and undermine U.S. security. The United States would suffer greatly if it has to fight after China attains equality or superiority. On this view it is better to start the war at a time and under conditions most beneficial to the United States. A second policy would be to *contain* China's future power potential by pushing for an independent Taiwan and helping to arm Taiwan so that it will be able to counter China without primary reliance on U.S. forces. The policy of containment might have any number of components, but they would include limiting institutions that give China's economy certain benefits compared to America's economy and maintaining strong military alliances with Japan, South Korea, and many other states in East Asia. It might also include increasing cooperation with India, though this would require careful balancing so as not to disrupt U.S.-Pakistani relations, which are central to U.S. counter-terrorism policies.

A third policy would be to maintain the status quo and pursue a gradual and limited *reduction of tensions* while *continuing to compete* with China. On this view the United States should avoid major changes but focus on competing with China more vigorously than in the past. It should let the forces of supply and demand work to the advantage of America's superior productivity and insist that China comply with international laws and norms. Otherwise, if China succeeds in violating international laws pertaining to financial transactions, trade, copyright, intellectual property, and the like, it will gain an unfair advantage. A fourth approach would be to work to *integrate* China further into major international institutions and the world economy. The aim would be to create both a more prosperous and more democratic China in the future. This policy would include U.S. support for bringing China into regional Asian organizations, though the process would have to be managed in a way that promotes Japan's role and prevents Japan from being dominated by a nondemocratic China.

Rationales

Political analysts have discussed a wide variety of rationales that may be used to justify different U.S. policies toward China. One is that **(RC1) All states seek hegemony**, although only a few have the resources to achieve it. While China has been very poor for centuries, its economic standing has changed in recent decades. Many in the West worry that China is acquiring the resources to pose a challenge, as evidenced by the fact that **(RC2) in the past decade China has exhibited dramatic and sustained economic expansion**. For decades China allowed itself to fall behind other large states in military acquisition and preparedness as it focused on developing its civilian economy. But now the concern over China's economic expansion is heightened by the fact that, **(RC3) over the last decade, China has been improving and expanding all aspects of its military**. The rapid economic growth of China is seen as especially dangerous because **(RC4) China has the world's largest population**. In the foreseeable future China will most likely have the resources to challenge the United States in Asia. Because of China's ability to close the gap with—or even surpass—the United States, China will seek to restructure security and trade relations in Asia, and possibly beyond, to create a system more to its liking. At the time, China would be willing to go to war with the United States to achieve its goals. So **(RC5) a leading state is better off fighting a war against a rising challenger while it is still superior rather than after the challenger catches or surpasses it**.

China is a communist state whose political system has changed little since the Nationalists were defeated in 1949. While most of the communist world turned democratic, China did not. **(RC6) China's internal repression has not abated**. In 1989, at the very height of the process period when most communist and totalitarian systems were reforming or collapsing, China showed, by violently crushing pro-democracy protests, that it has no intention of reforming for a long time to come. China's economic liberalization has had little impact on the political structure of the government. And **(RC7) the ideological rigidity of communist doctrine in China shows that there will eventually be a conflict with the ideologically incompatible West**. The cold war between the United States and the Soviet Union eventually reached an end. The Soviet Union disappeared and did not continue to coexist with the democratic West. A general statement of this problem is that **(RC8) communist states cannot coexist with democratic states**. As a communist and revolutionary state, China has very different aims from states that support and benefit from the existing international system. In this sense China qualifies as a "revisionist" state. And **(RC9) revisionist states are more willing to go to war** because their radical aims are difficult to achieve peacefully.

The United States' relationship with China has improved steadily in the past forty years. China has been granted MFN status by the United States and was finally brought into the World Trade Organization (WTO). China's foreign policy behavior has similarly moderated since this process began. While China supported Communist military operations in Korea (1950s) and Vietnam (1950s–1960s), it had hostilities with the Soviet Union (1969) and later attacked

Vietnam itself (1979). **(RC10) Over the past twenty years, since China has been brought into the world economic system, it has been peaceful**. A recent indication of China's good behavior in the international community is the decision by the International Olympic Committee to award Beijing the honor of hosting the 2008 Olympic Games. Since the efforts to work cooperatively with China over that period have been so successful, they should be extended and expanded because **(RC11) states that derive benefits from their positive role in international institutions will continue to behave in a cooperative way**.

The post–cold war era has shown that **(RC12) the world has changed radically in the past fifteen years**, which goes to show that **(RC13) further transformation of the international system is possible**, including great power relations. So, it is best to try to shape the changes consciously in ways that will create a better world. Working with China to bring it into many international institutions will lead China itself to transform in ways that will create a more peaceful and cooperative world. Since the world has learned that such changes are possible, **(RC14) all states have a moral obligation to create a better world**, and we must work to create this new and better world.

There is nothing inevitable about how China will view the United States in the future. So the size of the Chinese economy and its material capabilities are less important than whether it sees the international system, and the United States in particular, as either hostile or friendly. **(RC15) How we talk about China creates the atmosphere within which China understands its own role in the system**. Cooperation with China will be useful because **(RC16) the integration of outsider states helps to socialize them into the norms of the system's leaders**. China's capabilities are rising. But even today China has a massive army and nuclear weapons. A war now, for example, over Taiwan, would have a serious possibility of escalating to all-out war. Both states have sizeable nuclear arsenals capable of causing immense destruction. **(RC17) War between two nuclear-armed great powers would become so destructive that virtually no intended goal would be worth the costs**.

We can see that most of the general rationales—that is, theoretical principles—may be applied in somewhat different ways to the case of China. How they are applied will depend largely on the specific empirical evidence available. This combination of general theoretical principles and empirical data suggests particular policy choices in the three cases we have looked at. But the dependence on empirical evidence is more prominent in the case of U.S. policy toward China because the period of greatest concern about China's behavior is neither the recent past, as with Iraq, nor the immediate future, as with North Korea, but the next twenty years. The events of that period are still well off in the future, which leads to a wider set of possible assumptions about the actual conditions that will prevail. As there were with Iraq in 2002, there are different estimates of the real dangers that North Korea poses to the United States based on differing interpretations of the evidence about North Korea's capabilities and intentions at the moment. But those differences are compounded when analysts have to project their effects ten or twenty years into the future, as with the case concerning China.

Table 1.3 China rationales and policies

Rationale*	Policy 1: Attack China	Policy 2: Contain China	Policy 3: Reduce Tension	Policy 4: Integrate China
RC1 All states seek hegemony.	X	X	X	
RC2 *In the past decade China has exhibited dramatic and sustained economic expansion.*	X	X	X	X
RC3 *Over the last decade China has been improving and expanding all aspects of its military.*	X			
RC4 *China has the world's largest population.*	X			X
RC5 A leading state is better off fighting a war against a rising challenger while still superior, rather than after the challenger catches or surpasses it.	X			
RC6 China's internal repression has not abated.	X	X	X	
RC7 The ideological rigidity of communist doctrine in China is incompatible with long-term peace with non-communist states.	X			
RC8 Communist states cannot coexist with democratic states.	X			
RC9 Revisionist states are more willing to go to war.	X			
RC10 *Over the past twenty years, since China has been brought into the world economic system, it has been peaceful.*		X	X	X
RC11 States that derive benefits from their positive roles in international institutions will continue to behave in cooperative ways.			X	X
RC12 *The world has changed radically in the past fifteen years.*				X
RC13 Further transformation of the international system is possible.				X
RC14 All states have a moral obligation to create a better world.				X
RC15 How we talk about China creates the atmosphere within which China understands its own role in the system.				X
RC16 The integration of outsider states helps to socialize them into the norms of the system's leaders.			X	X
RC17 War between two nuclear-armed great powers may become so destructive that virtually no intended goal could be worthwhile.		X	X	X

*Italics indicate factual rather than theoretical rationale.

Whenever decision makers formulate policy, they must have facts, causal beliefs, and values. They make certain basic background assumptions about all three, which means that not everything that guides policy choice needs to be explicitly stated. In the case of values, they assume, unless otherwise stipulated, that the goals or values of foreign policy prominently include promoting national security. When considering policy toward China, decision makers do not need to state, for example, that China has a huge population. They might want to be explicit about economic growth since there have been periods when the PRC has experienced severe economic problems as well as, like in the present, rapid economic growth. These unstated assumptions are more likely to be in the factual category, as causal and value claims are more prone to dispute between proponents of different theories. The explicit rationales for policy refine and revise these assumptions or might add entirely new content to our thinking about facts or theory; since the assumptions are not always correct, new evidence can force us to revise them. And new theories may lead to redefinitions of, for example, what "national security" is.

Since multiple rationales are needed to formulate a particular policy, any individual rationale by itself might support several, but not all, policies. In the case of China policy, we have a good example of a rationale that can be used to support all four of the policies identified, namely RC2. (It might not support some policies other than the four noted, such as those that would require treating China like a declining state.) But the dramatic economic expansion can be used by realists who believe that conflict will eventually occur, that it is better to engage in the conflict before the adversary reaches full relative capability. It could be used by a liberal to show the possibility of extensive joint gains and support cooperation even more powerfully. And it could be used by a constructivist to argue that the rapic growth constitutes a major change in the structure of the system; so consciously directed norms of behavior are more likely to take root than when the system is in a static phase.

Depending on the other elements, one rationale may well support several possible policies. For example, RC2 could be used to support any of the four we have delineated in this chapter. It would depend on what other beliefs the policy maker has, as to how RC2 would affect thinking.

Rationales RC1 (which states that all states seek hegemony) and RC6 (which states that China has not improved its poor record of respecting human rights) could be used to support thee policies: preparations for war, containment, or the reduction of tensions. RC10 (that China is now a member of the global economy) and RC17 (that great power war is too destructive for anyone to benefit) could each be used to support any of three policy options other than war, thus not the same exact three as RC1 and RC6. And two others, RC11 (which says that institutional benefits will influence states to use the institutions more) and RC16 (which says that states that are generally outside of the rules of the system become more socialized to operate within the norms of the system if they have been integrated into it), could be used to support either the third or fourth policies, those of reducing tensions or working to integrate China fully into the international system.

Conclusions

It is clear from the discussion of the three policy problems that each solution is based on specific rationales. Whether the assumptions should be accepted will depend on whether we are willing to accept some general claims of the rationales. Such claims can only be grounded in a theory of IR. Most of the rationales depend on beliefs about cause-and-effect relationships in world politics, which brings us to the question, which theory of IR should be accepted? Chapter 2 begins the examination of which theory is the best.

CHAPTER 2

Policy Decisions and Theories of International Relations

Theories of IR try to find the causes and conditions that lead nations into conflict sometimes and cooperation at other times. Theories are proposed to answer questions such as, why don't states live together in harmony? Why do some states build arms and threaten each other during peacetime? Why do some states go to war? And why, in general, is there so much conflict in the international system? This chapter summarizes the most prominent types of theory and then looks at how they would or would not support the various policy options toward Iraq, North Korea, and China presented in Chapter 1.

Theories and Their Uses

In showing how IR theories serve as the intermediary that links policy making to debates over metatheory, we need to consider alternative theoretical approaches. This chapter looks at three: political realism, liberalism, and constructivism. Political realism and liberalism are long-established theoretical approaches. Constructivism is relatively new—some have questioned whether it is a theory, a metatheory, or both. The substantive IR theory of constructivism is considered in this chapter and the metatheory is considered in Chapter 4.

This chapter presents outlines of the three theoretical approaches noted but only in outline form in order to show how they differ on some of their theoretical principles. We can thus show that the metatheory debates between naturalist/rationalists and interpretivist/reflectivists have a bearing on how scholars and policy makers should rationally choose among competing policy solutions. There are textbooks that enumerate the competing theoretical approaches in much more detail.[1] The aim of this book is to show why the metatheory debates are relevant to those who seek policy solutions. In order to do so we will offer only a brief view of policy options and theories sufficient to set the stage for the more detailed exposition of contemporary metatheory debates in Chapters 3 and 4.

Policy makers are able to decide rationally among the available competing options *only when* they have a theory, empirical evidence, and values or goals. As we will see, some theories used to justify policy actions include moral values moral values and some do not. When they do not specifically include values or goals, we will assume that American policy makers choose policies based on the most basic goals Americans elect their leaders to fulfill, those of protecting the borders of the country and promoting the security and prosperity of American citizens. Figure 2.1 illustrates this relationship.

For example, think about the disagreements between political candidates Senator John F. Kennedy and Vice President Richard M. Nixon in the 1960 presidential campaign. They took different positions on how to treat China, which at the time was using its artillery to attack two islands held by the Nationalists.[2] But the two presidential candidates *agreed on the goals* of protecting U.S. national interests, credibility, and allies. Their difference was over the best means for achieving those goals, which was, therefore, a difference between the "cause-and-effect" theoretical principles they accepted. Vice President Nixon held that allowing China to control the islands between Formosa and the mainland would cause U.S. allies to question the commitment of the United States to defend them; Senator Kennedy did not.

In 2004 Senator Kerry and President Bush disagreed on foreign policy matters, including how to deal with North Korea, which had indicated in 2002 that it had nuclear weapons. The United States and North Korea (along with Japan, South Korea, China, and Russia) were engaged in Six-Party Talks, which had no one-on-one U.S.-North Korea component. The two candidates disagreed on cause-and-effect consequences of adding a set of talks directly between the United States and North Korea. Bush and Kerry agreed on the goal of maximizing the security of the United States and its allies, and they agreed that the best means to reach that goal would be to prevent North Korea from developing a nuclear arsenal. But they accepted different theories about the effects of certain policies. Senator Kerry believed that North Korea would simply continue moving toward nuclear weapons tests if the United States did not go along with its demand for direct negotiations. President Bush insisted that North Korea would be less likely to test and build a nuclear weapon if the United States refused to talk directly with North Korean officials and instead forced them to deal with the five other parties together. As with Nixon and Kennedy, the two candidates

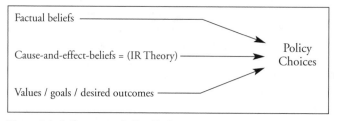

Figure 2.1   Influences on Policy Choices

agreed in detail on the goals but disagreed on the causal principles, which led them to different policy preferences.

We should also note here that theories and policies are related in at least two important ways: testing theories and guiding action. These correspond to the use of theories by political scientists, on the one hand, and policy makers, on the other. Political scientists apply various theories that have cause-and-effect principles to one or even many cases. Most studies of political science use the policy decisions of leaders and states to test competing theories to see which offers the best explanation of the greatest number of cases.

The second way that theories and policies are related, which the next three chapters of this book try to trace out, is outlined by Figure 2.1. Decision makers may choose a policy when they have a set of factual beliefs about conditions; a set of cause-and-effect beliefs about how states interact, which are the core of a theory of IR; and a set of objectives, goals, or values, which may be part of the theory. So decision makers use the causal beliefs of the theory by applying them to the particular circumstances to find a way to achieve the goals of the state.

Figure 2.2 gives a simple schematic idea of how "naturalists" who adopt the scientific approach to IR might envision the process. We see that if two decision makers were to begin with different sets of factual beliefs, they might choose different policy options, even given the same values. We also note that proposed causal principles should be subjected to scrutiny and tested before they are made the basis of policy actions. (Chapter 3 looks at naturalism and examines the elements of Figure 2.2. Chapter 4 criticizes some of the conclusions and especially

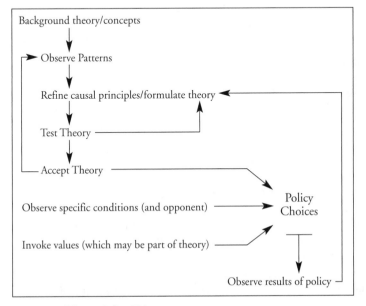

Figure 2.2 Theory, Policy, Values

considers the implications of the dotted line connection between theory and observation.)

Theories, Action, and the Problem of Collective Action

Theories

Since this chapter deals with theories, we begin with a rough characterization of what a scientific theory is. According to most philosophers of science and practicing natural and social scientists, a theory is (1) an organized set of propositions that specifies the boundaries of the part of the world it seeks to account for its domain; (2) includes general principles (either universal generalizations or probabilistic generalizations) encompassing key factors or variables that help researchers to organize observations (that is, to describe the part of the world in the domain of the theory); (3) explains (often understood as "causally explains") the patterns or regularities stated in the generalizations; and (4) generates predictions, which may be probabilistic or deterministic. This last claim about prediction is disputed by some philosophers of social science and will be questioned in the two succeeding chapters. It is important to note that all of the social sciences, though not necessarily the natural sciences, are ordinarily seen as providing only probabilistic rather than universal deterministic general truths. This issue is considered further at the end of the next section.

Predicting and Preparing Actions

All policies are actions aimed at bringing out certain results or conditions in the future. In order to see why this is so, take as an example the idea—widely discussed in 2002–2003—that attacking Iraq will help to reduce terrorism aimed at Western countries. Rationale R3 states that a democratic Iraq will be more peaceful than it had been and will lead to a more peaceful Middle East. So invading Iraq and removing Saddam Hussein will increase peace in the Middle East. Whether it is reasonable to accept this rationale depends on whether it is justified by any of the theories we accept. What is it about the way the world works, according to the theory, which leads a rational policy maker to expect that the chosen policy will cause the desired outcome? The connection is usually referred to as the "causal link." This book offers a brief overview of the concept of "causality" and the problem of providing a satisfactory analysis of it at the end of Chapter 3. The causal claims we believe to be true give us the link that connects our evidence to various beliefs about the future—these are beliefs about whether we can expect the policy (attacking another country to install democracy) to lead to the desired outcome (a more peaceful Middle East).

Let us think about how the theory relates to the policy. Consider a country, A, whose leader is considering attacking country B. The leader of country A decides to order an attack on B because B has started wars in the past that sometimes drew in A. In that case, the outcome of a new attack will (probably) be greater security for A in the future. The leader accepts the statement, "If we attack country B now, there will be more peace in the world and our soldiers will be less likely to go to war again in that region in the coming years." There are three crucial points to consider about this belief. The first and most obvious is that the action of attacking B makes no sense if leaders do not truly believe the statement to be true.[3]

The second point is that the statement deals with a near term action (attacking B) and draws a connection to a somewhat later result (more regional peace, security for valued ally, economic revival, or reelection). So the action makes no sense unless the government decision makers believe predictions such as, "if this action is performed now, there will be a later benefit"—all of which are *predictions*. Why would anyone believe that an action performed now (invading B) would produce a desired result (more peaceful regional relations) a year from now? The answer is usually presented in terms of causality, which is explained more fully in Chapter 3. The leaders must believe one or another of these predictions. Many policy makers do not recognize how impossible rational policy making becomes if they do not believe in the possibility of predictions. The term "prediction" is used in this book to refer to any statement or belief about the future that can be defended by a reasoned argument.[4] Predictions have been controversial, as some theorists do not believe predictions are possible in the social sciences. If they are right, the policy-making role of social science theory is greatly reduced. This important point is developed further in Chapter 3 and revisited in Chapter 5.

Anarchy and Collective Action

When a nation-state or locality faces problems like urban sprawl, declining air quality, or inadequate highways, the government takes steps to solve it. There are usually financial costs to the solution. For example, when faced with the problem of increasing pollution, a government might commission studies or purchase public buses that emit less carbon monoxide and other pollutants, both of which have financial costs. Some regulations, like mandating air pollution devices for cars, which the United States began in the 1970s, do not have costs to the government directly. Individuals pay the direct costs, and for that reason they might want to "cheat." In the case of the United States in the 1970s, some motorists, upset about the rising price of gas (over thirty-five cents per gallon!) and the decreased gas mileage resulting from the pollution-control mechanisms, chose to remove or disable the devices to save gas. However, there were strong disincentives to cheat because the government forced cheaters to pay huge fines. As a result, few people disobeyed the law. Whether the costs are paid by a government's treasury with tax revenues or by citizens directly, a government can use its hierarchy of authority, including the ability to fine or jail violators, to ensure that the problems are solved.

When problems arise in the international system, like increases in trade barriers, state sponsorship of terrorism, or diplomatic crises that endanger the peace, there is no straightforward way to go about solving them, even if governments recognize that many people and nations might suffer as a result. One major obstacle is that, in contrast to national and local governments, the international system has no centralized, legitimate, overarching authority with the right to impose decisions on the members of the system.

Some people think of the UN as such an entity but it is very far from it. The UN members are nation-states and UN decisions are made by the members, not by some independent UN body. If most member states do not like a proposal, it will be defeated. The UN is a group of members deciding how to treat themselves, not a distinct authority over and above the members. This is most obvious in the UN Security Council, the chamber that makes the most important decisions about war and peace. China, France, Russia, the United States, and the UK are permanent members and have the power to veto any proposal. The five permanent members may do anything they like in world affairs without having to worry about the Security Council taking action against them—as long as they have a representative present at the meeting to cast the veto.[5]

All governments of nation-states consist of a hierarchy of authority, while international systems have no such hierarchy. In this sense they are anarchical. "Anarchy" does not suggest that the system is chaotic or disordered. There is no contradiction in a system lacking hierarchy but also having order. Collective action is thus fundamentally different in domestic politics and international politics. Some theorists say that the most basic difference between the two is that domestic politics is hierarchical and international politics is anarchical.

We should make clear here that the term "hierarchy" refers to a legitimate form of authority from the top downward. "Anarchy" is what there is when there is no such top-down hierarchy of authority. It is the presence of many separate units (nation-states) in the system, each with equal legitimate authority though perhaps not with equal material wealth or power. The system of states is one of anarchy where each nation-state is fully "sovereign." No state has the right to interfere in the internal affairs of another state. *Sovereignty* in the international system, as understood since the Peace of Westphalia in 1648, is regarded as having *a monopoly on the legitimate use of force within a territorially bounded area.*

Theories of IR deal with a number of important issues regarding the nature of the international system. The way a theory is structured gives us implicit answers to some of the questions about what should be included in a proper theory. For example, the structure of the theory tells us whether the theorist thinks that social science theories should include or exclude moral concepts. IR theories offer substantive answers for each of the eight questions summarized in the next section.

Eight Features of Contemporary Theories

We turn next to the theories that most contemporary scholars support. Almost all major theorists today fall into one of the categories of theory outlined in the remainder of this chapter. As noted, the theorist must deal with some of the central questions of conflict and cooperation listed at the beginning of this chapter.

What Is the Proper Level of Analysis?

Theories include an idea about what sort of actor or unit of analysis is most effective in explaining IR. We will consider three groups but there are more. Each of the three theories might emphasize either the particularities or general features. Each theory says that we will be best able to understand world politics past and present, and perhaps future, by focusing our attention on one of the various possible kinds of units.

First, some theories focus on the role of people, either by emphasizing the differences between individuals or the general similarities among them. An example of the former is: "Hitler was a very violent individual," or "Hitler took advantage of Britain in 1939 because he saw British leaders as unusually passive." An example of the latter is, "All individuals rationally pursue their interests," or "The rational decision in 1990 for Iraq was to attack small, weak, wealthy Kuwait."

The second type of theory emphasizes the nature of particular types of states—democracies, communist states, or theocracies—or the nature of states in general, which is that they either have a monopoly on the use of force within their borders or seek to survive or maximize power. An example of the former sort of explanation is, "The crisis between the UK and Iceland in 1975–1976 over cod fishing was resolved peacefully because democracies have specific conflict resolution mechanisms that they externalize and thus they are more peaceful when dealing with other democracies." An example of the latter is, "Holland joined the European Union because gaining the right to vote on initiatives and consulting in a large group of more powerful European states would give Holland more power in world affairs and to pursue self-interest, where 'interest' is defined in terms of power." A related question at the state level arises over whether all states are considered to be alike internally and only the state's external features (their actions toward others) are relevant, or whether the internal political, economic, and social characteristics of the state (democratic, totalitarian, socialist, capitalist, Judeo-Christian, Confucian, etc.) are relevant.

The third type of theory deals with the international system, either the characteristics of particular systems, such as the Greek system 2,500 years ago, or the cold war system of the twentieth century, or the nature of the international system in general, such as anarchy. An example of the former is, "Because there were so many city-states in ancient Greece, wars were frequent—this is explained by the fact that the numerous city-states formed and often changed alliances, which increased the chances of a major miscalculation of the effects of various diplomatic maneuvers." An example of the latter is, "War is an enduring feature of the international system because the inherent anarchy renders impossible a powerful conflict-resolution mechanism that would decrease the world's experience of war."

Each of these three types of theory selects where to focus attention to produce the best explanation (on the individual, the state, or the system). These distinct foci of study are sometimes called "levels of analysis." Thus when we ask the question, on which type of actor or level of analysis should we focus to get the best explanations of the world? We will find that some scholars answer by focusing on the individual, some on the state or society, and some on the international system.

Are States Unitary Actors?

The typical state is made up of many agencies, bureaus, offices, and people. But we ordinarily talk about the state as a single thing, saying "England defeated France at Agincourt," or "The Soviet Union signed the Anti-Ballistic Missile Treaty in 1971." Many theories treat these statements as appropriate. They hold that the state acts as an identifiable single entity in the realm of world politics. Other theories hold that we must understand smaller units, like specific bureaucracies, or even the ideas and actions of individual people. Still other theories hold that we must view the state only in the context of the international system. So we will see differences on this question as we compare theories.

Do States Generally Act Rationally?

Some theories hold that states or leaders act rationally. There is, however, some debate about the proper definition of "rationality." It is typically used to refer to the most effective means of achieving the goals of the actor (individual decision maker or state). An actor is rational if, given the information available, the path chosen is the most efficient one to achieve the goals or at least is not less efficient than others considered. Those who define the term along these lines do not consider whether ends might themselves be irrational. Must we accept whatever goal the state chooses and then evaluate the rationality of the state's behavior only with regard to the means chosen to reach it? If so, we are stuck accepting without question the rationality of the goals of Pol Pot or Hitler, however brutal, inhuman, and repugnant they might be. On this definition we may only evaluate rationality based on whether actors chose the most effective means to achieve them.

Scholars who define rationality in this means-ends way, however, do not rule out that the ends might be evaluated on moral grounds. Rationality does not imply that the decision maker has access to all the information, knowledge, or intelligence that she might or should want. Some authors also add that actors must make an effort to gather accurate information and intelligence. It is widely accepted that any theory in the social sciences has to account for decisions that are made with a degree of uncertainty about the facts of the case, since most decisions are in fact made under those circumstances. But authors like Snyder and Diesing (1977, 81) regard it as irrational to make decisions without any effort to learn about important real-world conditions.[6]

Some theories not only assert that actors are rational but also tell us what the goals of actors are or should be (e.g., all states seek survival; all states seek to maximize power; all leaders seek to stay in power; all states seek to improve citizens' standards of living). In these sorts of theories the instrumental paths chosen are evaluated as rational in light of how efficient they are at achieving the goals imputed to the actors.

Do States Have Fixed Preferences and Identities?

Most theories of IR assume that all states have a set of goals that they seek and that these goals or preferences drive the major decisions that states or other actors make. Examples might include those previously cited—survival, maximizing state power, preserving leaders' continued power. That is, if a theory holds that actors try to maximize power or wealth, the theory regards them as having a preestablished set of objectives. For a theory that focuses on states as key actors, if we observe new states created, as happened frequently in the 1990s with the breakup of Yugoslavia, the Soviet Union, and Czechoslovakia, it would imply that the new states will also pursue the goal of maximizing power. We will see later in this chapter that some very recent theories take a different view and hold that the preferences of states might change over time as the state interacts with others and as the preferences and character of other states in the system change.

Do States Always Expect Conflict?

This question is closely related to two others: Do states evaluate policies using a framework of relative gains (rather than absolute gains)? And, are states' interests in fundamental conflict with one another (as opposed to fundamental harmony)? These three basic questions are closely related in that most theories that answer "yes" to one of them are almost certain to answer "yes" to the other two. And most that answer "no" to one will answer "no" to all. Some theories explain international activity by holding that states always seek to gain an advantage over one another. The idea here is that states use a *zero-sum* understanding of political interaction. They do not accept the possibility that all sides can gain meaningfully. A state would rather no one gain than see its rival gain more than itself.

Theories differ from one another with regard to how they see the basic interests of states. Some theories claim that if states acted on their *true underlying interests* and bad leaders and bad institutions were removed, the world would be harmonious. They hold that what is best for one state is actually what is best for all the other states in the system. These include peace, prosperity, free trade, and human rights. Other theories reject this view and hold that the underlying structure of interests is fundamentally one of *conflict* rather than harmony. On this view it is normal and natural for states to make their plans with an expectation that there will be conflict. States will arm themselves and pursue trade, arms, alliances, and other policies based on their belief that they might find themselves in conflict with any other member of the system. The idea of "expectation of conflict" is an important one because, as some theorists argue, IR would be substantially different if states did not always expect conflict. These theorists claim that arming, spying on one's rivals, resisting trade with them, building hostile alliances, and so forth can actually make conflict more likely. Thus they hold that the expectation of conflict becomes a *self-fulfilling prophesy*.

Is There a Chance of Overcoming the Violent Effects of Anarchy?

This question is closely related to two others: Is there, or can there be, progress in history (as opposed to a continuation of the repeating cycles of war)? And is there an analogy between domestic and international politics? These questions are related just as those of the last section were. Theories tend to answer "yes" to all three questions or "no" to all three. With respect to the first, some theories hold that, because of the nature of international politics, history will continue to look the way it has looked since the world was first divided into states as political units—namely, it will exhibit *cycles of war*, exhaustion, preparation for more war, and then more war. Other theories hold that *there is or can be progress*; that is, they hold that either things have gotten better over time or the obstacles that have prevented them from getting better could be reduced or removed. They conclude that such obstacles are not inherent in the nature of the international system.

With regard to the latter, many theorists agree that the anarchical nature of the system is an impediment to peace and cooperation, but they differ on whether and how this anarchy can be overcome. Some see the possibility for greatly increasing cooperation in the international system, either by getting rid of anarchy altogether or by instituting practices or regimes that counteract the effects of anarchy. Other theories provide reasons why anarchy cannot be erased and why the features of anarchy that promote or permit conflict cannot be altered. Some hold that while anarchy is, by definition, the absence of hierarchy, in different possible historical contexts the characteristics of the anarchical system might vary. There are conceivable anarchical systems that are more cooperative than the current system and others that are less. These theories maintain that there is nothing in the definition of "anarchy" that ensures that the system will be conflict-inducing and war-prone.

On the last point, some theories hold that the actors within the domestic system (people) are very much like those within the international system (states), and for that reason the systems themselves might be made to be more similar.[7] Other theories hold that there are essential differences between people and states that render the analogy very limited or hold that the analogy is only useful to help us see how the international system can never be made to resemble domestic systems.

What Is the Relationship of Moral Principles to Theories?

All theories make general statements about the behavior of leaders, states, and/or systems. In addition to these empirical generalizations, some theories include moral precepts about what leaders or states ought to do. There are three possible ways in which moral values might be included in a theory: not at all, in a purely descriptive (that is, non-prescriptive) way, or as a normative element of the theory. On the first approach, theories steer clear of any mention of moral values. They talk about what observable conditions cause wars, currency revaluations, or successful trade negotiations, and draw connections between the various factors. On the second approach, theories mention moral values but only by describing a society. They treat values only as factual subject matter. Theories of this sort avoid endorsing the society's values in any way. An example statement would be the singular statement, "Chinese society accepts Confucian values," or the generalization, "states that adopt Confucian moral values engage in less imperialist behavior than states that do not." These theories talk about moral values, but they do not tell us which values are the best ones. This is simply a description and avoids either endorsing or condemning the values. The third way is found when a theory adopts a set of values and includes them as imperatives in the theory. Such a theory might include statements like "leaders must always obey international law" or "leaders have an obligation to expand a state's power as much as possible."

These three categories exhaust the possible relationships between IR theories and moral values. But there are other sorts of values. Thus the relationships of the second or third categories might be applied to these non-moral values. For example, a theory might endorse as a value any of the objectives discussed in the previous subsections, stating that leaders have an obligation to pursue that value. The value might be those of expanding power, offering consistent set of policies, or seeking all the relevant information reasonably attainable before making a major decision.

Chapters 3 and 4 look at values about proper methods of enquiry—philosophical theories about what sorts of scientific theories we should adopt. The discussion covers what one *should do* in order to expand knowledge, that is, how to satisfy "epistemic norms." A theory with epistemic norms does not tell us what we must do to be moral but only what we must do in order to be rational, to seek the truth, or to be scientifically correct.

How Important are International Institutions?

Contemporary theories differ sharply over the role of international institutions. There are three answers to the question of how important institutions are. One is that they are not important, and unilateral action can be effective and legitimate without the existence of or support of institutions. Theories that adopt this answer denigrate reliance on institutions and contend that states damage their interests and security by relying on them. A second answer is that institutions are important in making policies work more effectively. Theories that adopt this answer make the empirical claim that institutions promote cooperation or allow states to achieve policy objectives more effectively but do not include any normative claim demanding that policy makers have an obligation to use them. A third answer, adopted by some theories, is that institutions are essential to provide legitimacy to certain sorts of policies, especially the use of armed force. On this view institutions should be developed and used because it is morally wrong to undertake certain sorts of actions, like using force, without acting within the legal and normative bounds of the international system, which only institutions can confer.

Political Realism

Political Realism and the Eight Dimensions of Theory

Political realists regard international relations as a struggle to *gain advantage* over rivals. For realists, each state sees others in the system as potential rivals. Proponents of realism trace the roots of many realist principles back two and a half millennia to the works of the Chinese strategist Sun Tzu and the Athenian commander Thucydides, historian of the Peloponnesian war. Other seminal realist thinkers include Niccolo Machiavelli in the sixteenth century, Thomas Hobbes in the seventeenth century, Hans J. Morgenthau in the post-World War II years, and Kenneth Waltz today. Although there are important differences between various realist theories, as realists they all generally share the following answers to the eight questions listed in the previous section.

Realists like Machiavelli, Hobbes, and Morgenthau and their present day followers view the state as the *most important unit of analysis* in the development of a theory of IR. They argue that there are far too many individuals in a modern nation-state for a theory to be able to account for each one; that leaders' behavior, under similar circumstances, does not vary greatly; and that theories, in any case, have to simplify to produce explanations. An important element of political realism is that all states are seen as motivated in similar ways. Whether they are democratic, socialist, Confucian, capitalist, or Islamist makes no difference. From the point of view of IR theory, it is more important to study the foreign policy behavior of states than the internal structure or character of states.

Political realists agree that to get accurate explanations the most useful simplification comes from *treating the state as a single unit*. Moreover, political realists do not think that the many other actors in world politics like banks, corporations, political parties, and terrorist groups are nearly as significant as states. So while some accuracy in smaller details is lost (just as it might be by not looking at the actions of each individual within a state), the loss of accuracy resulting from overlooking the nonstate actors is small and the simplicity gained is great.

Different realists also generally accept that *the state should be treated as a rational actor*. While there are variations in how some specific states behave in particular circumstances, on the whole there is a great similarity among actors in their behavior when they have similar constraints, similar opportunities, and similar information about those constraints and opportunities.

Realist theorists treat states as having a *fixed set of preferences and goals*, which do not change as the international system evolves. The fundamental identity of the state is similar for all states. What the state seeks—to survive and to expand power as much as possible—is the same for all states at all times. All states evaluate options in a zero-sum framework. They believe that anything their rivals gain endangers or weakens them. Because states compete for goods of which the world has a fixed quantity, like territory or gold, they *expect conflict* over these goods.

Realists emphasize the states' struggle for power, and they claim that there is a fixed total amount of power in the system. *It is not* possible for everyone to get more power at the same time, in the same way that it *is* possible for every state to increase in population or even gain more wealth at the same time. Realists hold that states thus see their relations with one another in a zero-sum framework. Realists see "power" as the centerpiece of what states compete for and as the central concept that theorists should use to compare one state with another.

The term "power" *appears* to function in sentences the way "wealth" and "population" do. We might choose to study the increase or decrease in population of eighteenth-century Prussia. We can do so without looking at anything going on outside of Prussian territory. We can imagine a population increase in Prussia occurring at the same time that there is a population increase in all of the major states of Europe in the eighteenth century. The term "power" appears to function in the same way. But it does not. We cannot imagine a simultaneous increase in the power of all the European states in the eighteenth century. Gaining power requires gaining influence over others. So if one state gains power, then other states must be more prone to being influenced. Whenever we speak of power we are speaking of a relationship. If states calculate increases in power, they are calculating how to gain relative to their rivals.

Imagine the following payoff matrix as state A ponders war. "Cooperate" represents not attacking; "defect" represents striking immediately. State A knows that if it attacks, B will counterattack. Both sides will suffer much damage, but having struck first, A will have a big advantage in winning the war. The calculation is identical for state B. If both sides strike simultaneously, both will be seriously and similarly damaged and neither will gain an advantage over the other. The numerical values represent an index of the overall value of the state's military, economic, and social infrastructure.

The top left (cooperate-cooperate) cell is the best outcome in absolute terms for both sides. However, for relative gain-seekers in state A, the best outcome is the bottom left (defect-cooperate). The reason is that B has suffered twice as much damage as A. In relative terms, even though A is materially weaker in an absolute sense, if state A cares only about relative standing, A has become

Table 2.1 War initiation payoff matrix

		State B	
		Cooperate (Withhold attack)	**Defect** (Attack)
State A	**Cooperate** (Withhold attack)	**10,10** (C–C)	**5.5** (C–D)
	Defect (Attack)	**5,0** (D–C)	**1,1** (D–D)

stronger compared to B. Thus if A evaluates policies by reference to relative gains, the best strategy is to strike (defect), since the relative gains of defecting are +5 or 0, depending on what B does. The worst case—A defects—is 0, which is equal to the best case—A cooperates.

The contrast with an actor who evaluates the available options in terms of absolute gain is clear in this matrix. In absolute terms the best outcome is C-C, in which case there is a strong incentive to try to work with B to bring about that outcome. On an absolute gain framework, state A would prefer a cooperative outcome as it could retain the highest value, 10, in that case. On relative gain analysis, there is no strong reason to seek cooperation except perhaps to try to dissuade B from defecting, so that A gains 5 rather than 0 in the D-D cell.

Realists generally agree that world politics is best understood by focusing on states as the agents of change and action. There are, as noted, other sorts of actors that various theorists emphasize, such as international organizations, transnational corporations, banks, terrorist groups, and churches. But for realists the focus should be on the state. In their view the other sorts of actors have only minor effects on the major processes and outcomes one observes—such as war, peace, alliance formation, and trade pacts. The states coexist and interact in a system of anarchy, that is, without legitimate hierarchy of authority comparable to that within a state. In the anarchical system there are inequalities of power but not of rights, duties, and obligations. All full-fledged states have the same rights; no state or actor has the legitimate authority or right to dictate internal policies to another state. In every era one or more states have "great power" status. If they are able to influence the actions of others, it is a result of threats and force of arms and not of right or legitimate authority.

Many scholars note that an anarchical system lacks any mechanisms for preventing escalation of conflicts. Anarchy is a feature that permits, and perhaps even promotes, escalation of conflict. In an environment where there is a domestic government, individuals get along with one another because there are rules and laws that people obey—this is either out of a sense of obligation as citizens or a sense of fear of the police and the courts. The hierarchy of legitimate authority in the state imposes order on the individuals. In contrast, in an international system of sovereign states, no one state has the right to rule others. Thus cooperative behavior is difficult to achieve. The lack of hierarchical authority, that is, the presence of anarchy, in the international system, leads states to believe that they risk being taken advantage of if they act cooperatively. For this reason many scholars think of anarchy as having effects that promote, or at least permit, conflict to escalate until it results in major war.

Political realists see states as maximizing *relative gain*, which means that the great powers of a system at any given time are on a collision course with one another. Because realists also see anarchy as a defining feature of international politics, which entails that there are no powerful mechanisms to derail states from their collision courses with one another, they see the state system as unchanging and as giving rise to periodic great power wars. The realist expects recurring conflict among rival powers and does not see any solution for the problem of war, because anarchy is a major cause of war and the effects of anarchy cannot be limited.

Realist theories are quite clear in the way they view history as a series of repeating *cycles of war and peace*. They hold that states expect conflict, arm for conflict, and engage in armed conflict when challenged or when an opportunity for gain arises. When one side finds that it is no longer in its interest to continue to fight, it capitulates and begins to work within the constraints the defeat imposes on it to regain what it has lost. For realists, the lack of any hierarchy of authority in the international system allows this cycle to continue without any feasible *prospects for overcoming anarchy* and the effects of anarchy.

Realists argue that there are some *parallels between domestic politics and international politics*. But they also argue that there are crucial differences. In particular, they do not believe that anarchy can be overcome. As Hobbes put it, in domestic politics all individual humans living in a primitive state of nature are in grave danger; even the strongest individual is vulnerable to others ganging up on her to rob her of her goods or kill her. So every rational individual will give up some autonomy in order to escape the anarchy of the state of nature and live in a society with a governing sovereign. The government has legitimacy only because every person in the primitive state of nature benefits. In contrast, international politics will always feature one or more actors in the system that will resist the creation of a world government. Since these particular actors are not truly vulnerable, they will not benefit from a world government; they only stand to lose autonomy and freedom of action under hierarchy. The great powers will never consent to an arrangement that weakens their ability to pursue self-interest and power. Thus anarchy and its effects will not, according to this theory, be overcome.

Realist theories do not rely on *moral values* or prescriptions. Instead, they emphasize the pursuit of the state's material and security interests. Some realists do seem to advocate other sorts of values. They imply that leaders have an obligation to maximize the state's interests and may treat this obligation as a moral imperative. But realist theories are generally seen as offering descriptions, explanations, and prehaps predictions, not moral prescriptions.

Different theories and various solutions for improving the ills of world politics involve creating new institutions or organizations. Realists hold that such solutions cannot work. States are the primary agents of world politics and the states that benefit the most from the system—the most powerful—will not give up their power by creating *institutions* designed to take over the functions of regulating the system that are already preformed by the great powers. Realists acknowledge the creation of many multi-national bodies, but they deny that such bodies have an impact on states' behavior. Military alliances may be viewed as institutions, broadly defined. But they are of a special sort in that they form the foundation for what many realists hold to be foreign policy strategies to protect national security; alliances are not the sort of international institutions that liberals or idealists propose to solve the world's problems. Realists see the use of alliances as part of the zero-sum (or relative gain) framework that they emphasize and that liberals and idealists criticize.

For realists who follow Machiavelli's position, the state needs no justification for action beyond the pursuit of its own interests. Most theorists prior to Machiavelli argued that the justification of state behavior must be grounded in some higher authority, such as the Will of God or universal moral principles. Machiavelli's writings were revolutionary in large part because they offered justifications for the state that did not rely on anything over and above the state. Realists do not maintain that international institutions are important in themselves as ways to justify state behavior. There may be exceptional cases where the support of the institution is helpful to persuade other states to support a given state's actions. But this is a matter of convenience for a state, and as realists see it, an international institution cannot bestow legitimacy in any inherent way.

The aim of this review of theories is to show how contemporary metatheory debates are important for anyone who wants a full grounding for policy decisions. For this purpose the book considers only three theories rather than offer an exhaustive survey. And within those three there are several different versions. We need only to sketch the three theories and their variations in order to carry out the main task of this book, which is to show how theories affect our choice of policies and how a metatheoretical or philosophical account will affect our choice of theories. The next two sections simply note the relationship between classical realism, neorealism, and democratic realism (also known as neoconservatism).

Classical Realism and Neorealism

The previous discussion of political realism drew upon principles that are widely accepted by many sorts of realists. We should also note some difference among those who are categorized as "realists." Many contemporary realists focus more on systems of states than on individual states. Systemic theories are very important today and their relationship to classical realism must be noted. The structural or systemic realists, known as neorealists, claim that one of the first great realist thinkers, Thucydides, was ultimately a structural thinker. They say he believed the cause of the twenty-seven-year long war between Athens and Sparta to be a result of the shifting balance of power or, as it is now more often termed, distribution of capabilities. These authors see the same struggle for power at the state-to-state level, but they are interested in explaining the behavior of systems of states rather than individual states. *Defensive* or *positional* neorealists like Kenneth Waltz see balancing as pervasive at the state level, but argue that the anarchical character of world politics can only be fully appreciated when one looks at the system as a whole. Systems behave the way they do because of the states' continual process of balancing, which creates a sort of equilibrium between states over time. Waltz, in particular, holds that a *bipolar system* (one with exactly two great powers) is more stable and less likely to give rise to a major power war than a *multipolar system* (one with three or more major powers). This is because of the different sorts of great power balancing that are possible under multipolarity. Others like Karl Deutch and J. David Singer argue the reverse (Waltz 1979; Deutsch and Singer 1977).

Offensive neorealists like John Mearsheimer argue that states compete for power and are willing to risk war rather than give up the search for power. Mearsheimer includes at least five propositions as the core of neorealism, namely (1) that the international system is anarchic, (2) that states have offensive capabilities, (3) that states can never be fully certain that they will not be attacked, (4) that states desire to survive, and (5) that states are rational. Defensive neorealists see states as more willing to maintain the status quo if the state's own security can be protected; offensive realists see states as more aggressive and expansionist (Mearsheimer 2001). Both see anarchy as a central, defining feature of international politics and as a chief cause of war. Other major, contemporary, structural realists would include Stephen Walt and Stephen Krasner.

One of the main attractions of structural realism or neorealism is that its central principles are very simple. Waltz begins by identifying the three defining features of a "political structure": (1) *ordering principle*, (2) *function of units*, and (3) *distribution of capabilities among the units* (1979). A political structure like the government of the United States has many units within it (three branches of government) and each of the units has a specifiable function. These may be very different from the functions of the units within the Chinese government but similar to those of the French government. Likewise, the functions of the units of the Chinese government may be quite similar to those of the North Korean government. This factor tells us something about which countries are likely to behave with other countries. There are two other defining features of "political structure," as well.

With respect to ordering principle, Waltz says that in all domestic political structures (national government of China, municipal government of London, etc.) there is a hierarchy among the units. In all international systems, there is an anarchical order among the units; the ordering principle is therefore one of "anarchy." The final defining feature is the relative distribution of material capabilities or resources among the various units in the system. When all three factors are considered, it is possible to explain the similarities and differences of the actions of governments throughout history. For example, the UK and Italy will behave more alike (since they are similar on all three features) than the UK and North Korea (since they share only hierarchy). For Waltz, states seek to survive and compete. The existence of states that do not have these goals would be unusual and brief because states that do not strive to survive and maximize power are quickly eliminated from the system by those that do.

In the case of international political systems, all systems are made up of states as the units; classical realists and neorealists downplay the significance of institutions and other nonstate actors. The units thus all have the same functions: survival, accumulation of power, etc. The systems all have the same ordering principle—anarchy. The difference between one international system and another then resides entirely in the third feature, distribution of capabilities. Some systems have one great power, some have two, and some have three or more. A system with two great powers (for example, Greece in 430 BCE) will be more like another system with two great powers (such as the global system of 1975) than like a system with three or more great powers (such as the European system in 1914) or a system with one great power (such as the global system of 2007). The theory explains the behavior of systems rather than states and does so with great simplicity, because it avoids the complications of numerous variables.

Some of the recent work on this theory has pointed out that (C1) Realism, with its emphasis on state's pursuing self-interest, is sometimes criticized for being unable to be "falsified"—whatever a state does may be argued after the fact to have been believed by the leaders to be in the state's interests (see Chapter 3). Because of Waltz's focus on the three chief principles, neorealism is widely seen as having the virtue of great simplicity. The theory has been questioned on the grounds of its lack of specificity of both its key principles and its predictions.

We next turn to the way in which someone who endorses realism would be likely to make policy decisions. But we must bear in mind that the decision to adopt one of the available policies will depend on the acceptance of a set of goals along with both theoretical/casual propositions and a set of factual beliefs. A particular theoretical orientation such as realism might advocate military action in one case and no action at all in another case, *depending on the facts of the matter.*

Democratic Realism

The Doctrine
Democratic realism, more commonly referred do as "neoconservatism," is another approach that draws on realism. It deserves attention because of its influence on President George W. Bush and several of his top advisors. The term "neoconservatism" usually refers to a broader set of principles not specifically focused on IR or foreign policy. Some of the leading intellectuals who have advanced these principles include Francis Fukuyama, Robert Kagan, Charles Krauthammer, and Irving and William Kristol. The most influential political actors who support it have been Donald Rumsfeld, Paul Wolfowitz, Douglas Feith, and Richard Pearle.[8]

Democratic realism differs from classical and neorealism much more than the latter two differ from one another. For example, while democratic realism uses several realist principles, it also adopts some key liberal or idealist principles.

Democratic realism's proponents present a doctrine that is an amalgam of realism and liberalism—two theoretical approaches that are generally thought to be incompatible. Democratic realists select only specific principles from each and go so far as to add moral elements that reflect various idealist principles. Like classical realists, democratic realists stress the importance of power in the international system and they doubt the value of institutions; they focus their analysis on the state, which they treat as distinct from the various entities that constitute it (individuals, agencies, etc.). The state is also considered to be distinct from the international system of which it is a part.

Democratic realists differ from classical realists in several important ways. One difference is that democratic realists do not regard the forces of nationalism in the world to be as powerful as the desire among peoples for democratic rights (see Mearsheimer 2005). This is a factual claim that can be subject to tests. A second difference from classical realism is that democratic realism makes claims about how the behavior of democratic states is different from that of nondemocractic states, for example by being more peaceful or at least more peaceful toward other democratic states. This "democratic peace" hypothesis is a core principle of liberalism. Another major difference from classical realism is that democratic realists inject an important moral claim into their theory, namely that the United States should act for moral purposes and that it will be successful if it does so.[9]

Fukuyama offers four principles that have guided democratic realists and neoconservatives. The first is a concern with democracy, human rights, and the internal politics of states. This principle fits well with liberalism but opposes realism and neorealism. The second is a belief that American power can be used for moral purposes, which is closer to liberalism and idealism than it is to realism. The third is a deep skepticism about the ability of international law and institutions to solve serious security problems, which accords with realism and neorealism. And the fourth is a skepticism about ambitious social engineering, since such efforts often lead to unexpected consequences that can undermine the initial purposes (Fukuyama 2006, 4–5).

Democratic realists usually agree with realists or liberals or both on the eight dimensions of IR theories. However, they diverge from both on the moral dimension. Realists and most contemporary liberals can state their theories without overt reference to moral values, whereas the moral dimension is very important for democratic realism. The first two of Fukuyama's four principles draw on moral notions.

Democratic Realism as a Legitimate IR Theory: The Question of Testing
Scholars in the field of IR today do not regard democratic realism or neoconservatism as a legitimate theoretical approach to IR despite the fact that it may have played the role of "theoretical guide" to foreign policy decisions for some prominent officials in the Bush administration. There are at least three main reasons—all connected with testing—that lead scholars to discount democratic realism as a theory of IR. This could, of course, change in the future if the doctrine is reformulated and subjected to appropriate scrutiny. The reservations scholars have at this point concern whether the theory of democratic realism has been specified in a clear enough way to be tested, whether the theory has in fact been tested by scholars in the academic literature, and whether it deserves further consideration given its purported failure to the extent that it has been tested.

One reason scholars have questioned democratic realism as a theory of IR focuses on the fact that proponents of democratic realism have not published their views in scholarly journals of IR. Rather, these views have been published almost exclusively in newspapers, popular journals, or the publication outlets of advocacy groups, like the Project for a New American Century or the

American Enterprise Institute. In contrast to popular journals, scholarly journals in IR (and other fields) use a process of anonymous peer review to test and scrutinize new ideas in the field. This process is intended to scrutinize and evaluate, using widely accepted standards, any new hypotheses and theories. Democratic realism has not gone through this process. Authors who do not support democratic realism have also not tried to formulate it in a way that would allow them to test it. There are only a few articles in IR journals that have sought to examine democratic realism. The authors of these articles include Tunç (2005), Nuruzzaman (2006), and a very brief note by Mearsheimer (2005). Furthermore, the first two focused specifically on the use of the doctrine by American proponents of the invasion of Iraq and have not attempted to test any general propositions of democratic realism.

Specifying democratic realism is hard also because there is no definitive text on democratic realism in foreign policy that provides a focus for discussion comparable to the way that Morgenthau's *Politics Among Nations* or Waltz's *Theory of International Politics* do for classical realism and neorealism. In the debate over what principles lay at the center of democratic realism, proponents have taken Krauthammer's February 2004 lecture at the American Enterprise Institute as a starting point of discussion (see Krauthammer 2004). However, it is important to note that some scholars who define themselves as neoconservatives do not agree with all of Krauthammer's views (see Fukuyama 2004).

The second reason focuses on the fact that democratic realism has not been formulated in a way that would allow for rigorous testing. Some of its principles do appear to be ones that we could subject to tests, but these are mainly principles drawn from realism and liberalism. The unique principles, at least as democratic realism is understood at the present time, are not the sort that could be tested, since they are moral imperatives—that is, statements that say what ought to be done. One example would be Fukuyama's second principle, which is that America should use its power for moral purposes. There is no way to test whether or not this claim is true. As a result, some adjustments need to be made in the way democratic realism is understood, otherwise it cannot be subjected to social science tests. In Chapter 3 we consider in more detail what sort of testing is required.

A third reason why scholars have not treated democratic realism as a full theory of IR is that if we regard it as testable in its current form, it would be testable by a single case: Iraq. That is the only time it has been put into practice. Mearsheimer's article does consider it as testable by the Iraq case, the one case where its principles were followed by policy makers. And Mearshimer clearly states that democratic realism failed, and failed spectacularly, in Iraq. Almost nothing that was predicted by the administration's main neoconservatives occurred. Mearsheimer concludes that it should not be used as a guide to further policy nor should it be considered to have a status above other discredited theories.

Realism and Policy Options

Iraq

Most realists argued against an invasion of Iraq. Some were in favor not because they held different principles, but because they held different factual beliefs about the initial conditions of an invasion, especially facts about the costs and benefits (discussed at the end of this section). But the overwhelming majority of realist theorists in the academic world opposed war in Iraq. One reason is that they believe the benefits of a democracy in the Middle East to be minimal, at best, both because they do not necessarily believe that democracies are more peaceful than nondemocracies, even in their dealings with one another, and because they did not think that a government that truly represents the sentiments of the Iraqi people would be friendly toward America.

In a letter that appeared as an advertisement in the *New York Times* on September 26, 2002, three dozen scholars, many of who are prominent realists, made six main points (Art, et al. 2002):

1. No one has shown evidence that Iraq is cooperating with al-Qaeda.
2. Saddam Hussein could not use nuclear weapons, even if the had them, without suffering massive U.S. or Israeli retaliation.
3. An attempt to conquer Iraq could spread instability in the Middle East, threatening U.S. interests.
4. Iraq could use chemical and biological weapons or urban combat tactics that would impose significant costs to U.S. forces.
5. Even if victory comes easily, the United States has no plausible exit strategy. Because its society is deeply divided, the United States would have to occupy and police Iraq for many years to create a successful state.
6. Al-Qaeda poses a greater threat to the United States than Iraq does, and a war with Iraq will reduce the United States' ability to fight al-Qaeda by increasing anti-Americanism and diverting resources.

Many realists thought that a government that truly represents the sentiments of the Iraqi people may be even more anti-American than Saddam Hussein's government. They reject rationale R3 that states a democratic Iraq would be more peaceful toward the United States. They reject factual rationales such as R1 that says Saddam Hussein transfers money and weapons, at least in any significant degree, to terrorist groups, including al-Qaeda—point 1 of the previous list— and rationale R2 that claims Saddam Hussein has a nuclear weapons program that will soon be able to produce a weapon. And they accepted rationale R10, which says a war in Iraq would tie down the U.S. military and make other threats to use force less effective, point 5 of the previous list. Moreover, many realists accepted R14, that is, they did not think Saddam Hussein posed any significant threat to the United States, since twelve years of sanctions that strangled his economy and his ability to build any sort of weapons that could endanger the United States. These realists did not see any threat-relieving benefit of an invasion, because they did not believe that Iraq posed any real security threat to the United States (see Mearsheimer and Walt 2002; Mearsheimer and Walt 2003).

Realists regard military force as a legitimate policy tool, but they advocate using it only when it will enhance the power of the state. To see this we can turn to the most important realist of the past fifty years, Hans Morgenthau, and note that he argued against escalation of the war in Vietnam on the grounds of the high cost and limited benefits to the United States (Morgenthau 1967). Even a great power has finite resources, and realists like Morgenthau opposed squandering them when there is no likelihood of a substantial benefit. Mearsheimer draws a parallel from Vietnam to Iraq (2005). Mearsheimer has stated that realists who focus on the nation-state as the key actors in IR see the forces of nationalism as having the most powerful effects on state action. He says that nationalism in Vietnam, which meant opposition to America's involvement, overwhelmed positive feelings of liberation from an unwelcome political system. People oppose domination by outsiders more than they oppose an unjust domestic ruler. In Iraq, Mearsheimer argued, the people would resent foreign domination of a Western (and non-Muslim) society more than they would be grateful for liberation from the unjust and violent rule of Saddam Hussein.[10]

Virtually all academic IR theorists in the realist camp opposed going to war in Iraq, arguing that it would hurt rather than help American interests (as the letter cited indicates). However, as Figure 2.1 shows, realism will lead to avoidance of an invasion *only* when combined with a particular view of the relevant facts and certain values. The value we are assuming is that of advancing American national interests. In the case of Iraq there were some realists, especially some in the Bush administration, who viewed the facts differently from most. For realist policy makers who believed that Saddam Hussein was on the verge of developing nuclear weapons, the invasion option appeared more worthwhile than it did to those who held the same theoretical view but believed Iraq had no substantial unconventional arsenal or nuclear program. So the factual beliefs (that may be either true or false) influence which option a reasonable decision maker will choose.

In the Iraq case, as with many important decisions, the president's advisors were divided on the best policy choice. The group was split between classical realists and democratic realists (neoconservatives). The two groups disagreed on whether an invasion of Iraq was good or bad for U.S. interests, especially without broad support of the international community and the UN. In foreign policy speeches and debates during the 2000 campaign, President Bush described himself as a realist, meaning classical realist, on foreign policy. When Bush took office, the self-described realists in the administration, such as Secretary of State Colin Powell and National Security Advisor Condolezza Rice, resisted suggestions in early and mid-2001 to target Iraq. Powell and Rice worked in the administration of President George H. W. Bush, whose foreign policy is often seen as following explicitly realist principles.

Their realist commitments are evident from the foreign policy of the first President Bush, who went to war against Iraq in 1991. At that time the president did not believe that a war inside Iraqi territory, with the aim of ousting Saddam

Hussein, was in the U.S. interest because of the anger it would create in the Muslim world and because of the high costs (Bush and Scowcroft 2002). Realists opposed an invasion of Iraq in 1991 and continued to do so in 2001–2003re. Perhaps because of their realist perspective, they paid little attention to the role of nonstate actors, including al-Qaeda, and downgraded the Clinton administration's efforts to track and destroy al-Qaeda (see Clark 2004). They did not regard al-Qaeda as a threat comparable to that posed by hostile states, at least until the attacks on September 11, 2001.

The Bush administration entered office in 2001 with a group of democratic realists who had been advocating an invasion of Iraq ever since Iraq attacked Kuwait in 1990. During the 1990s many of the people in this group worked together in Washington with The Project for a New American Century to develop and lobby for the doctrine of democratic realism (that is, neoconservatism). According to several accounts of the decision-making process prior to the Iraq invasion, the attacks on the World Trade Center and the Pentagon gave the democratic realists an advantage within the administration (see Daalder and Lindsay 2005; Woodward 2006).

After September 11, the democratic realists were able to persuade the classical realists that there were grave dangers posed by states that support terrorists groups, especially by offering safe havens, financial support, and even weapons. They argued that Iraq might be in a position to offer such support, especially financial help and weapons transfers. The terror attacks on the United States allowed them to push some of the realists to observe new facts or at least reevaluate old ones. They were not necessarily converted to democratic realism. But they came to see some of the facts in a different way and concluded that the cost of leaving Saddam Hussein in power was much greater than they previously believed. In general the way some of the key policy makers who had been regarded as realists throughout their careers came to endorse the invasion option underscores the way in which Figure 2.1 illustrates the process of choosing a policy.[11]

North Korea

There are many versions of realism and, depending on the factual claims that particular realists accept, a foundation may be found for any of the first three policy options previously noted toward North Korea: military force to bring about regime change, diplomatic and economic isolation, and containment. Some realists hold that states do not make significant internal changes (regime changes) on the basis of moral suasion or external pressure; only force will be likely to work. Realists hold that this emphasis on regime survival means that leaders will not give up power unless they are forced out. Thus military force, such as air strikes, would be the only way to bring down the North Korean regime; no level of escalation of economic pressure and sanctions will succeed. Thus U.S. interests would be advanced, in the view of many realists, by forcible destruction of the regime of Kim Jong-il.

Realists do not believe that international systems experience progress; rather, patterns recur. When conditions change behavior changes, but the changes do not transform the system from one set of rules to another. Because patterns endure until conditions change, Realists observe that the pattern of containing North Korea has worked ever since the end of the Korean War, thus it is likely to work in the future. Some realists add that even if it were to acquire nuclear weapons, there still would be no incentive for a rational North Korea to initiate a war that it knows will result in its utter destruction. Realists hold that North Korea has behaved badly, and bad behavior should not be rewarded with improved relations and concessions from the United States and South Korea. Some realists, notably Kenneth Waltz (1981), argue that as states acquire nuclear weapons they are rationally forced to behave more cautiously because they know that other states cannot dismiss their actions as harmless and as unlikely to have consequences. These realists hold that the rest of the world will more closely scrutinize the behavior of a leader who possesses nuclear weapons. For these realists, isolation or containment are most likely to lead to peace and the advancement of U.S. interests.

China

Realists generally expect the United States to come into conflict with China. As this book has repeatedly noted, theories help us choose a policy only after we have a set of goals and beliefs about the specific conditions. Most realists look at the conditions and are struck, just as liberals are, by the rapid growth in China's economy. What do realists make of China's economic growth? Realists who believe it will continue worry about conflict with the United States. A minority of realists are not concerned about future conflict because they believe the Chinese economy will soon slow down or even decline. There are several lines of argument that lead them to expect conflict. One is the relationship of industrialization and economic power to ambitions in foreign policy. They note that when a state develops industrial might, it acquires grand foreign policy ambitions.

For example, they note that when Great Britain developed as an industrial power and experienced rapid economic growth, it also built a very powerful military force, the Royal Navy, and challenged other states over much of the globe. The rise of France as an economic power brought with it an attempt to dominate Europe under Napoleon and also an empire in Africa and the Middle East. Germany experienced rapid economic growth as a result of industrialization and unification and proceeded to build a military designed to challenge Britain and France, which led to two world wars. Japan's economic growth after its defeat of Russia in 1905 led to a highly ambitious foreign policy and an empire in the Pacific. And the industrialization and economic growth of the United States led to conquest across North America, adventurous foreign policy actions in Central and South America, and hundreds of military bases spread across the globe.

The mechanism for this process can be described simply. Leaders will seek to expand territory to suit the purposes of the leadership, since they tend to believe that holding more territory and controlling more people gives them more power. If they do not choose this policy path, they may be challenged by someone who promises to pursue it and to spread the wealth to key groups in exchange for their support. In weaker states those making such promises will fail to fulfill them. But in states whose power exceeds its territorial holdings, ambitious leaders will succeed.

China is not only large in population and economically successful, but it fits into a category of countries that IR scholars call "rising powers." Some realists argue that the historical record shows that these are the most troublesome and instability-producing countries. Such countries endured a period when the rules of the system were established, which usually occurs after a great power war. The rules deal with how border disputes are settled, what states are permitted to do, what rules govern trade, and so on. If these rising powers were weak at the time, then the sorts of rules that would give them advantages were probably not incorporated into the system. China was a weak and desperately poor state in 1945 when the last great power war ended. As a rising power today, China will desire changes in the rules of the system. And such states, when the reach a certain point of capability, feel that they can get what they want by military means. So realists argue that these rising powers are difficult to satisfy.

In the case of China, as noted in Chapter 1, the biggest injustice that the post-World War II system produced was the world's willingness to treat Taiwan as a separate entity (even though it has been described in different ways legally). Most of the world has accepted that Taiwan may disregard the laws of the People's Republic of China, make independent decisions about its own economy, purchase weapons from foreign countries, and so forth. Realists thus believe that China will be working to bring the now-affluent Taiwanese into the PRC one way or another. If Taiwan does not agree to the PRC's terms, the PRC will use violence. The arms that the PRC is developing rapidly, which many realists say will be used to intimidate Taiwan into submitting to the rule of the PRC or to invade if intimidation fails, create further problems in Asia. Other countries, especially Japan, cannot be sure that all of those weapons are being built solely for the purpose of intimidating Taiwan and not for intimidating them as well.

Some realists claim that states wish to dominate the world but acknowledge that because of the size of the globe and the vast oceans, this is a practical impossibility. Thus the ultimate goal that states can realistically pursue is to become a true hegemon in their own region and to develop military and economic means to prevent any other state from becoming a hegemon in any other region (see especially Mearsheimer 2001). On this view China will seek to become a hegemon in East Asia and the United States (like any hegemon) will try to preserve its hegemony in the North American system and at the same time prevent any other state from becoming a hegemon in that *or any other* region. Those realists clearly expect that the United States will face a direct conflict with China. Some of the recent works that deal with the challenge that China will pose for the United States in the coming decades have ominous titles like, *The Coming Conflict with China* (Bernstein and Munro 1997), *Playing with Fire: The Looming War with China over Taiwan* (Copper 2006), *Hegemon: China's Plan to Dominate Asia and the World* (Mosher 2000), and *The New Chinese Empire and What it Means for the United States* (Terrill 2003).

Thus realists who believe China will be able to sustain its economic growth believe that conflict with the United States is almost certain. The United States should pursue policies that advance its own national interests, which means creating the most favorable conditions for the eventual conflict with China. They would either advocate isolating China from the benefits of trade in the world economy—which they say China is taking unfair advantage of anyway, such as by artificial currency rates—or by specifically preparing for a war with China that is to come.[12]

Liberalism

The Liberal Tradition and the Eight Dimensions of Theory

The tradition of liberalism has roots far in the past. Historians, philosophers, jurists, and theologians have written about international politics, viewing it as capable of exhibiting cooperation, harmony, peaceful co-existence, and world government. Immanuel Kant, Adam Smith, and John Stuart Mill are considered some of the seminal thinkers in the liberal tradition of politics and economics. In IR, liberals often draw on Kant's 1795 essay "Perpetual Peace." Liberals reject many of the principles that realists endorse and adopt a much more cooperative image of world politics.

Liberals typically agree with realists that states pursue their own self-interest in a rational way. But they disagree with realists by holding that states do not define their self-interest in terms of a zero-sum framework. Liberals hold that states look at their options in terms of absolute gain. Thus when a liberal looks at national leaders evaluating options in a crisis, as in Figure 2.2, the liberal theorist would expect a leader to consider absolute gain and thus seek the top left, C-C, outcome. They also differ with realists by arguing that some governments are flawed and do not represent the true self-interest of the state but rather pursue private self-interest.

Until about the mid-eighteenth century, liberals emphasized that the goal of liberty would be undercut by the actions and interference of government. Liberals analyzed political issues by stressing that an enlightened human being was capable of recognizing her best interests and pursuing those interests in a way that need not infringe on the rights of others. Liberals believed outside interference in actors' harmonious pursuit of their interests would create conflict and problems. They held that this principle applied both to politics (freedom of expression, association, religion) and economics. And they believed that it applied on both the state level and the international system level. Liberal political theorists believed that justice would be achieved if liberty could be maximized and the elements of government could be kept in balance. Thus government structures devised in the eighteenth century stressed checks and balances. The U.S. constitution is a notable example, using precisely this mechanism as it seeks to create domestic tranquility and harmony.

With respect to economics, limited interference by the central government would allow each actor to produce what was most needed in each society. If producers were to make goods that were not needed, prices would fall and profits would decline; there would thus be an incentive for them to stop or reduce production until supply declined enough to cause a price increase sufficient to make producing the goods profitable once again. Supply and demand will stay in balance as long as producers have enough information about markets, are enlightened in producing what would benefit them, and are allowed to make their own decisions about what to produce and how much. The notion of the "invisible hand," developed by the eighteenth-century liberal economist Adam Smith, captures this image of economics.

The liberal view in IR was similiar. In the late seventeenth and most of the eighteenth century the world was often seen as one of balance. There were roughly a half dozen great powers that aligned and realigned over time, as conditions changed. States would seek their own self-interest rather than the overall good of the system as they aligned to create the smallest coalition that could protect their national security. But the result would be that the system would stay in balance. This parallels to the way in which individual economic producers, in seeking to maximize their own profit interests, end up keeping the overall economic system stable. Once states' full sovereignty was recognized in 1648 the Peace of Westphalia, ending the Thirty Years' War, it appeared that large-scale war in Europe would be prevented. Relative peace will prevail if outside forces like the Catholic Church are banished from world politics (which was largely accomplished by the Peace of Westphalia) and states simply do what they ordinarily do, that is, form alliances and reform alliances when conditions change.

By the late eighteenth century, liberals had to rethink both their domestic and international theories, especially regarding the conditions that lead to harmony and cooperation. Outside intervention was increasingly seen as necessary for, and not an obstacle to, balance and harmony in the system. On the domestic side, the industrial revolution made it harder for producers to switch from one product to another and for individuals to compete against larger firms. More government regulation was seen as necessary to keep a competitive balance. On the international scene, the balance of the great powers came to an end, not by the Church interfering from the outside but by the conquest of much of Europe by one great power, Napoleonic France. Thus liberals came to prefer more regulation on the domestic side and intervening institutions on the international side.

Realists dismiss the importance of institutions, arguing that anarchy is basic to all international systems and allows the powerful states to achieve outcomes they favor in a way proportional to the amount of power they have. The existing rules, norms, institutions, or organizations in any system were created by the great powers to serve their interests. The outcomes achieved when institutions are used are essentially the same as what would result if there were no institutions. Liberals strongly disagree with realists on this and emphasize that peace and cooperation are more likely in some international systems than in others. The rules, norms, and institutions that exist have an effect on prospects for cooperation.

Liberals believe that the conflict-promoting effects of anarchy can be reduced or overcome by the right sorts of institutions. Those who are referred to here as "liberals" are more likely to see the need to create institutions as a matter of national self-interest, for example, to help prevent destructive wars. Liberals admit that anarchy has no mechanisms to reduce the likelihood that disputes between states will escalate to war but hold that there is nothing preventing enlightened leaders from creating violence-preventing institutions. States' interests are not fundamentally in conflict. If appropriate institutions are created, states will be able to communicate, negotiate, produce agreements, and expect compliance, and all parties will benefit from these developments. The underlying interests of states are in harmony. The effects of anarchy that promote, or at least permit, conflict to escalate can be overcome; a solution would allow states to act on the underlying harmony of interests among them.

While realists assume that one state's gain is a rival state's loss, liberals see many situations in which two or more rival states all improve their situations. One of the clearest examples was the super-power nuclear standoff during the second half of the last century. By the late 1960s both the United States and the Soviet Union had the capacity to wipe out most of the population and industrial capacity of the other side and its allies, and neither side had anything beyond negligible defenses able to stop an attack if the other side chose to launch one. But if one side should attack, the other would be able to deliver a retaliatory strike inflicting almost as much damage. Why did neither side ever attack during the decades when doing so was well within their reach? Liberals would say it was because both sides considered absolute gain. Even though the side that absorbs the first strike would probably be a bit more damaged than the side that launched the first strike, neither side viewed the exchange as beneficial. Each side preferred to accept rough equality of power with the other.

Liberal theories have a range of different *units of analysis*. Some theories focus on the individual level, some on the state level, some on the system level, and some include nonstate actors. For those theories, the different types of states—democratic, socialist, authoritarian—will adopt different foreign policies, which is a point realists deny. Some of the most widely held liberal theories today differ from traditional liberal theories by emphasizing the system as the unit of analysis. They are generally referred to as "neoliberal" or as "neoliberal institutionalist" theories. The most influential proponents are Robert O. Keohane, Joseph Nye, and Lisa Martin. According to neoliberalism, a system with certain types of regimes, which operate across the system, will behave differently from a system that is otherwise similar but lacks those regimes. The term "regime" refers to "a set of rules, norms, patterns of behavior and decision-making procedures around which actors' expectations converge" (Krasner 1982, 186). These theorists stress the efficacy for the promotion of cooperation of international regimes.

According to neoliberal institutionalists the effects of anarchy can be mitigated by the development of the proper sorts of regimes. Regimes facilitate cooperation by reducing "transaction costs" and by spreading accurate information more evenly throughout the international system. Knowing they have better information, states will have to worry less about miscalculations, which could lead a cooperative action to produce an unwanted outcome. Keohane and Nye (1977) also argue that the realist focus on power is mistaken; there are different "issue areas" other than the military-diplomatic area, like energy, textiles, and telecommunications. And states that are powerful, and get their way, in one issue area may not be as powerful in another area. Realists hold that states that dominate in a way of military power will get their way in other areas. Keohane and Nye argued in the 1970s that states like Japan and Saudi Arabia, which were exercising major influence in industrial trade and energy, respectively, and causing the United States and European states much trouble, were negligible military powers. They concluded that there is no overarching hierarchy of issues; states with power in one area will have an ability to shape affairs in the area that is not a reflection of its military power.

Liberals agree with realists that states generally behave *rationally* and that *states' identities and preferences are fixed*. Indeed liberalism generally assumes that states do behave rationally, but the goals they rationally pursue are different from what realists posit. Still, liberals and realists agree that states have fixed identities and rationally pursue an enduring set of goals.

Liberals do not believe the world must remain as it has been—a series of wars followed by periods of exhaustion and rebuilding for the next war. Some argue that the cycle has already been broken, and great power war might already have been rendered obsolete. So liberals hold that *progress is entirely possible*. They hold that states can continue to create an increasingly peaceful world, which, although anarchical, need not be one of open hostility. Cooperation under anarchy is possible; indeed, it is rational. Liberals adopt the "democratic peace" claim that mature democracies do not go to war against one another. Thus they have argued that the world will become more peaceful as more states become democratic. In general, it is in a state's interest to look for ways to cooperate under anarchy, which is illustrated by the superpowers' nuclear standoff during the cold war.

Liberals take issue with Hobbes's realist argument about the impossibility of overcoming anarchy and of making the *international* political system more like the *domestic* political system. Many plans for world government have been put forward over the centuries. Some advocate a gradual strengthening of the system of international law that now exists, while others advocate a more abrupt transition to hierarchy. Liberals are more likely to seek international institutions as a way of creating new incentive structures to induce states to cooperate rather than a system of international law modeled on domestic law.

Wealthy countries that provide foreign aid and financial support to poor countries are common in the twenty-first century. Realists argue that these actions are insignificant because they constitute such a small portion of resources, as measured by the gross domestic product (GDP) of even the most generous states. The three most generous donors are Denmark, the Netherlands, and Norway, which give respectively 0.93 percent, 0.83 percent, and 0.76 percent. The United States is the twenty-first most generous and gives just 0.05 percent of its GDP. Realists do not believe that states act altruistically on important questions. They admit that minor policy decisions of this sort may not be based strictly on national-interest calculation. Some realists, however, contend that even foreign aid donations serve national interest goals, since they are often intended to induce the aid recipient to take a more positive attitude toward the donor—or at least to avoid becoming too friendly with the recipient's rivals. For example, the Soviet Union offered aid to Egypt in order to prevent Western powers from having free access to the Suez Canal. Similarly, after 1979 the United States offered aid to Egypt to promote stability in the region by reducing conflict between Israel and its most dangerous adversary, Egypt. This in turn would reduce the chance that oil deliveries would be disrupted again, as they had been a few years earlier when Arab oil producers instituted a boycott.

Liberals differ sharply from realists on the question of what renders the behavior of states *legitimate*, especially as concerns the use of force. For liberals it is important that states behave according to existing norms and laws. Thus unilateral or multilateral military action is not legitimate and should not be tolerated unless it is approved by the authorizing international body, or is clearly within the bounds of accepted norms and laws, such as self defense.

Liberalism and Idealism

Idealism has a great deal of overlap with liberalism. The two are essentially the same on five of the eight dimensions listed previously and are not far apart on two of the remaining three. The clearest difference regards the *role of morals*. Many of the same figures are considered seminal in both traditions, such as Kant as a theorist and Woodrow Wilson as a practitioner. Thomas Aquinas and Saint-Simon also injected a moral element into theories of inter-state politics.

Like all of the other terms for theories, "idealism" is used loosely and there is no consistent distinction between it and "liberalism." The most prominent difference, as just noted, is the explicitly moral component of idealism. Idealists generally hold that human beings have moral obligations that cannot be escaped under any circumstances. They believe that the responsibilities of a leader of a nation-state might increase because of the leadership position, but that the leadership position never excuses a person from the obligation to act morally. Often liberals and idealists will agree on the best solutions to policy problems in international relations, but the liberals typically justify them by emphasizing that it is in the long-term self-interest of the state to adopt those policies, while idealists are more explicit in injecting a moral dimension.

Idealists believe that the *moral motivation* to create a better world is sufficient to guide major policy decisions. The right leaders with the right understanding of their duties, obligations, and responsibilities can reach accord. For idealists, foreign aid shows that it is possible for states to commit resources simply for the purpose of doing what is right and helping others. With the right leaders and the right institutions, these altruistic actions could become much more widespread.

Since idealist theories generally include moral imperatives and since most moral theories hold that individuals most clearly have moral obligations, they often operate at the individual level. It is harder to make the case that states, bureaucracies, or systems have moral obligations. Idealist theories are also more likely to emphasize human rights as an important part of international relations, but in their view institutions can be effective. The absence of proper systemic institutions in the world at any given time often leads authors to a system-level focus. Realists, especially the many who focus the analysis on states, cannot easily fit the importance of human rights into a theory of state-to-state behavior.

There is a third, rather minor, difference between liberal and idealist theories on "rationality." Idealists do not look at material means-ends considerations in the way that realists and liberals do. Idealists say that states sometimes follow a value-laden ideology or that they follow moral imperatives. These may be pursued "rationally" in a broader sense of the term. These theorists also hold that preferences, goals, and components of identity are fixed. (C2) Realists have criticized liberalism for not being able to account for the larger events of the past century; realists and behavioralists criticize idealism for its reliance on moral principles, as such principles cannot be proved with certainty or even established in a way that elicits broad approval. Proponents of idealism emphasize that its stress on bringing moral values back to IR theory is a strength of their view.

Liberalism and Policy Actions

Iraq

Liberals differed from the unilateral approach to the invasion of Iraq taken by some realists. Liberals generally argued that an invasion should be a cooperative effort among many countries or should not be undertaken at all. They pointed to the model of the 1991 war against Iraq in Kuwait in which the UN Security Council authorized the war and the United States built a coalition against Iraq that consisted of nearly three dozen members of the coalition, including many from the Middle East. France and the UK had major combat roles and, perhaps more importantly from the United States' point of view, coalition members other than the United States paid 88 percent of the financial cost of the war. In contrast, the unilateral invasion of Iraq in 2003, even with the ground forces role of the UK and with token material support or verbal approval of other countries, was not a truly cooperative effort. In a number of cases, rather than the coalition members paying the financial costs, the United States offered financial inducements to other states to join the coalition, that is, to allow the United States to use bases on their territory or even to provide verbal support. Some of the American financial offers were rejected, most notably by Turkey where bases were very important to U.S. logistical plans.

Some liberals believed that there were both internal and international justifications for removing Saddam Hussein from power and creating a democracy in Iraq. They placed a high priority on the human rights of those individuals who were seriously oppressed under Saddam Hussein; democracy, if it could be instituted, would create the conditions for their liberation. (Idealists other than pacifists do support the use of armed force under some circumstances. It was

President Wilson who enthusiastically led the United States into World War I.) Liberals also took seriously the view that democratic states do not usually, or ever, go to war with other democracies. They thus believed that the cause of peace would be advanced if Saddam Hussein were removed from power. But liberals held that the war would be illegitimate without sanctioning of the authoritative international legal body, which in this case was the UN Security Council. Since the UN never passed a resolution specifically approving the use of force by the United States and coalition members against Iraq, most liberals regarded the war as illegitimate. Liberals and idealists often supported the use of force if it should be sanctioned by the UN but not otherwise.

North Korea

In the case of North Korea, liberalism may be used most directly to justify containment or the sunshine policy. Liberal theories embody principles such as the benefits of interdependence, multilateralism, avoiding worst-case planning, and the idea that enlightened citizens will choose democracy. According to liberals, interdependence reduces the incentives for war and conflict. The sunshine policy advocates increasing the interactions with North Korea, which provide benefits it will eventually come to rely on. Once North Korea comes to expect these benefits, the threat of removing them becomes a fulcrum on which the United States and allies can gain leverage to influence North Korean behavior to be more cooperative and to obey international norms. The liberal principle of multilateralism bolsters the sunshine policy approach by holding that the many states working together in institutions to promote North Korean cooperation will be more effective than if individual states try to do so unilaterally. The threat of removing benefits is far more effective if the benefits of interaction with many countries are at stake rather than punishment solely by the United States.

Liberalism also allows a state to avoid the costs of worst-case planning. By advancing the ideas that all rival parties should offer incremental concessions and increasingly significant confidence-building measures, all parties come to know more about the others' capabilities, strategies, and intentions. This in turn allows the United States, South Korea, and Japan to plan for a somewhat narrower range of possible actions by North Korea, which reduces the most extreme of the worst-case scenarios. The United States and its allies will save money by having fewer dangerous scenarios to plan for, and they will have a decreased chance of escalation to war resulting from misinterpretations of the other side's actions and intentions. On these grounds a liberal may advocate the sunshine policy.

Finally, the general liberal principle that enlightened citizens will demand democratic rights and liberties. If North Koreans see what is going on around them they will see that other systems are better and how they would benefit from living under a different, more democratic system. This aspect of liberalism also helps to ground the sunshine policy. Only through increased interactions with the outside world can North Koreans come to see what the rest of the world is like.[13]

China

Liberals are hopeful that the future will hold greater cooperation between the United States and China. They regard all states as having the potential to work together for mutual benefit. They regard peaceful relations as highly likely if three processes continue, namely democratization, international trade, and integration into international organizations and institutions.

On trade they note that the value of goods and services moving between the United States and China has increased from $1 billion in 1980 to $120 billion in 2000 and then to $240 billion in 2004.[14] There has also been a great deal of U.S. investment in China in recent years. Between 1990 and 2000, U.S. investment increased from $354 million to $9.58 billion. Liberals cite China's entry into the WTO in 2001 as evidence supporting both the proposition about international organizations and the proposition about economic interdependence and trade.[15] The trends are running powerfully in favor of greater trade and financial interdependence. China has also gotten very busy joining a variety of international organizations (see Richardson 1994).

Liberals believe that international cooperation is possible but difficult to achieve because of distrust, uncertainty, and the security dilemma. If state A cannot know what state B is planning, then A must prepare for the worst, which could drive B to prepare to counter A's preparations. Liberals believe that membership in international institutions can do a great deal to reduce this sort of uncertainty and the tension it produces. Liberals are generally very happy to point out China's extensive involvement in institutions over the past decade. China has come to play a role in Asia-Pacific Economic Cooperation (APEC), Association of Southeast Asian Nations (ASEAN), the East Asia Summit, and, in 1996, the Nuclear Nonproliferation Treaty (NPT). Overall China's membership in international organizations (including both IGOs and NGOs) has gone from 71 in 1977 to 1,163 in 1997. If China is a central part of the existing international system, it will be less likely to work to overturn it, either by peaceful or violent means. Thus liberals hold that China's gaining a large stake in the existing international order in East Asia will keep it working to maintain stability. The many organizations that include both the United States and China have been leading to better and more cooperative relations between the two states, and will continue to do so.

People desire control of their own lives, according to liberals, and living under a democracy greatly helps to achieve that control. Liberals accept that democratic states are very unlikely to go to war with one another. So if China were to democratize—and some liberals argue that it is (see Rowen 1996)—it would be very unlikely to go to war with the United States. The relationship would be much like that between the United States and other major states, even nuclear-weapons-possessing states like the UK, France, and even Russia.

Liberals hold that the process of democratization, economic interdependence, and international institutions, not only promote peace individually but also reinforce one another with regard to their effects on peace. For example, greater economic integration demonstrates the need for democratization because investment will continue to flow from democratic industrial states only if states like China encourage more widely available communication and the free flow of information. The latter makes tyrannical rule more difficult and enhances the rule of law, which is essential for the enforcement of contracts. Great powers can get along well if they are all democratic. Thus liberals would recommend a policy of engagement and concessions to push China to continue democratization. Democratization will come sooner or later to China, and they hold that it will be sooner if China is brought into international organizations and the world economy. As China democratizes it will enter what liberals call the "zone of peace" inside of which states like Canada, the Netherlands, the UK, and the United States do not even consider military force against others.[16]

Constructivism

Constructivism was initially developed in the social sciences and in IR as a metatheory. After the first decade in which authors published self-consciously constructivist works in IR, critics charged that constructivism had provided little in the way of substantive knowledge, or even hypotheses, about the behavior of states or state systems. However, since the mid-1990s a number of authors have taken up the challenge and tried to apply constructivist principles to IR in a way that will produce a substantive theory of behavior. The argument against constructivism as an IR theory is that it has not yet emerged from its origins as a metatheory about how the social sciences operate. However, the extensive efforts to develop substantive constructivist principles over the past decade warrant that it be taken as an IR theory.

This section looks at the principles proposed by current constructivists. (Whether a scholar could abandon or loosen some of them and still remain a constructivist is considered in later chapters.) Constructivist scholars argue that the international system is "socially constructed," that is, consists of the ways in which human beings think and interact with one another. They hold that the international system, because it is socially constructed, does not have an existence distinct from human conceptions of it. Constructivists claim that there are also important sociological and cultural dimensions of any international system. Constructivists say that IR theorists have been led into error by having ignored this sociological dimension. In their view the social relationships exist alongside material factors, such as territory, armies, arms, and gold in the treasury. Constructivists also hold that the *identities and preferences* of the actors are *shaped* in part *by these structures*. They come from beyond the political realm that IR scholars study and are not fixed or unchanging. The specific cultural characteristics and norms of a society shape how actors in that society choose to act. Instead of conceiving all states as acting on the same set of goals, constructivists hold that the goals can change and that the political or strategic culture of a state might affect its behavior.

The term "constructivism" in IR is applied to two very different sorts of enterprises. One is the development of a metatheory that tells us what social science theories can and cannot do. The other, which this section will consider, deals with the development of a substantive theory about how the international system behaves. On the metatheory side, there are disagreements within constructivists about how much IR is like the natural sciences. In the United States the dominant constructivist metatheory has attempted to permit natural science-like theorizing. Other versions of constructivism reject scientific-style theorizing and stress the interpretive nature of social science and other sciences. Those versions are more explicitly normative and are skeptical about what empirical theory can achieve. In this section we consider the substantive principles presented by authors who describe themselves as constructivists. The view that constructivism is essentially a metatheory will be considered in Chapter 4, as constructivism is treated as a challenge to philosophy of science doctrines of naturalism, rationalism, and materialism.

An array of recent theories in IR such as poststructuralism, neo-Marxism, reflectivism, and some versions of feminism share constructivism's central insight that systems of IR are, at least in part, socially constructed. Sometimes the entire array of theories is termed "critical international relations." The most influential exponents of standard or American constructivism are Emmanuel Adler (who incidentally is not an American), Nicholas Onuf, John Gerard Ruggie, and Alexander Wendt. Two claims that separate constructivism from the traditions of realism/neorealism and liberalism/idealism, according to Wendt, are that social structures have both material and social components and that the identities and preferences of the actors result from several influences, including these social structures. This chapter takes the influential version of Wendt as sort of constructivism to be described.[17]

Scholars in the constructivist camp agree with liberals on the possibility of states maximizing *absolute gain*, the applicability of the *domestic-international analogy*, the possibility of *overcoming* the peace-constraining *effects of anarchy* and the importance of *institutions and legitimacy* in international behavior. The most recent wave of constructivist theories embraced a good deal of naturalism and consider norms and moral values as variables to help describe and explain behavior. Other constructivists agree with idealists that theories should be developed to serve moral purposes, particularly those of social justice and liberation of oppressed social groups. Wendt has especially noted the liberal theoretical tendencies of constructivists and has tried to build a bridge between constructivist metatheory and liberal IR theory. Constructivists hold that the internal constitution of a state, including the way its leaders and population understand and describe the international system, is highly relevant to how the state will behave toward others.

Constructivism accords with realism in accepting the principle that the *international system is anarchic*. Constructivists agree with realists on several other points: that states have offensive capabilities; that states can never be fully certain that they will not be attacked; and that states desire to survive. But the way in which constructivists understand the international system is different from realists and neorealists. Constructivists agree with liberals that when certain norms and regimes are present, many of the difficulties of cooperation that anarchy brings with it can be overcome.

Constructivism is unique among IR theories in having been developed from the ground up by its supporters beginning with philosophical and methodological foundations. One of the most influential constructivists, Emanuel Adler says that constructivism consists of "a three-layered understanding—(1) involving metaphysics, (2) social theory and (3) IR theory and research strategies" (2002, 96). The first two are considered in the next two chapters and the third in this chapter. (See also the four-layered typology, "Four levels and a Discipline," of Jørgensen 2001, and Chapter 4.)

Like contemporary versions of liberalism (neoliberal institutionalism) and realism (neorealism), the most popular constructivist theories operate on the system level of analysis. All emphasize the importance of understanding international systems in order to understand world politics. However, constructivism sees itself as "more structuralist" than neorealism in that Waltz's neorealism, for example, relies heavily on the (very individualist) analogy with micro-economics to show how systems behave (Wendt 1995). Some recent scholars have emphasized that constructivist theories can operate at levels other than the system level.

A major difference between constructivists and all other sorts of theorists (realists and liberals) is the constructivists' conception of the nature of *systems and agents* in world politics. States' *identities and preferences are neither fixed nor unchanging* and differ from one state to another. Rather, states' identities and preferences are influenced by the character of the particular international system that they constitute. The international system is, in turn, shaped by the particular features of its states. The identities and interests of the states and the characteristics of the international system influence each other—they are thus said to be *co-generative* or *mutually constitutive.*

Constructivists stress that the capabilities are only a part of what theorists must take into account; they must also consider *shared knowledge* and *practices.* What the actor is—its identity—is shaped by its knowledge, beliefs, and expectations. We can imagine systems in which actors do not *expect conflict* and see how such systems would differ from those in which states had a clear expectation of conflict. Constructivists here take up the insight of English school authors Hedley Bull, Herbert Butterfield, and Martin Wight who argue that there may be different forms of anarchy. An anarchical system with states socialized the way Waltz describes, that is, to expect conflict (Hobbesian anarchy), is only one of various possible ways in which anarchy might develop. There may be other forms of anarchy in which states try to cooperate when they can (Lockean) or in which they see a clear harmony of interests among them (Kantian).

Two particular examples are helpful in illustrating the constructivist view that the international system has a social character in addition to its material character. The first is that after 1990 the United States and the Soviet Union ceased beaving strictly as rivals after doing so since 1945. But they changed not because there was a war or any sudden material change in the system (and such abrupt change is usually the result of war), but because they began to *believe* that the cold war was over; that is, they began to think about the international system differently. It was a change in the body of "shared knowledge" that changed behavior and the system. While constructivists regard the material distribution of power as important, beliefs, ideas, and values can also change states' behavior and, in turn, the character of the international system.

The second example is a comparison of the U.S.-UK relationship and the U.S.-North Korean relationship. If the UK builds new nuclear weapons the United States does not have to worry about what to do to counteract that development. However, if North Korea were to develop a large arsenal of nuclear weapons, the United States would be very worried and would either try to dissuade North Korea from deploying the weapons or try to develop defensive systems to protect against them. The material capability is just as real in both cases, but the reaction of U.S. policy makers is completely different. The conclusion constructivists draw is that the difference is not a result of the material changes, since we are imagining the material capabilities to be equivalent in the two cases, but of how policy makers think about the material changes.

We note that (C3) constructivism pays much closer attention to norms and values than other contemporary versions of realism and liberalism. This is seen as a strength by many of its supporters. Some of the critics have attacked constructivism's record of having produced very little in the way of specific substantive principles that are falsifiable. This is changing, however, as constructivism has recently gained many more adherents who are now employing its principles to develop empirical propositions.[18] Chief criticisms of the three theories are summarized in Table 2.2.

Constructivism and Policy Choices

When faced with policy choices constructivists would presumably aim for those that support the goals and moral norms the theory endorses. Policies must add to

Table 2.2 Principle criticisms of major IR theories

C1	Realism	with its emphasis on states pursuing self-interest, is sometimes criticized for being unable to be "falsified"—whatever a state does may be argued after the fact to have been believed by the leaders to be in the state's interests.
C2	Liberalism	is unable to account for the large events of the past century; realists and behavioralists criticize idealism for its reliance on moral principles, which are difficult to prove with certainty or even in a way that allows wide agreement. Proponents of idealism emphasize that its stress on bringing moral values back to IR theory is a strength of the view.
C3	Constructivism	pays much closer attention to norms and values than other contemporary versions of realism and liberalism, which has led some critics to argue that constructivism's record thus far has produced very little in the way of specific substantive principles of international behavior.

shared knowledge in such a way as to help create a more peaceful and egalitarian world, resist hegemonic control, and advance human emancipation. Theories and policies should both be designed to further those ends. Constructivists' desire to create new shared knowledge[19] and beliefs that would contribute to such goals.

Iraq

In the case of Iraq, four policy choices were outlined in Chapter 1. Given what has just been said about the theory of constructivism, a policy maker who adopts that theory would not choose the first option—unilateral invasion—since it lacks grounding in law or norms and "constructs" a norm in which hegemonic powers use force against weaker ones. The second option would seem possible, assuming continued noncompliance by Iraq, since a multilateral attack on Iraq with authorization of the UN would support the norms that constructivists endorse, such as the promotion of a system in which force is used only when it is authorized by a legitimating international body. This option also offers the emancipation of oppressed groups inside Iraq. The third option, that of increasing the monitoring of suspected Iraqi weapons production and storage sites, is also consistent with constructivism, since it, more than any of the other options, would add to the store of shared knowledge in the international system. The fourth option, doing nothing, would not be appealing to a constructivist policy maker. If the leaders believed that international law was being ignored by Saddam Hussein, something should be done. Constructivists hold that ignoring violations of international law seriously weakens it. And international law is one of the most important ways in which the right sort of shared perceptual framework can be created. Two important constructivists in particular have written extensively about law in this regard, Kratochwil (1989 and 2006) and Onuf (1989 and 1998).

Constructivists would choose either the second or third option, perhaps leaning toward the third—disarmament though increased inspections. Invasion would be less appealing because of the powerful way in which high-profile and high-impact behavior shapes how people, leaders, and states think about world politics. It reinforces the notion that force of arms is an acceptable way of solving problems. Using force and killing innocent civilians lends legitimacy to the idea that the use of violence is acceptable. While there may be some cases where there are no other reasonable options, in March of 2003 a big increase in the monitoring system was available as an alternative.

North Korea

Ordinarily each theory is consistent with more than a single policy choice. However, in the case of the four options laid out for U.S. policy toward North Korea, constructivism is more consistent with the sunshine policy than with any of the other three policies. There are two general principles of constructivism that relate to policy: the effect of state action on the sociological character of the system and the role of shared knowledge in opening up secure options. Constructivists argue that security dilemmas arise in only one type of anarchical system—the Hobbesian system. There may be other anarchical systems with different sociological characteristics. Other systems may be more Lockean or Kantian. Every action either moves the system toward one sort of sociological structures or reinforces the existing structure. The sunshine policy of greater interaction with, and less isolation of, North Korea was justified by the claim that, as North Korea becomes more fearful of its military vulnerability, it will take more steps to reduce those feelings of vulnerability. Acting on such a rationale is justified by the constructivist claim that the sociological character of systems can be changed by the actions of the units of the system.

Constructivism also holds that greater trust and confidence in other states within the system reduces the need for worst-case scenario planning. If states do not have to plan for such dire situations and scenarios, then they might offer incremental concessions and perhaps negotiate confidence-building measures that increase cooperation. The sunshine policy is thus justified by general constructivist principles, one of which overlaps with the liberal justification for pursuing confidence-building measures.

China

Constructivists tend to see China as a potential strategic partner of the United States and the West, if the proper norms are instituted, though some constructivists may dissent on this point (see Chapter 1 and Friedberg 2005, 37–39). Constructivists believe that specific choices made over a long period affect the character of the system. Different international systems may have their own cultural norms and characteristics, and specific states may have their own identities and cultural traits.

For constructivists, how the international system operates depends largely on the process of socialization of the various member states, especially the most influential members. If a state has a culture of isolation, it may be harder to engage. The traits of states and systems endure for long periods, but they are subject to gradual change. When constructivists consider China's identity, culture, and norms, they note significant shifts in the past several decades, especially since the death of Mao Zedong.

During Mao's lifetime China worked closely with other socialist states, such as North Korea, North Vietnam, and, until the 1960s, the Soviet Union. We noted that relations with the Soviet Union were good during the Chinese civil war, after 1949, and up through the late 1950s, but started to decline in the 1960s. China also developed a strategic relationship with non-socialist Pakistan in order to keep pressure on India, China's enormously populous neighbor to the south. The United States' courting of China, marked by Kissinger's and then Nixon's visits to China in 1971–1972, was a watershed in opening China up to the rest of the world. The process of opening to the world accelerated after Mao's death and still more with the end of the cold war a decade later. Since the end of the cold war China has moved rapidly into the world trade system and international organizations. On the strategic military side, China has accepted two important nuclear arms control agreements: the Nuclear Non-proliferation Treaty and the

Comprehensive Test-Ban Treaty, which has been interpreted as a sign that China is more of a *status quo power* than a *revisionist power.*

Constructivists note that, while China is behaving more like a status quo power that accepts the existing norms of the international system, it nevertheless has a distinctive political and strategic culture. The history of China as a great power—at one time the greatest economy in the world—affects how China sees its place in the world. China should then be expected to behave in ways that are different from Thailand, Cambodia, or Vietnam. Asia might develop into a hegemonic system with China as leader, which would give China the chance to set the rules of the system based on its interests. This project could go relatively smoothly for China, constructivists hold, especially if China works at it within the many existing global and Asian international institutions. The task for the United States would then be to facilitate the continued shift of China from a revisionist to a status quo power. Constructivists say that the United States should engage China and reassure China that great powers can work together for mutual benefit, much as the United States and Germany or Japan do.[20]

Conclusion

This chapter has shown in the first two sections that causal principles are possible in IR and that they are needed for predictions, which in turn are needed if IR theory is to have any empirical usefulness for policy making. The chapter then laid out eight dimensions on which theories may resemble or differ from one another, which are summarized in Table 2.3. While some of the theories share certain principles, no two theories are identical on all dimensions.

This chapter laid out three different theories (but did not attempt to show which one should be accepted over the others). The next chapter deals with the general process of choosing one theory over its rivals. It looks at various criteria

Table 2.3 Dimensions of competing theories

Dimensions of Theories	Realism	Liberalism	Constructivism
Level/unit(s) of analysis	System state	System state, nonstate	System state, mutually constitutive nonstate
Unitary actor assumption	Yes	Yes	No
Rational actor assumption	Yes	Yes	No
Fixed preferences of actors	Yes	Yes	No
Relative/absolute gain framework Expectation of conflict	Relative	Absolute	Absolute
Possibility of progress or cycles of war	Cycles	Progress	Progress
Role of morals	No	No	Yes
Value of international institutions	No	Yes	Yes

of theory choice and possible methods of application. It points out that any application of general criteria will also require that we gather enough empirical evidence to test the theories. Actual choice among theories, which requires gathering up and sifting through the empirical evidence and then applying the criteria to the theories, is left up to the reader.

The debate over the war in Iraq was considered in light of the theories of IR outlined. Three general policies were described in Chapter 1: invade Iraq, drastically increase inspections under the threat of an invasion if there is significant noncooperation from Baghdad, and avoid discussion of military action. This chapter considered the rationales for the policies—that is, the reasons that could motivate someone to support them. The rationales were then located in general principles, either causal or moral, which in turn were part of a theory of IR. These are summarized in Table 2.4.

Table 2.4 Rationales for policies in Iraq and causal principless

Policy	Rationale	General principle	Theory
Invade unilaterally	**R3** A democratic Iraq would be more peaceful (democratic domino effect).	Democracies are peaceful.	Unclear (democratic realism)
Invade unilaterally, invade multilaterally	**R4** Saddam Hussein is a dictator that cannot be deterred.	Dictators are impossible to deter.	Realism (democratic realism)
Invade unilaterally	**R5** The UN chain of command has flaws and weaknesses.	Only unilateral action is reliable.	Realism
Inspections, invade multilaterally	**R7** An attack on Iraq is legal only with the support of the UN.	States must act lawfully.	Liberalism, constructivism
Inspections	**R8** Cooperation in restraining Iraq helps to aid cooperation in the war on terror.	Cooperation provides the basis for more cooperation.	Liberalism, constructivism
Inspections	**R9** Information on Iraq's weapons of mass destruction improves efficiency.	War should only be a last resort.	Liberalism
Inspections, no military action	**R11** War against Iraq is only a last resort.	War should only be a last resort.	Liberalism, constructivism
Inspections, no military action	**R12** A return to Western imperialism should be avoided.	Imperialism is immoral.	Liberalism, constructivism
Inspections, no military action	**R15** Killing Iraqi civilians should be avoided.	Killing noncombatants is immoral.	Constructivism
Inspections, no military action	**R16** Attacking Iraq legitimizes war.	War reinforces war norm	Constructivism

Table 2.5 North Korea: Policies, rationales, and general principles

Policy	Rationale	General principle	Theory
Attack	**RK2** There is no other way to get Kim Jong-il out of power.	Leaders do not surrender power.	Realism
Attack, isolation	**RK3** North Korea rejects global norms and will not reform.	States that reject norms do not reform.	Realism
Attack, isolation	**RK4** It is immoral to negotiate with human rights abusers.	The means do not justify the ends.	Idealism
Isolation	**RK5** The communist economy will collapse without aid.	Communist economies are inefficient	Liberalism
Isolation, containment	**RK7** Deterrence has worked for fifty years.	Patterns continue until conditions change.	Realism
Isolation, containment	**RK8** North Korea's bad behavior should not be rewarded.	Rewarding bad behavior encourages more bad behavior.	Realism, liberalism
Containment Sunshine policy	**RK9** Give North Korea the benefits to lose; carrots will become sticks.	Interaction leads to dependency, which leads to cooperation.	Liberalism
Containment, sunshine policy	**RK11** Unilateral U.S. punishment undercuts the coalition.	Multilateralism leads to incentives for good behavior.	Liberalism
Sunshine policy	**RK12** With more fear, North Korea will take military steps.	Reducing fears reduces the security dilemma.	Constructivism
Sunshine policy	**RK13** Incremental concessions and confidence-building measures produce cooperation.	Confidence reduces worst-case planning.	Liberalism, constructivism
Sunshine policy	**RK14** If ordinary North Korean citizens learn more, they will demand reforms.	Citizens that are aware of the world tend to demand reform.	Liberalism
Sunshine policy	**RK15** North Korea will be more restrained if it gets nuclear weapons.	Nuclear proliferation lowers the chances of war (deterrent).	Realism

The four policies for dealing with North Korea, which were described in this chapter, are each justified by a set of rationales, causal principles, and theories. The rationales and the general theoretical principles and theories from which they are derived are summarized in Table 2.5.

Table 2.6 provides the policies, the rationales that help justify them, the general theoretical principles, and the theories that relate to U.S. policy options for relations with China.

Table 2.6 China: Policies, rationales, and general principles

Policy	Rationale	General principle	Theory
Prepare to attack, contain, ease tensions	**RC1** All states seek hegemony.	States seek to maximize power.	Realism
Prepare to attack	**RC5** War is better while ahead in power.	States seek to maximize power.	Realism
Prepare to attack, contain, ease tensions	**RC6** China is still repressive internally.	Democratic peace theory	Liberalism* (Marxism, democratic realism)
Prepare to attack	**RC7** The ideological rigidity of communist doctrine in China is incompatible with long-term peace with non-communist states.	Ideological compatibility is relevant to cooperation.	Liberalism* (Marxism, democratic realism)
Prepare to attack	**RC8** Communist states cannot coexist with Democracies.	Ideological compatibility leads to cooperation.	Liberalism
Prepare to attack	**RC9** Revisionist states are more willing to go to war.	Democratic peace theory	Liberalism
Ease tensions, integrate	**RC11** Economic integration leads to peace incentives.	Kantian triangle	Liberalism
Integrate	**RC13** Further transformation is possible.	Systems can be transformed.	Liberalism, constructivism
Integrate	**RC14** There is a moral obligation to improve world.	It is imperative to advance.	Constructivism
Integrate	**RC15** Descriptions create social conditions and reality.	Socialization of the system	Constructivism
Ease tensions, integrate	**RC16** Integration socializes outsiders.	Socialization of the system	Constructivism
Contain, ease tensions, integrate	**RC17** War between nuclear states is irrational.	States behave rationally.	Realism, liberalism

*The principle support for these rationales comes from theories that are mentioned in this chapter but not from the three that are given the central focus. Realism, liberalism, and constructivism do not exhaust all possible IR theories.

The last step in choosing the best policy toward Iraq or North Korea is to investigate how one chooses the best theory. The next two chapters proceed to consider that task, the complications that make the task a daunting one, and some of the responses to critics who would argue that the task is impossible to carry out.

CHAPTER 3

International Relations and Scientific Criteria for Choosing a Theory

Chapter 1 looked at U.S. policy options toward Iraq, North Korea, and China and the rationales for them. Chapter 2 laid out today's major contending theories of IR and showed that, with a particular set of factual beliefs, those who advocate a particular theory are more likely to support some of the policies in these cases and oppose others. Thus, given the set of factual claims, which option policy makers choose depends on which theory they accept. An answer to the question, which policy is most likely to succeed? hinges on the answer to the question, which theory is best? However, before we can determine which theory is best we must answer the question, how do we determine which is the best theory?

International Relations and the Philosophy of Science

The answer to the question, how do we determine which is the best theory? does not come from the study of IR or social science but from philosophy. For centuries philosophers have posed questions about how to decide which of various competing theories is best. Those who study the theory of knowledge (or "epistemology") ask questions like, What is knowledge? How do we recognize the truth? How do we know when we know something? How do we know when one body of statements (or theory) should be accepted over its rivals?

Many philosophers regard science, especially the natural sciences (like physics, astronomy, chemistry, geology, botany, zoology, physiology, and microbiology) and the subset of physical sciences (physics, astronomy, chemistry, and geology) as the greatest achievement of systematic human knowledge. Science is usually viewed as a purely rational attempt to develop a body of certain or highly reliable knowledge based on rigorous procedures of observation and logical reasoning. Scholars in the *philosophy of science* have attempted to explain how these fields accomplish the expansion of knowledge, how scientists can and should reject old theories in favor of new theories, and how they might improve their practices.

What is the connection between the natural sciences and IR? Those who have written about IR over the centuries have made use of methods drawn from military strategy, ethics, legal theory, diplomatic history, and the like. Few people prior to the twentieth century applied the concepts and methods of modern science to problems of IR. In the 1960s some scholars argued that the failure of the field of IR to solve key problems and to make progress in the way physicists have done stems from IR's failure to adopt the elements of scientific theory just noted. Some like J. David Singer argued that the subjective elements of IR and other social sciences, as they have been studied in the past, have prevented progress. The problem is that as long as there are aspects of IR theory that are subjective, such as claims about right and wrong, people will differ on those aspects of theory. As long as moral claims and other subjective propositions are part of the body of IR theory, there is no way that people, even if they have a common language and common set of observations, can come to the agreement needed to develop universally accepted conclusions about which answers are right.

Thus Singer and others argued that the empirical theory that IR produces should be parallel to natural science theory in that it should be objective and free of moral judgments. People might use moral judgment in *applying* the theory to policy problems, but the empirical side of social science theory must be free of moral imperatives, moral assumptions, and moral content if there is ever to be *progress* in IR theory. We will return shortly to the attempt to remove subjectivity from IR.

We are interested here in social sciences, especially IR and political science. Philosophers of the social sciences have explored the crucial question of how those sciences are similar to and different from the natural sciences. We want to know how old theories in the social sciences get replaced by newer and better theories. The authors who look at the question of theory choice in the social sciences are, of course, interested in how it is—and should be—similar to or different from theory choice in the natural sciences.

Some authors who study these questions agree with Singer that the sort of reasoning involved in, and the structure of, social science theories may be understood as a parallel to those in the natural sciences. These authors are called "naturalists." Some authors believe that there are fundamental, even radical, differences between the proper study of nature and the proper study of society. This last group includes "hermeneuticists," "interpretivists," "poststructuralists" and "Critical Theorists." Some of these approaches are constructivist, as explained in Chapter 2. Those who reject any parallel with the natural sciences are "anti-naturalists." Semi-naturalist authors reject several of the supposed parallels but admit several others. This chapter will consider primarily varieties of naturalism to see how far the parallel can be pushed. The next chapter looks at anti-naturalists.

In order to understand the claims about possible parallels to the natural sciences, we must first consider what the natural sciences are generally understood to be. We then look at one prominent attempt to make IR as rigorous as possible and then move on to three sets of criticisms of this attempt. The first set of criticisms comes from scholars who believe that we can account for the natural sciences in a way that includes progress and the accumulation of knowledge over time. The second comes from critics who contest that "progress," in the usual sense, is possible only in the natural sciences. The third group of critics, considered in Chapter 4, are anti-naturalist who assert that the standard view of the natural sciences, whether it is right or wrong, is irrelevant because the social sciences are fundamentally different.

Comparison with the Natural Sciences

The natural sciences have been admired through the centuries by scholars in all fields, because they seem to be able to attain truth and certainty. Their success has generally been ascribed to the procedures and methods used in those disciplines. Thus investigators have reasoned that the best path to truth and certainty in their own fields lies in adopting the same procedures as the natural sciences. Over the years they have been impressed by how, for example, the advances of Newton's new principles in the seventeenth century were quickly accepted throughout the scientific world. In the twentieth century, investigators in other fields were also very impressed when the natural scientific community adopted Einstein's superior theory when it came along, even though physicists had complete confidence in Newton's theory for more than two centuries. Many argue that the considerations that led physicists to choose Newton's theory over its competitors in the seventeenth century were largely the same as the considerations and criteria that led physicists to choose Einstein's theory over its competitors in the twentieth century. What, then, are these considerations?

Characteristics of the Natural Sciences

In order to determine whether IR and the social sciences are genuinely parallel to the natural sciences, and thus within the scope of scientific methods, we have to be specific about what natural sciences are. While there are various ways to list the standard characteristics of the natural sciences, we note nine here.

First, (NS1) science is based on observation that uses our senses and the senses are generally reliable, although not perfectly so. Thus precautions like repetition must be taken to correct for possible sensory error. Second, (NS2) this requires that the world actually displays regular patterns of behavior. Third, (NS3) the regular patterns can be quantified. Fourth, (NS4) scientific theories involve causal explanations and causal mechanisms. Fifth, (NS5) by creating different conditions artificially, investigators can draw conclusions about the world outside of the experiments. Sixth, (NS6) scientific theories make use of two different types of terms: "observation terms" that refer to entities directly observed and "theoretical" terms that do not refer to what is directly observed. Seventh, (NS7) the investigation is "objective" in the sense that the behavior investigators observe is the same whether it is being observed or not; that is, the observation does not

Table 3.1 Characteristics of natural science

NS1	Science is based on sensory observation, and the senses are generally reliable, although not perfectly so.
NS2	Characteristic NS1 requires that the world display regular patterns of behavior.
NS3	The regular patterns of N2 can be quantified.
NS4	Scientific theories involve causal explanations and causal mechanisms.
NS5	By creating different conditions artificially, investigators can draw conclusions about the world outside of the experiments.
NS6	Scientific theories make use of two different types of terms, "observation terms" that refer to entities directly observed, and "theoretical terms" that do not refer to what is directly observed.
NS7	The investigation is "objective" in the sense that what the behavior investigators observe is the same whether it is being observed it or not; that is, the observation does not alter the behavior.
NS8	The domain is "objective" also in the sense that different investigators would make the same observations; what is observed does not depend on the personal traits, religion, nationality, or ideology of the investigator.
NS9	Reliable (though not necessarily infallible) predictions will be justifiable from the theory.

alter the behavior. Eighth, (NS8) the domain is "objective" also in the sense that different investigators would make the same observations; what is observed does not depend on the personal traits, religion, nationality, or ideology of the investigator. Finally, (NS9) reliable, though not necessarily infallible, predictions will be justifiable from the theory. Let us consider each in a bit more detail.

The nine characteristics fit together neatly in the traditional empiricist account of natural science. On this view the scientist observes events; notes various regularities; measures the regularities (quantifies the relationships); offers various (causal) explanations for them; and then performs experiments to determine which of various competing regularities are true. The theory's descriptions and causal explanations make use of both observational terms and theoretical terms. All aspects of the theory are objective in that the results of the investigations do not depend on any individual-specific aspect of the investigator and the processes observed would occur in the same way even if there had not been any investigator present. They create complexes of regularities to explain complex phenomena, which constitute theories. Competing sets of regularities or theories are tested against one another, whenever possible, by means of experiments. The theories that are not contradicted by the tests are retained and those that are contradicted are either revised or discarded. The best theories will be able to generate predictions that are reliable—or at least more reliable than the predictions of any rival theory.

Let us try to be more specific about what is involved in each step in this process. We *observe with our senses* one specific event, say a ball rolling off the edge of a table, and notice that it is followed by another specific event, such as the ball falling to the floor. We observe this sequence over and over again and then postulate a *regularity*. We notice that under some conditions this does not happen. For example the ball does not fall to the ground when the ball is on a table in a ship traveling through outer space. There are then *initial conditions* for the regularity to hold, like being near to Earth, which must be noted. We also might measure the time it takes for the ball to drop to the floor and use the measurements to state the regularities in *quantitative terms*.

We also expect that a truly scientific enquiry must be *objective*, that is, *observer-independent* in at least two specific ways. One is that we believe that the investigators' observations provide them with knowledge of how nature functions. That is, we believe that the sequences of events observed would happen the *same way if the investigators were not there* to observe it. The ball rolling off of the edge of the table would fall to the floor in the same amount of time whether or not there was someone watching and measuring. A second form of objectivity we expect of science is that *if the conditions are replicated by another investigator, they will produce the same results*. The particular characteristics of the investigator such as hair color, marital status, religion, political party affiliation, and moral code do not affect the observed outcomes. So if another investigator repeats the procedure, say observing the ball rolling off of the same table, we believe that it will likewise fall to the floor and will do so just as fast.

After a regularity is formulated and quantified, the scientist takes several further steps. One is to ask why the regularity holds, that is, what *causal mechanism* there is. The causal mechanism is what assures the scientist that the many times the first event is followed by the second event was not mere coincidence. Gravitational force may be postulated as an explanation. Secondly, the scientist will seek other regularities to add to the first to produce explanations of more complex phenomena that have been observed. Some of the new regularities might help to explain the initial regularities (for example, "balls always fall to floors when they roll off of tables" is explained by the more general regularity that "all unsupported objects near the surface of the earth fall to the earth.") A system of laws is thus developed, each with causal explanations.

Once a regularity is observed and formulated, scientists want to know if it is true as stated, true but in a more limited form, or not true at all. They try to create the proper conditions to find out. Then they observe what happens. Similarly, there are also cases where two different regularities or complexes of regularities are offered by different investigators and only one can be true. How do scientists come to a conclusion about which that is? What scientists want are particular observations under particular conditions. Thus they might want to create the right conditions and observe what happens. This leads to *experimentation* in the natural sciences. Because of their subject matter some natural sciences like physics, chemistry, and many branches of biology are capable of lots of experiments, while others like evolutionary biology and plate tectonics are limited in the experimental conditions they can create. The system of regularities with initial conditions and causal explanations are often regarded as the core of a "scientific theory."[1]

A traditional element of scientific theories is that when they are fully formulated with their descriptions and causal explanations, they will require the use of "theoretical terms." In other words, some of the propositions in a theory require terms that do not refer to observable entities. As logical positivists saw it, the sentences of theories deal with observable phenomena. Some use terms that do not clearly refer to observable phenomena but are abbreviated ways of saying things that could be rephrased in purely observable terms, though they would require much more effort and explanation to do so. Sentences of that sort are either true or false. Then there are statements that use terms that appear to refer to things that human beings could, even in principle, never observe.

For example, the explanation of why objects with mass attract one another is a result of an unobservable gravitational force. While the existence of gravity is posited to explain various events that we observe, the force itself is not observable. The term "gravitational force" is thus a theoretical term. There is no way to revise or rewrite the important statements about gravity that could say the same things in purely observational language. Some philosophers of science hold that all scientific theories have such terms and that they are to be sharply distinguished from "observational terms" like "pen," "table," and "floor."

Before leaving the subject of the traditional nineteenth- and twentieth-century views of science, we should mention also foundational theories of knowledge and the deductive-nomological (d-n) model of explanation. They are not as close to the core view of science as the nine points just described, but they are nevertheless often associated with it. Foundationalism is especially relevant because of the first point—the alleged reliability of the senses. But historically, many non-empiricists also endorsed foundationalism. Science makes use of observations of the empirical world, and those observations rely on the senses. While our senses can mislead us on occasion (there are famous examples), if we recheck using different methods, we eventually can come up with reliable statements about the empirical world. For many, but not all, scientists and philosophers throughout the history of modern science, their belief in the reliability of sense perception made a foundationalist theory of knowledge possible. According to this view, natural science is based on a firm foundation of observation and logic. Foundationalist theories of knowledge have been dominant throughout the history of philosophy, at least until the late twentieth century. Foundationalism is a way for philosophers of science to satisfy their desire to conceive of science as a structured body of knowledge that carries with it as much certainty as possible.

There are many ways to formulate specific foundationalist theories of knowledge. While the theory of Plato is very different from those of Leibniz or Chisholm, what they have in common is that the body of knowledge begins with something that is known with certainty and is then built on that foundation by means of pure logic and other reliable methods of reasoning. Foundationalist theories are used by various philosophers to account for different sorts of knowledge, such as metaphysical, moral, mathematical, logical, as well as empirical and scientific. Foundationalist philosophers of science argue that if scientists and philosophers were to begin with what is known and were to use only the most reliable methods of accepting other claims (i.e., following rules of logic) then they would be able to develop a larger structure of knowledge. Philosophers like Bertrand Russell developed mathematics purely out of logic, a project known as "logicism." Those who hold that there are other methods of developing knowledge are known as "anti-foundationalists."

The deductive-nomological or "covering law" model of explanation was developed by Carl Hempel, one of the most important logical empiricists of the twentieth century. The deductive-nomological model states that a scientific explanation must have a particular form. The scientist states the set of initial conditions (C) of the event (E). The scientist next states the relevant regularities or general laws (L). These two sets of statements, C and L, must be known to be true for the explanation to be a genuine explanation of event E. In this sort of explanation the event E follows without fail from C and L. The form of reasoning involved is called "hypothetico-deductive," because it involves deriving a deductive conclusion from the premises and checking the observed outcome of the experiment or case study to see if it conforms to the expectation deduced from the covering law and initial conditions. This sort of reasoning uses general laws to derive expectations about what should happen if the law is true.

The deductive-nomological model is deterministic in that it gives predictions that tell us if the initial conditions occur then, given the covering law we have accepted, the expected outcome must occur. However, much of natural science and virtually all of social science deal with probabilities rather than deterministic certainties. The deductive-nomological model can be adapted for what Hempel called the "inductive-statistical (i-s) explanation." If the laws are probabilistic they might say "when conditions C occur, events of type E are 80 percent probable." Instead of giving us a deterministic expectation of E, the explanation would then give us an expectation that E is 80 percent likely, when conditions C arise. These traits taken together make up our standard, traditional conception of science.

Criteria of Theory Choice in the Natural Sciences

There are many criteria that scientists have been said to use by historians of science and many that have been recommended to scientists by philosophers of science. This chapter will consider eight of the most widely discussed criteria:

1. Internal consistency
2. Coherence
3. Simplicity
4. Corroboration/Range
5. Falsifiability
6. Concreteness
7. Fecundity
8. Methodological conservatism

Internal consistency is the requirement that all statements of the theory are mutually compatible; we must not be able to derive any formal contradictions from any combination of statements within the theory. *Coherence* is the requirement that the propositions of the theory fit together not just in a way that avoids formal contradiction but creates a meaningful whole. *Simplicity* requires that a superior theory will, compared to its rivals, have fewer laws or laws that postulate fewer entities or causal mechanisms that are less complex. *Corroboration/Range* is the breadth of different events and kinds of events that can be inferred from the laws of the theory. (The idea of *explanatory power* is sometimes associated with range and sometimes with a combination of simplicity and range, which tend to work against one another.) These first four are the most widely accepted throughout the history of science.

Many other criteria have been proposed and debated. The next four listed are more associated with particular philosophers or approaches than the first four and are subject to more debate. However, they are included here because they have, nevertheless, been widely adopted. *Falsifiability* is the requirement that we be able to imagine certain experimental outcomes or other specific conditions that, if we encountered them, would lead us to give up the theory. *Concreteness* is the requirement that the theory represent reality in a direct way. This criterion is questioned by various philosophers, especially instrumentalists. *Fecundity*, which has been proposed relatively recently, is the goal of a theory leading us to consider events that we have not previously thought about. A theory that rates highly on this criterion will lead us to new ideas and to look in new places for observations, which in turn will lead us to propose hypotheses or laws. *Methodological conservatism* is the requirement that a new theory fit as closely as possible with the older theory it is replacing. If our old theory postulated entities a and b and we have two new theories, one that postulates entities a, b, and c and another that postulates entities d, e, and f, we should choose the former over the latter.[2]

The preceding are the most widely discussed. But we should note three others. In the social sciences there has been considerable debate over the claim that theories must be value-free. Some have used their position on this question as a requirement for a good theory. So naturalists will insist on the proposition that a good theory must be *value-free*, at least in the sense that moral or other subjective propositions not be a part of the theory. However, some of the IR theories and metatheories we will consider, especially in Chapter 4, demand that a theory is only acceptable if it fulfills certain anti-naturalist criteria, such as that a good theory must *pursue moral goals*, like equality and must *advance human emancipation*.

Logical Positivism and Logical Empiricism

The most influential school of philosophy in the early twentieth century was logical positivism, which argued for both foundationalism and empiricism. Proponents offered rigorous arguments for most elements of the traditional conception of science, with two important differences. Logical positivists argued that knowledge must start with a foundation of observation and must be built up by logical inference. Inspired by the revolutions in physics, mathematics, and logic taking place at the beginning of the twentieth century, they argued that the new methods of reasoning would allow a structure of knowledge to be developed on a secure foundation. They wanted philosophy to progress in the way that physics and mathematics had, which required eliminating many traditional questions asked by philosophers. They held that disagreements endured because these questions are unanswerable and thus they viewed the answers proposed over the centuries as literally meaningless. The views of logical positivists largely overlapped with, and were closely connected to, those of the philosophers known as "logical empiricists," discussed later. While the specifically positivist tenets were debated and abandoned some years ago, there are many philosophers today who defend logical empiricism.

At the turn of the last century, empiricists like Bertrand Russell focused on the study of observable phenomena and rejected what could not be observed. Russell was, in part, reacting against the highly elaborate systems of metaphysics, which postulated a wide range of unobservable entities (such as Absolute Spirit) that accounted for many aspects of the world, including science. As their predecessors in the seventeenth and eighteenth centuries did, empiricists of Russell's generation tried to rely as far as possible on observation and the laws of logic. The logical positivist and logical empiricist schools were inspired by Russell's work as well as by Einstein's development of relativity theory.

The logical positivists who met regularly in Vienna to debate these questions came to be known as the "Vienna Circle." The group included philosophers, natural scientists, and social scientists. Their initial goals were to find out how pure natural science and pure mathematics were possible. Some then sought to expand those methods into the social sciences. One of the most important figures in this school, Rudolf Carnap, eventually came to hold that philosophy was the logical investigation of the many possible formal languages (Carnap 1937). Logical positivists and logical empiricists placed the understanding of language at the center of their enterprise, believing that so much wasted effort over the centuries had been a result of a misunderstanding of how language works and how ideas and meanings are conveyed.

Logical positivists came to hold that "verification" was a central feature of science and of any meaningful discourse in philosophy or elsewhere. If a statement or theory could be verified, it was meaningful and worthy of attention. If the available empirical evidence verified the theory, it should be retained. This would eliminate many of the philosophical systems of the mid- and late nineteenth century, like the "Absolute Idealism" of Hegel and the systems of Fichte and Bradley. In order to make sense of the revolutions in physics, mathematics, and logic, the logical positivists embraced several key ideas about which theories were valuable and why. These ideas made use of the principle of verification, the "analytic-synthetic distinction," the "fact-value distinction," and the unity of science.

Carnap held that empirical knowledge has "elementary experiences" as its basis, which are expressed in "protocol sentences." He and his followers argued that all science is reducible, through logical analysis, to statements about elementary experiences. The task of distinguishing analytic from synthetic sentences was crucial for the empiricist orientation of Carnap and most of the Vienna Circle. Logical empiricists—like positivists—did allow for a subjective component to science, along with the objective. Objective elements are the observations that investigators make, while subjective elements are the definitions formulated and the conventions chosen. Different investigators might choose to formulate different definitions. Authors noted that Einstein's theory of relativity showed that we could choose one sort of geometry of physical space, say Euclidean, and formulate laws of motion and universal forces to conform to it. Or we could choose non-Euclidean (curved) geometry of space and formulate a different (and, as it turns out, simpler) set of laws, like Einstein's. But they argued that the different systems are not equally good on philosophical grounds; there are good reasons to accept Einstein's non-Euclidean theory.

The fact-value distinction was central to logical positivists' thinking because of their view that arguments over moral or value judgments could not be settled on empirical and logical grounds (the only solid grounds there are)—they believed that the inclusion of value judgments in any field of study would prevent progress. Hume argued that there is a clear distinction between the two terms and the statements that include them. He said that whatever we discover about what "is" can never permit us logically to draw any conclusions about what anyone "ought" to do. Emile Durkheim, a founder of sociology in the late nineteenth century, argued that when we study a society we might observe the prevailing values in the society. However, we observe them as facts and we do not endorse or oppose them as true statements about what is right and wrong. Max Weber, another significant figure in the development of twentieth-century social science, argued that, as social scientists, we must separate our studies of "what is" from our beliefs about "what ought" to be done. Both men would agree that a statement like, "Danish society in the twenty-first century holds that cannibalism is morally wrong" is a descriptive statement of fact about the people of Denmark and does not imply that the particular investigator who asserts it must also hold that cannibalism is wrong.

Finally, logical positivists strongly endorsed the idea of a single method for all sciences. They believed that all scientific knowledge is developed with the same sort of enquiry, observation, and analysis. The Vienna Circle included several social scientists who carried the scientific project into sociology. While they did not discuss the field of IR, the application of methodology of physics and formal logic to sociology would apply equally to IR. This approach is highly naturalist, in the sense defined at the beginning of this chapter.

Progress in science and human knowledge would then be possible, according to logical positivists, when scholars stopped wasting time on fields that deal with inherently unanswerable questions. In the view of logical positivists it was essential that it should be possible to state a precise and rigorous rule for separating meaningful questions from the meaningless. As noted, after years of discussion, the key seemed to be that the unanswerable questions and the attempts to answer them were, in a literal sense, meaningless. Questions in logic, natural science, and some philosophical questions were meaningful. Questions in metaphysics, ethics, religion, and elsewhere were not. The core task was then to find out how to separate meaningful statements in the languages of philosophy and science from the meaningless ones. As noted, logical positivists argued that what makes a statement meaningful is that it can be verified. Logical positivists defended "the verification criterion." They came to identify the meaning of a statement as its method of verification. If a statement did not have any method of verification, which was the case with sentences like "The Almighty is omniscient" and "The Absolute Spirit is unfolding," then they believed that it simply did not have any empirical meaning and should be eliminated from scientific and philosophical discourse. The famous example Carnap gives is Martin Heidegger's discussion of "the Nothing," where he says, for example, "the Nothing nothings" (Carnap 1959, 69–70).

Finally, logical positivists were committed to the "unity of science." This idea was interpreted in slightly different ways by different people, but it included, at the very least, a scientific method that would apply to any investigation that could be called science. This is a powerful form of naturalism. Most also held that it would include a set of observations that could be used by all sciences. The logic of scientific enquiry would allow these observations to be used to build up more and more complete scientific theories. The most extreme view of the unity of science, which some adopted, held that there would ultimately be a single all-encompassing science that would explain what happens in both the natural and social worlds, and would include physics, chemistry, biology, psychology, economics, politics, and so on.

Three points on which the traditional view of science sharply contrasted with the logical positivists' view stem from the treatment of "theoretical terms." One consequence of the logical positivists' view is that, while *laws* may be true and false, *theories*, taken as wholes, are neither true nor false. They are evaluated based on other considerations. Second, and closely related, the things that theoretical terms appear to talk about may or may not be real. The inherently unobservable entities that theories invoke are useful for various purposes of illumination or prediction, but our acceptance of a theory does not assure us of the existence of things that the theory appears to talk about. Third, logical positivists generally rejected the use of the notion of "cause" or "causal mechanism."[3]

International Relations and the Natural Science Analogy

Some scholars have argued that the social sciences work in a way parallel to the natural sciences, and the scientific method could be applied to IR. The use of scientific methods to test IR claims was strongly advocated by J. David Singer, Melvin Small, and their colleagues involved in the Correlates of War (COW) project. In the 1960s they argued that many of the IR issues debated at that time were essentially the same as those debated centuries earlier, since neither side had defeated the other. This is a situation that we do not find in the natural sciences. As noted, the prevailing theories of physics in the mid-seventeenth century were challenged by Newton and his followers. Newtonian principles were soon accepted and remained standard in physics for over two hundred years. Most of the debates of 1650 had been settled by 1700. When the Newtonian view was challenged in the early twentieth century it was not challenged by a centuries-old theory but by a very new one, namely Einstein's theory of relativity. Investigators examined the evidence, applied widely accepted standards of scientific reasoning and criteria of theory choice, universally rejected the old theory, and embraced the new theory. This is regarded as a clear example of scientific progress.

Singer and many like-minded scholars in IR (and in other social sciences) asked why the history of debates in natural sciences like physics has been so different from the history of debates in IR. One answer Singer defended was that the social sciences failed to follow the example of the natural sciences by focusing only on what is objective. Singer and others advocated a reorientation of IR methods to make them more objective and thus more like the natural sciences. This would include a focus on using observable behavior as evidence rather than intentions or values. They were often called "behaviorists" or "behavioralists." Their project also sought to make the observations much more precise, which would make it possible for different investigators to conduct the same tests on hypotheses.

An example helps to illustrate how these scholars make their case. One of the key theoretical claims in IR deals with "democratic peace," which generally states that democratic government or lack thereof makes a difference in how war-like states are (Kant 1989; Babst 1964; Babst 1972; Doyle 1983a; Doyle 1983b; Russett 1993). Are there really similarities between the theoretical claim of democratic peace and the scientific method? In the eighteenth century, Kant offered an argument about what would be necessary for the world to become peaceful, which included the condition that all states in the system must adopt republican constitutions. This was based on Kant's ideas of freedom and justice, but not on observations of existing states, because few real republics existed in Kant's era or before. Dean Babst published two papers noting that, in the two centuries since Kant wrote, many democracies have been formed and many wars have been fought, but in all that time no two democracies have ever gone to war against one another (1964; 1972).

Several years later, Melvin Small and J. David Singer argued that rigorous scientific-style tests could settle the matter (1976). They set out to test the claim that democratic regime type makes a difference in war-related behavior. They could not set up experiments like physicists do, since it is impossible to put democratic and nondemocratic states into different sorts of pairings, create potential conflict situations, and observe them to see if there are any patterns in the wars fought (especially patterns indicating that democratic states go to war less often than nondemocratic states). Some natural sciences have similar limitations. For instance, astronomers might test a hypothesis by analyzing older data in a new way. They cannot set up alternative solar systems or galaxies to see how they will behave or conduct laboratory tests to create interesting conditions in the same way that physicists and chemists often can. And those who study botany or evolutionary biology might test a hypothesis or law by looking at data or specimens that have already been collected. What Small and Singer did was look at many cases from the past to see what happened in terms of war and peace.

Small and Singer (1976) looked at a great deal of data drawn from the previous five hundred years of war and peace. In order to do this, they used the COW database, which contains information on every country and includes variables such as what kind of government each country has, what kind of arms each has, whether or not each has engaged in war during any given year, and if so, against whom and for how long. They compared all the democracies in the world to all the nondemocracies and looked to see if democracies fought wars less often. They used general laws to derive a specific observable conclusion through deduction. By using deductive-nomological reasoning they deduced consequences (what one would expect to find) from the view that democracies are peaceful.

Small and Singer then analyzed the data and *measured* frequencies of war, which allowed them to see if the observed pattern matched the expected results. They concluded that there was no significant difference between the frequency of wars fought by democracies and by nondemocracies. They thus defended a realist position that wars are fought based on power considerations and not what type of governing regime is in place in a given state. They certainly maintained that their results were *objective*, both in the sense that any other scholars using the same data could apply the same mathematical tests and come up with the same conclusions and in the sense that the pattern would be the same whether or not anyone was studying it.

Other scholars thought about the basic claim that Kant had made regarding how a world of democracies would (as long as several other conditions were also met) come to be peaceful. These scholars began to consider that Babst's specific claim that democracies do not go to war with one another was closer to what Kant was saying than the more general claim studied by Small and Singer, that democracies fight fewer wars than nondemocracies. The scholars reasoned that democracies might be attacked by nondemocracies in which case the simple measure of how often democracies are involved in wars would not reveal much about whether they have a peaceful internal nature. The truth of the matter would be clearer if scholars tried to determine who started each war, as this would indicate whether democracies fight wars as innocent victims of nondemocracies' aggression or if they are themselves responsible for initiating violence. However, there are difficulties with this approach since it is not always easy to determine who started a war. A democracy might legitimately see a nondemocratic neighbor as threatening and even move to attack it rather than waiting to be struck first. In such a case, the democracy technically initiates the war by firing the first shot but is not the party responsible for the war occurring.

One of the classic examples of this situation is the 1967 Arab-Israeli War. Egypt and Syria were just about to launch a massive attack on Israel when Israeli leaders, seeing the troops massed, decided to strike the first blow in order to minimize the damage of the impending Arab assault. Although the Arab armies still inflicted heavy losses on Israel in the first days of the war, Israel soon reversed the course of the war and captured large portions of Arab territory—the Sinai Peninsula and the Gaza Strip from Egypt, the Golan Heights from Syria, and the West Bank from Jordan. (For an alternative, see Abu-Luhad 1970 and the essays that follow)

Scholars who wished to test the "dyadic hypothesis"—that democratic states are peaceful toward other democracies—divided all pairs of states, or dyads, into three possible categories: two democracies, one democracy and one nondemocracy, and two nondemocracies. These scholars proposed that if we look at the frequency of war in each of these three categories of dyad, those with two democracies will have the lowest frequency.

Several groups had, for other purposes, been collecting data on the factors tested by democratic peace hypotheses. The groups included the COW project, Freedom House, and the Polity project. This turned out to be a significant advantage for making progress in the democratic peace debate. The reason is that it is always possible for a scholar who seeks to establish a particular position and who has to "code" data to test a result, even without intending any bias, to code difficult cases in a way that makes it more likely that the desired result will be established. Coding data requires someone (often a graduate student) to study the history of each case and make interpretive judgments about the case. Some coding decisions are easy, like the population of Great Britain in 1900 was thirty-eight million. But some are more difficult, like how important the UK and Iceland regarded the stakes on a fishing rights dispute on a 1–10 scale or how democratic Iran is in 2007 on a 21-point scale.

In the case of the debate over the democratic peace hypotheses, there had already been many scholars who had coded the particular variables needed to test the democratic peace hypotheses. When the democratic peace debate intensified, the COW data, Polity data, and other data sets were available to all sides. These data sets could then be used commonly by both the liberal proponents and the realist opponents of the democratic peace hypotheses. This might well have made it easier for the two sides to reach some agreement. While there is still some debate, most scholars who currently publish in this area have concluded that the monadic hypothesis is not true, but the dyadic hypothesis is true. Jack Levy has gone so far as to say that the dyadic hypothesis, which states that democracies do not fight one another, is the one clear "law" that has been established in the field of IR (1989, 270).

A next stage in the research on democratic peace has been to seek *causal explanations* of the dyadic hypothesis. Kant offered explanations connected with the enlightened nature of states and leaders. In nondemocratic states the leaders do not bear the costs of war; that is, they do not do the fighting, they do not pay heavier taxes, and they are unlikely to lose power if they fight a wasteful or unwise war, even if it damages the interests of the state. In democracies this is reversed, since leaders are accountable to citizen-voters who are themselves responsible for fighting wars and paying the taxes to support them. Recent scholars have also proposed and debated many explanations. One is that, in a democracy, internal conflicts are dealt with through negotiation and compromise rather than by the stronger party issuing commands to the weaker party, which can become violent if there is access to weapons. These "peaceful conflict resolution norms" within democratic societies are "internalized" by individuals or group actors and show themselves in the state's dealings with others. Nondemocracies lack these norms, and when a crisis arises between a nondemocracy and a democracy, the democracy may be forced to abandon its more peaceful norms and resort to war in order to ensure its survival. Another explanation is that the leaders of non-democratic states might decide single-handedly to go to war and to launch a strike, while most leaders in a democratic state recognize the need to ensure that they have the support of the electorate or the legislature before taking action. If a conflict is between two democracies, then the leaders on both sides have to spend time trying to secure the necessary support, and the longer a crisis goes on without either party striking, the more likely that whatever anger inflamed the crisis will recede, allowing for a peaceful resolution of the crisis. Thus, the structure of the government within a state impels leaders to acquire public support, and when both sides in a crisis have this slow-to-react structure, it is more likely that violence will ultimately be avoided.

With this sketch of how the naturalist, or scientific, approach to IR has been put into practice by "behavioralist" scholars, we may now turn to the various challenges to it posed by different groups of critics.

Challenges to Logical Empiricism and Logical Positivism

Logical positivism dominated the philosophy of science and much of the core of philosophy from the 1930s until the 1960s and beyond. Most of the central claims of the approach noted have been modified or rejected over the past forty years. Most logical positivists came to accept the related doctrine of logical empiricism, which is still held today by some important philosophers. The way in which logical positivism shaped many debates over the years shows the depth of the approach and the brilliance of many of its proponents.

Logical positivists and early logical empiricists accepted a number of key claims. They include the following eight:

1. *Foundationalism.* Science was built upon a firm foundation of objective observation and strictly logical reasoning.
2. *Verification.* Theories in the natural sciences are different from others in that results from scientific reasoning can be verified and tested.
3. *Progress.* The idea is that theories are compared to one another, and the best theories move us forward from inferior theories, producing progress over time. The idea of progress raises the question, What sort of things or units (laws, theories, paradigms) are progressing over time?
4. *Objective comparisons of units.* Once the observations are made, different

competing theories (or whatever units of comparison are favored) may be compared on the basis of objective criteria so that we may see which one is correct.

5. *The objectivity of observations.* The progress that occurs is a result of our ability to observe the world in an objective way—all investigators in the same situation would report observing the same things.

6. *Discovery of reality.* Scientific knowledge accumulates over time as one theory gives rise to a better theory, resulting in progress toward the true nature of reality.

7. *Objective facts versus subjective values.* Objective observation is in part possible because personal traits like moral values do not influence what is seen.

8. *What the world consists of.* Science adheres to the strictly observable and empirical and, in this way, separates itself from nonscientific methods and topics like religion and magic and deals with the reality of the world about which science theorizes. Ultimately the best theory is chosen, because it is the one best supported by the set of available observations and most closely describes reality.

Each of these elements of the logical empiricist and logical positivist idea of natural science has been criticized since the 1950s. Let us consider them. As noted at the outset, there are three groups of critics whose ideas are important to understand contemporary debates about the nature of IR theory. The first group accepts logical positivists' and logical empiricists' ideas of "scientific progress" but finds errors in their arguments to account for it. The second group challenges the logical positivists' and empiricists' traditional ideas of how science operates and progresses. And the third group rejects any attempt to extend the methods and concepts of the natural sciences to the social sciences.

The first group of philosophers of science shared with the logical positivists the goal of creating the greatest possible certainty for science, mathematics, logic, and philosophy. These include, most prominently, Carl Hempel, Karl Popper, and Imre Lakatos. The second group finds fault with the logical positivist/empiricist conception of science. It includes N. R. Hanson, Wilfred Sellars, Ludwig Fleck, Thomas Kuhn, and W. V. O. Quine. The remainder of this chapter looks at the criticisms of these two groups. The third group, discussed in the next chapter, rejects the attempt to extend the methods of the natural sciences to the social sciences. Those authors oppose the naturalist conception of the social sciences and include some constructivists and most post-moderns.

Foundationalism

The logical positivists argued that certainty could only be achieved by building a structure of scientific knowledge on a firm foundation. They held that the foundational approach, as noted, was possible because science begins with both objective and certain statements about experience. They argued that these foundations could then be developed into a larger edifice of knowledge by rigorous logical reasoning using only carefully prescribed methods. There are several ways of criticizing foundationalism. One is to attack the objectivity and certainty of the observation reports. The other is to attack the possibility of rigorous, strictly logical methods of developing theoretical knowledge from them. Some of the criticisms of foundationalism were developed by authors generally in favor of the logical positivist goal of a rigorous and progress-engendering form of natural science. Two such arguments will be noted here.

Carl Hempel disagreed with the logical positivists' view of foundationalism and attacked it by criticizing the observational basis. Logical positivists argued that we begin with basic observations of the world, which could be expressed in what they called "protocol sentences." They argued that once the protocol sentences are accepted, science must continue to accept them. Protocol sentences form a foundation for knowledge that cannot be removed. Hempel disagreed. He argued that observation reports are always subject to at least some small degree of uncertainty. There is always a possibility that we are mistaken in what we take to be experience; our senses are imperfect. We could even be dreaming or hallucinating.

While the possibility that any particular observation report is wrong may be small, when we add many of these reports together as the basis for a scientific theory, the possibility of error is compounded. The result is a much higher probability that somewhere along the way one of them is false. Hempel maintained that because these reports are fallible, it must be possible for scientists to revise them on the basis of further study. There is a problematic gap between our subjective experience and any beliefs about the objectively existing world of physical objects that we derive from them. Hempel, who is one of the major figures in the logical empiricist school, held that scientific knowledge is the best sort of knowledge humans can develop, but aside from the strictly logical statements it admits (like a=a), scientific knowledge is always fallible. Hempel was thus a fallibilist and parted company with many other logical empiricists by rejecting a pure form of foundationalism.

The second general way to attack logical positivism's foundationalism is to attack the idea that there are purely logical moves that allow the building of a body of "certainty" from the observation reports. This position is generally taken to require categorizing all statements as either empirical (synthetic) statements or purely logical (analytic) statements. An analytic statement contains a subject (all bachelors, Socrates, the city of London) and says something in the predicate about that subject that does not add any information to what we know simply from our familiarity with the concept of the subject. The subject "bachelors" includes the idea of "being unmarried." So the statement "all bachelors are unmarried" is analytic because the full statement, including the predicate, does not add anything to the concept of "all bachelors." For logical positivists, if we are to be able to reason purely logically from our observation reports, then we have to be able to distinguish between analytic and synthetic statements. But there are criticisms of this project (see especially Quine 1953).

Verification and Scientific Discourse

The logical positivists were determined to erase all meaningless statements from science and philosophy. Their chief tool for doing this was the verification principle, which said that a statement was meaningful only if it is possible to conceive of a way to verify it. There may be no available means at the moment, but there is in principle some means. The meaning was, moreover, constituted by the method of verification. Logical positivism was substantially damaged by several criticisms leveled at the verification principle. One criticism raises the question of how we verify any general law. Take as an example Newton's law implying that "all physical bodies attract one another." We might observe the attraction in one particular case and then in another. No matter how long we repeat this procedure, we will not complete the task. We cannot even imagine observing all such cases. The law makes a claim about all cases, but it is in principle impossible to verify all cases. If we cannot make a claim about all cases then, on the verificationist view, the law is not meaningful. Few philosophers were willing to accept the verification principle if the cost was that we must regard Newton's laws meaningless.

We might similarly wonder how logical positivists would classify general principles that were central to their doctrine, like the statement that "all meaningful statements can be verified" or "all statements are either analytic or synthetic." It is difficult to see how the latter statement could be analytic (the concept of the predicate does not appear to be included in the concept of the subject). But at the same time it is difficult to see what evidence we could find to prove it true as a synthetic statement.

Karl Popper shared the logical positivists' goal of finding a basis for a secure, progressive notion of science. But he rejected the verification principle because it excludes some statements that were meaningful, including some metaphysics, and because it includes as meaningful some statements that were not meaningful. Popper shifted his focus to how we separate the scientific from the unscientific. This distinction he believed was more fruitful than the logical positivists' attempt to separate the meaningful from the meaningless. Popper wanted to know what makes genuine sciences, like astronomy, different from pseudo-sciences, like astrology. Popper developed the so-called *demarcation criterion*.

Ever since David Hume's attack on inductive reasoning, empiricist philosophers were uneasy with any reliance on induction. But there were no appealing ways around it. And scientific method seems to include in an essential way inductive reasoning—reasoning that moves from a finite number of cases to a general claim. Popper agreed with Hume that inductive reasoning leaves room for error, while deductive reasoning does not. Motivated by achieving greater certainty, Popper developed an account of science and scientific progress that relies on deduction rather than on induction. In formal deductive logic the rules of inference have names. If we start with the first two statements, then we are justified in inferring the conclusion.

If P, then Q
P
∴ Q

If Patrick is tall, then Lydia is short
Patrick is tall
∴ Lydia is short

This rule is *modus ponens*. No matter what "P" and "Q" stand for, the inference is always valid in the technical sense that if the first two premises are true then the conclusion absolutely always must be true. An equally valid argument is the following:

If P, then Q
Not-Q
∴ Not-P

If Lydia is tall, then Lydia is short
Monty is not short
∴ Patrick is not tall

This rule is called "*modus tolens*," and it is also a deductive rule of inference in deductive logic.

Popper developed the purely deductive scientific method of "*falsification-ism*." The basic idea is that any given theory will, if true, have certain specifiable consequences that will be observable. The method then is to propose bold theories that have a great deal of content and tell us a lot. We then try to falsify them. The idea that scientists try to falsify rather than confirm theories sounds counterintuitive. But Popper offers an explanation that has been widely accepted.

The process of falsification involves applying the theory to specific circumstances and deriving predictive consequences. We then observe whether the predicted outcome is actual. If the outcomes are not observably false, then we look further; we follow this procedure for all of the various rival theories, as well. We often have rival theories and try to falsify each of the theories. The more tests that our initial theory passes the more we may rely on it. But, strictly speaking, we do not prove the theory true. If the method is followed properly, we do eventually prove something, namely that its rivals are false. As investigators propose alternative theories, we derive consequences and look to see if the consequences are inconsistent with our observations. If so, we reject or revise the theory. As science moves forward the theory is tested more times and more rivals are proposed and eliminated, because they are inconsistent with observed results. As this process proceeds we have increasing confidence that our theory is right and thus that we are coming closer to the truth, even if we never quite reach it. That is, we never achieve absolute certainty about a theory being right but can achieve certainty that various rivals are wrong.

The methodology of falsificationism might sound counterintuitive, but it became widely accepted in the philosophy of science. For Popper we examine a general statement or theory and try to imagine circumstances that would force us to see that it is false; if we cannot imagine any such circumstances, then the statement or theory is flawed as science. In astronomy we can apply a theory to a specific set of conditions and draw out its predictive consequences about the movements of planets. We can easily imagine that astronomers observe movements of planets that do not accord with the theory. This has happened many times over the centuries and the theories were amended or rejected when better ones were proposed.

If the theory is true, then it will not be falsified; that is, the falsifying conditions that we can imagine do not in fact ever come about. But, to repeat, if we can imagine such conditions, then the statements or theories "have the capacity to be falsified" and thus are falsifiable. In contrast, when we think about astrology the predictions are typically so vague that no matter what specific events occur in actuality, that an outcome can be interpreted in a way that does not contradict the theory and we, therefore, do not have to reject the astrological theory. For this reason Popper argued that astrology is not a science. He argued that similar problems affect Marx's social theory and Freud's psychological theory, even though they are commonly regarded as scientific. Adherents of those theories make predictions based on the principles of Marxism or Freudianism. But if what happens turns out to be the opposite of what they predicted, they always find something within the theory, as it was formulated, that allows them to interpret the outcome as consistent with the theory. For this reason, Popper concluded that these theories are unfalsifiable and are therefore not truly scientific.

If we have two or more theories that are falsifiable and thus truly scientific, how do we know which is better? Clearly if one is falsified and the other is not, then the unfalsified theory is preferable. But what if neither of the two theories has been falsified through our tests and observations? Which one is to be preferred? Popper's answer is that we should accept the one that has more content— that is, the theory that tells us more or is "bolder." Clearly the idea of "content" or "boldness" is central to Popper's position. What does it mean to say that one law or theory has more content than another? Popper worked hard to answer this important question, which is closely connected to his demarcation criterion. For Popper, what makes a statement or theory scientific is that we can imagine circumstances that would lead us to reject it. There are more potentially falsifying conditions for some theories than for others, which means that they have more content. The more easily the falsifying circumstances might come about and the more they do not lead to falsifying observations of the theory, the more probable it is that the theory is true. So for Popper not only is a theory with more content more valuable because it tells us more about the world than a theory with less content, but if both have been tested and neither has been falsified, the theory with more content is still more likely to be true.

We can see Popper's point by considering two generalizations: "All planets in our solar system contain some aluminum," and "all bodies mutually attract." The second is a more sweeping statement. It says much more than the first. Popper explained that a statement has greater content if we can imagine more possible events that would contract the second principle. If the second statement is false, it will be much easier to find falsifying evidence. So our inability at any point up to now to falsify the second principle should give us a great deal of confidence that it is true.

Scientific Progress and the Unit of Comparison

Popper's picture of how science progresses was challenged by one of his students, Imre Lakatos. IR theorists rely on the methodological ideas of Imre Lakatos perhaps more than those of any other philosopher, so it is worth our while to look at his views in some depth. Lakatos accepted much of the basic Popperian outlook but made modifications significant enough for him to be regarded as a very important and original philosopher of science. Lakatos's view differed from Popper's in several ways, one of which pertains to the unit of comparison. According to Popper, scientists compare one theory to another; according to Lakatos, scientists compare something much broader and larger—a *research program*—that consists of a theory and the modifications of that theory made over time as anomalies are discovered, along with a set of supporting heuristic rules. Lakatos thus argued that we need to revise the logical positivists' and logical empiricists' conception of what sorts of units scientists test and compare. He said that when any major theory change takes place, what scientists are really comparing is not just a single theory but a research program.

Lakatos argued that in actual practice when a scientist encounters an anomaly, that is, a result that is contrary to the accepted theory, she will not simply discard the theory as falsified. Rather, she will rerun the experiment, check the equipment to make sure it works, make adjustments to the equipment, rethink beliefs about how the experimental equipment works and the like. Only after much work will she accept that the observations are truly inconsistent with the theory. At that point the scientist will still not discard the theory. What the scientist does in the vast majority of instances is to propose minor modifications to the theory. The modified theory might eventually encounter anomalies. At that point what typically happens is that further modifications are made. Popper sees the scientist as working in order to falsify the accepted theory, while Lakatos sees the scientist as trying to save, or salvage as much as possible, the accepted theory by amending and modifying it. According to Lakatos, Popper's view that a theory is rejected when falsified is not the way scientists actually operate, so it fails on descriptive grounds. Lakatos also believes that it is not the way scientists should operate, so Popper's account fails on prescriptive grounds.

Two questions immediately arise: Does any modification, even a small modification, of the older theory create a new theory? And is any modification of a theory acceptable as good science so long as it brings the theory into line with the troubling observations, that is, the anomalies? Lakatos answers "no" to both questions, and his notion of research programs helps to explain his answers. He holds that some modifications are minor and some are fundamental. Lakatos argues also that some modifications are acceptable and constitute good science; these are what we find in "progressive" research programs. But there are others that are unacceptable and constitute bad science. He calls them "degenerating" research programs.

With respect to the first question, whether all modifications create new theories, Lakatos answers that as the theories are modified, they form a series of related theories that are, as noted, part of a research program. Research programs have a core of propositions that give the essence or the key ideas of the theory. This is the *hard core* of the research program. In a good scientific research program these propositions are not modified. In addition to the hard core the research program also contains a *protective belt* of propositions, which insulate the hard core from falsification by new observations. These may be altered if anomalies are observed. The research program also includes rules to guide how the alterations are to be made, which Lakatos calls the positive and negative *heuristics*. The hard core of the theory would be the statements that form the essential character of the theory, like Newton's laws of motion and gravitation, while the protective belt includes statements added to help avoid falsification, such as Newton's explanation of how observations might appear inconsistent with the theory's expectations. These have to do with how the atmosphere affects our viewing of objects through telescopes and how the telescope itself works, which includes the possibility that there may be imperfections in lenses. If modifications are made to the hard core, it becomes a new theory and is part of a new research program. If the hard core is kept intact and the modifications are made elsewhere, then the new theory is a successor to the previous theory in the same research program.

With respect to the second question, whether any modifications that bring the theory into consistency with observations are acceptable as good science, we note that there are always many possible modifications that will accomplish this. Lakatos says that we may not use any adjustment or modification whatsoever for this purpose. He argues that progressive research programs have modifications that are acceptable and, in contrast, degenerating research programs make modifications that are unacceptable. Lakatos agreed with Duhem (and with Quine, discussed later) that it was logically possible to retain any proposition whatsoever, no matter what observations are recorded. But Lakatos agreed with Duhem also that science makes use of more than strictly logical principles; it requires the use of non-logical methodological principles, as well. On the basis of the latter, we can distinguish good science from bad science and conclude that some examples exist of theories that are salvaged by degenerating modifications in the protective belt, and these constitute bad scientific research programs. Such programs should be abandoned.

A progressive research program uses a powerful set of principles about how the world works to explain past events and to point our attention to events that we have not previously observed. These may be future events, which obviously have not been previously observed, or they may be past events that were never interpreted as relevant for the discipline at hand; investigators might not have understood their connections to and role in larger patterns. Newton's laws of motion and gravity formed the hard core of the Newtonian research program and constitute a very powerful theory. Their power is a result both of the extremely high content value, which is evident from the ease with which we can imagine possible observations that are inconsistent with them, and of their ability to withstand centuries of observations without being falsified and without having to be modified in ways that undercut the hard core.

There is also a directive to keep testing the research program—the positive heuristic—and a directive to avoid violating the hard core—the negative heuristic (see Nickles 1987). The heuristics give us ways to evaluate one theory against another as other accounts of science do. But they also tell us something about how to revise a theory and how to replace one theory by another within the same research program. Lakatos thus says that one research program is to be preferred over a rival not only if the theory it contains is better than rivals, for example by having greater content or a simpler form, but also if the research program revises the theory in the proper way, in accordance with the heuristic rules. One research program is to be preferred over another if it follows the heuristic guidelines and points us in the direction of new facts to be discovered. If small adjustments are made in the hard core in order to keep the research program in line with new observations, then the research program becomes narrower and degenerates.

Let us consider an example of how a progressive research program can guide us to notice facts or events that are unexpected in the older or rival theory. For example, astronomers in the Newtonian period would make an observation of the distances between two stars on a particular day at ten o'clock p.m., record that observation, possibly reexamine it to reduce the chance of error, and then move on to make other observations. An investigator might even think about the matter a day or two later and recheck the measurement when it is convenient, possibly again at ten o'clock p.m.. Astronomers prior to the twentieth century did not entertain the idea that the observed measurements of distances between stars would vary according to time of day. Thus they did not take measurements that would fit with the expectation that there might be a difference that could indicate a fundamental fact about astronomical measurement. Once Einstein's theory was proposed, astronomers did indeed begin to take measurements at different times of day to see if they would vary as Einstein's theory predicted. They did, which further corroborated Einstein's theory. The new theory prompted investigators to look for—and find—phenomena that no one would have looked for without having the theory to guide them. This is an important mark of a progressive theory and a progressive research agenda, as Lakatos describes them.

Let us consider an example in IR that some authors maintain is progressive (see Ray 2003; Chernoff 2004). The monadic hypothesis (democracies fight wars less than nondemocracies), and the dyadic hypotheses (pairs of states that are both democratic fight less often than other pairs of states), were previously discussed. We noted that there has been powerful empirical support for the dyadic hypothesis, which has led IR theorists to search for explanations. After considering the plausibility of those explanations, some scholars considered some of the implications (Siverson 1995; Bennett and Stam 1998). One implication might be that, if democracies make decisions in this different and more cautious way than non-democracies, then they would be less likely to fight wars that would incur large losses; thus they would be less likely to lose wars or suffer large casualties. These hypotheses were tested and found to be true. This is one reason to think about the democratic peace research program as progressive, in Lakatos's sense. This is not something that scholars would have been likely to think of or to take measurements of before the debate on democratic peace advanced as far as it did.

It is useful to contrast this with an example of a degenerating research program. Suppose a scholar looks at the many cases in which a large state defeated a small neighbor in battle and advances the principle that "the state with the larger economy will always win in a war." We might take this as the hard core of a hypothetical research program. This statement has considerable range and great content. It tells us with great simplicity something about all wars. Eventually a scholar points out an anomaly—Vietnam, with a small economy, defeated the United States. A supporter of the "large economy theory" then tries to save the theory by arguing that the principle holds unless there is an ocean in between the states at war in which case the smaller economy will win. This does help to make the theory consistent with the observations, but it reduces the content considerably and does not add any insights. It is especially unclear why the presence of an ocean would give the weaker economy an advantage.

A critic of the theory might then note another anomaly—that the United States, with a much larger economy, defeated Japan in 1945 despite an ocean between them. The defender of the large economy theory then revises the theory to say that the larger economy will win unless there is an ocean in between them, and if there is, it will be unpredictable who will win. This greatly reduces the content because it no longer says anything about any war where the main rivals are separated by an ocean. Still, there may be further anomalies. Someone might point out that Russia had a larger economy than Japan in 1905 but Japan defeated Russia. The defender of the large economy theory might revise the theory by saying that the side with the weaker economy will prevail if it is a Japanese-speaking society. This further reduces the boldness, or content, of the theory, and, again, it is not clear why a Japanese-speaking society would have any advantage. These modifications bring the theory in line with the observations, but they do so by making the theory apply to a smaller and smaller domain. The modifications reduce the content of the theory and do not produce new insights or stimulate us to look for new facts that we would not have noticed otherwise. Lakatos would say that this imaginary series of theories constitute a degenerating research program.

In sum, Lakatos's writings produce important criteria of what constitutes a good scientific theory. A superior theory is part of a research program that is progressive. In particular this means that any modifications to the research program are to the protective belt and not to the hard core, and it points us to new facts and phenomena. The account Lakatos proposed is, he believes, consistent with the idea that real progress in science can be made. Unlike the critics who reject the traditional account of science, Lakatos developed a view that said there are philosophically defensible criteria that allow us to evaluate and compare the merits of different "units of appraisal," namely research programs, and they allow genuine scientific progress.

The Objectivity of Comparing Theories or Paradigms

Another critic of the traditional logical positivists' ideas of scientific theory is Thomas Kuhn who developed his arguments in the 1950s and published them in full form in 1962. Kuhn's views closely reflect those developed in Germany by Ludwig Fleck in the 1930s (Fleck 1986). Like other critics of the traditional conception of science in the remainder of this chapter, Fleck and Kuhn did not believe that science was in fact objective or capable of genuine progress, as the term is ordinarily understood.

Through his studies of physics and the history of science, Kuhn developed an account of "theory change" according to which the unit of appraisal is the "paradigm." That is, what gets replaced as science moves on is not one theory by another or one research program by another but rather one *paradigm* by another. In a significant departure from the traditional view of science, Kuhn argued that when a new paradigm is adopted over an older one, the new paradigm is not "objectively better" and the process of making the change is not guided by rational principles. Kuhn said that progress would require a rational comparison of two or more competing paradigms. He argued that a genuine comparison would be impossible for two reasons: there are no objective criteria for comparison, and there are no objective grounds or data for testing the theories.

A scientific paradigm, according to Kuhn, is a complex that includes a theory along with its own framework for scientific theory evaluation. The theory contains substantive principles about the world and serves as an example of the sort of structure that a theory should have; that is, it is an *exemplar* of good science. The paradigm includes a set of criteria, which may be implicit or explicit, for evaluating theories. On Kuhn's view, each paradigm has a set of criteria that tell us what is a good theory.

The theory and the criteria develop in conjunction with one another. For example, because in paradigm A, theory T-A develops in conjunction with criteria C-A, the theory T-A will do well on criteria C-A, which were tailored to show T-A's superiority over alternative theories. But a second theory, T-B, in a second paradigm B, will score highly on the criteria, C-B, in the second paradigm given that criteria C-B were, similarly, tailored to its strengths. The result is that when two competing paradigms are compared, their merits cannot be fairly weighed against one another because the first theory will score highly on criteria included in its paradigm while the second theory will score highly on criteria included in its paradigm.

According to Kuhn, since any particular set of evaluative criteria is part of a particular paradigm, there is no basis outside of the various paradigms on which to compare the merits of different scientific paradigms. There is thus no objective way to compare the two theories, like Newton's and Einstein's, that are part of different paradigms (or two theories that are part of different paradigms). Kuhn refers to this as the *incommensurability of paradigms*. So one reason why paradigms are incommensurable, according to Kuhn, is that there are no paradigm-neutral criteria for a comparative evaluation of the competing theories. (The second reason is considered in the next subsection.) And the reasons why one theory eventually wins out over another do not result from strictly rational considerations but from psychological factors and from historical and sociological accidents, which are tied to power relationships in society.

If a new paradigm is successful, it will dominate a discipline for a period of time during which investigators in the field will practice *normal science*. They accept the philosophical foundations of the discipline and gather data, conduct experiments, and try to test hypotheses and refine the theories of the dominant paradigm. Only after anomalies develop will there be a *crisis*—a perceived need for a new paradigm, followed by a *revolution* when the new paradigm is proposed. The next new dominant paradigm will not be objectively better than its predecessor, as judged on philosophical, methodological, or logical grounds. The new great work will have important substantive science and either implicit or explicit criteria that are novel and that show why the new theory is to be preferred over the previous dominant theory. The newest one is, again, accepted because of the psychology of the community of investigators and the social institutions and power configuration of the discipline and the community.

Kuhn's study of the history of science led him to draw a sharp division between "mature sciences" and "immature sciences." He offered his account of paradigms and paradigm shifts as an explanation for mature sciences only. Immature sciences such as the social sciences do not work in the same way because there are no methods accepted throughout the discipline at any given time. So there can be no dominant paradigm. There are always competing theories and philosophical frameworks for evaluation, that is, competing philosophies of science. Investigators in immature sciences have to defend these philosophical foundations and methodological principles, which inhibits their ability to advance the substantive theory. The lack of a single method and philosophical framework allows investigators in an immature science to reconsider philosophical underpinnings more freely and does not bind them to a specific method and metaphysical outlook. However, the lack of a dominant paradigm of method and substance blocks substantive progress, because they have to try to persuade others in their field not only that their substantive findings are correct but also that their methods and criteria are superior.

Kuhn provides an extensive account of how the history of science fits the pattern of revolution, followed by debate over the revolutionary paradigm, followed by acceptance of the paradigm that has more powerful social and political supporters within the discipline and within the societies. The acceptance of a new paradigm is then followed by a period of normal, nonrevolutionary science. Kuhn's account is primarily a factual description of how scientific theory choice has historically operated in science. He does not offer what is offered by the other philosophical challenges to the standard view of science considered in this chapter, namely a better criterion of theory choice.[4]

Observation, Objectivity, and Theory-ladenness

Kuhn offers a second, very well known, argument for why paradigms are incommensurable and thus why science does not show rational progress. This argument was developed in the 1950s by Wilfred Sellars (1963) and N. R. Hanson (1958) and published in fuller form by both Kuhn and Paul Feyerabend in 1962. The argument seeks to establish that all observations are embedded in one theory or another. The view is that all observation is "theory-laden."

Kuhn's "theory-ladenness of observation" argument is again drawn from his study of the history of science and focuses on the nature and function of the language of scientific theories. According to Kuhn, the meaning of a scientific term in a theory is created or defined by the whole complex of substantive and methodological principles taken together. Terms acquire their meanings by their role in the full statement of the theory and not by some isolated definitions that may be separated from the full statement of the theory.

Each theory has theoretical and observational terms. The meanings of the terms of theory T1 are given by the principles and methods of that theory. But the meanings of the terms of a rival theory, T2, are given by the principles and methods of the rival theory. So even if the two theories use what look like the same terms, upon deeper reflection, Kuhn argues, we can see that the meanings are different. The term "mass" has a different meaning in Newtonian physics than it has in Einsteinian physics. The fact that we use the same word "mass" in both cases is almost as much coincidence as the fact that we use the same word to talk about the "grounds" of a hospital and "grounds" of coffee. When we look at the world, we are observing whatever we see in the physical world through the "lens" of the theory we accept. We might switch to accept another theory. When we do so, we "see" the world in a different way. This includes not only our theoretical concepts but also our reports of directly observable events. Thus the logical positivist notion that there are purely objective terms that allow us to report our sensations or experiences is impossible, according to Kuhn. The world cannot be examined in a truly objective way.

Kuhn says that a comparison of two paradigms requires that an investigator be able to think about both together so that they can be compared by applying relevant objective evidence. All of the evidence is interpretable only through acceptance of a theory and is thus theory-laden. Moreover, the two (or more) paradigms cannot even be conceived or thought of at the same time. An investigator can conceive of one paradigm or another, but she cannot conceive of both together. Consider the analogy using the familiar drawing of a square with a second square overlapping it and just above it and to the right; four diagonal lines

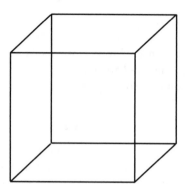

Figure 3.1 Double image cube

are drawn between the corresponding corners of the two squares (see Figure 3.1). A viewer can look at the bottom square and think of it as the foremost surface and the upper square as the rear surface. A viewer can interpret the diagram the other way, imagining the upper square is the closer surface. The point of the analogy in the context of our discussion of Kuhn is that the viewer can hold one interpretation or the other but cannot hold both interpretations in her mind at the same time. She can shift back and forth, especially with practice, as much as she likes. But it is always a choice between interpreting the lines one way or the other. Kuhn holds that a scientist can interpret the available evidence through the mediation of one theory or through the mediation of another theory. But it is a matter of shifting back and forth between the two theories. There is no framework external to both theories that allows the investigator to compare them objectively.

Increasingly True Representations of Reality

The notion that one generation of theory supersedes another on the grounds that it is a more comprehensive representation of reality is a basic idea of the traditional notion of science. It is one that almost all philosophers of science have endorsed. Popper and Lakatos refer to a superior theory as including all of the true content of the older theory and adding more content. There have been attacks on the claim that science progresses toward objectively better theories. The most prominent attack comes from the arguments developed by Kuhn's notion of the incommensurability of paradigms.

The core of the idea arises in a straightforward way from the criticisms laid out in the previous two subsections. One described Kuhn's argument that we cannot truly compare one paradigm to another; we noted that this argument aims to show that there is no objective sense in which the newer theory is a "better" one. Only if the newer one is better can we argue that science is progressing. Kuhn does argue that typically newer theories can do various things that older ones cannot, especially in terms of solving puzzles. But progress in the way it is traditionally understood by philosophers of science does not occur.

Objectivity and Moral Content

The distinction between moral-value statements and factual statements was drawn in the mid-eighteenth century by David Hume (discussed in Chapter 2 in connection with the concept of "causality"). Logical positivists and other empiricist philosophers believed that facts and values could be neatly distinguished. Factual statements describe the world by telling us what it is like while value statements prescribe action by telling us what the world should be like. Hume argued that no matter how extensively we describe how the world *is*, we will never be able to draw any conclusions about how the world *ought to be*. Thus value statements constitute a separate domain from science. This gives the study of values a more secure place in intellectual enquiry, as it cannot be "reduced" to discussions of reality. It also gives the sciences the ability to pursue rational theories without being infected by the subjectivity of values.

There are two major lines of argument to attack the fact-value distinction. One is to argue that all apparent value statements are, upon deeper analysis, really factual. So we can find out which value claims are true and which are false in much the same way we do with ordinary factual statements. A second way is to argue that all apparent factual statements are, upon deeper analysis, really value statements.

With respect to the first, someone might argue against the distinction by holding that value claims are of precisely the same sort as fact claims. That is, in essence, they are factual. Moral theorists have offered many definitions of "moral goodness" over the centuries. If one such theorist defined "moral goodness" as "pleasure" (as hedonists have) or as "what provides the greatest usefulness to the greatest number of people" (as utilitarians have) then she would be able to state claims about morals that could be verified by the same sort of methods as statements like "snow is white." This sort of moral theory is sometimes called "descriptivism" or "ethical naturalism." (The latter term has nothing to do with the "social science naturalism" this book investigates.)

The second strategy is sometimes advanced by arguing that science makes "presuppositions" that invoke values (see Putnam 1975). If the presuppositions of science make use of moral values, then science itself is not free of values. We must remember that the attacks on the fact-value distinction are discussed here because they are part of an attack on the objectivity of science. These attacks show at least three limitations on the arguments against the objective and value-free nature of science. First, they show only that (A) science is not value free; they do not undermine the fact-value distinction. And for our present purposes, the important question is whether or not science is value free, not whether the fact-value distinction holds. Second, these arguments do not succeed in showing that (B) *none* of the statements of science (e.g., physics or chemistry) individually are purely factual. But, a third point is that (C) the argument that science is not value free does not exclude "ethical naturalism" or "descriptivism." On this sort of theory of morals, value statements turn out to be factual. So it is still possible to hold that, even though we might conclude that science inherently includes values, the value statements in science are still objective and factual.

Among the issues connected with presuppositions, we note that all investigators in both the natural sciences and social sciences have to choose which problems to study. No individual can choose to study all possible problems. The decision about which problems or questions to investigate, like any other choice humans make, is shaped by that person's values and priorities. The choice to conduct research on leukemia rather than on Parkinson's disease is a choice that is made on the basis of one's values. No matter how objective scientists' experiments are, the mere fact that some choose to devote their lives to studying leukemia rather than Parkinson's disease is a development in science that stems from individual moral values.

A purely logical argument against the fact-values distinction, which was offered by A. N. Prior, asserts that it is possible to draw a conclusion that has value terms from premises that have none. The argument runs as follows.

A deductively valid form of argument is:

1. P
∴ 2. P or Q

That is, if we know (P) Nicolas Sarkozy is president of France, then we know with certainty that either (P) Nicolas Sarkozy is president of France, or (Q) Parker Posey is president of France. No matter what the statements P and Q are, we also know that if P is true, we may infer P or Q. Consider then the argument, (P) Nicolas Sarkozy is president of France, therefore, (P) Nicolas Sarkozy is president of France, or (Q) people are morally obligated to give 50 percent of their income to People for the Ethical Treatment of Animals. In Prior's example, the premise, P, which has no moral content, is the sole basis for the conclusion P or Q, which does have moral content. A disjunction like P or Q is true if even one of its components is true. So, as long as we know that proposition P is true, then even if Q is false, the proposition P or Q is true and logically follows from P.

Some philosophers object to this critical argument by claiming that it offers only a trivial objection—one that stems more from a feature of deductive logic than from the relation between facts and values. We could add any absurd statement as Q and it would equally follow. (Prior's own choice for a Q was "All New Zealanders should be shot.") Some have sought to defend the fact-value distinction from this logical argument by noting that the argument could be offered no matter what sort of proposition Q is. Thus, they protest, the argument does not show anything in particular about the relationship between statements of fact and those of value.

Consider also the argument that when we are confronted with two scientific theories, we have to choose between them. If our choice is not random, it must be based on a set of rational criteria that philosophers of science have developed. The philosophers consider various alternative sets of criteria and come up with what they regard as the best set. The decision of which set is best is a way of telling us that some theory, given the available evidence, is better than other theories. That is, we should value one more highly than the others. This is sometimes called an "epistemic value" or "epistemic norm" (mentioned in Chapter 2). Science cannot proceed without any values, it must invoke epistemic values. A defender of the distinction might argue that there is no problem admitting values to science as long as they are not moral values. Rational discourse among philosophers and historians of science could potentially lead them to a clear view about epistemic values. The history of disagreement about values is most obvious when we are talking specifically about moral values, which seem to be irreconcilable. In contrast, choices among epistemic values may turn out to be as reconcilable as various other choices theorists have successfully made throughout the history of science.[5]

Along the same lines we may add two more points. One is that the individual investigators have to make subjective decisions drawn from their personal value systems as to when there is "enough" evidence to support a hypothesis or theory. Empirical statements or theories can never be fully proven beyond any possible doubt. So some subjective and evaluative element must be involved to conclude that a particular claim should be accepted. Second, critics argue that all human researchers have human moral codes, which produce tendencies to interpret evidence in ways that are shaped by those subjective codes. This is inescapable so long as science is conducted by humans and not robots (and may be a problem for robots, too, if at some point they are built to be capable of designing and interpreting the research).

The Debate Over What Reality is Made of

Positivism, Empiricism, Underdetermination, and Conventionalism

Positivism and Empiricism

Scientific discourse involves talk about things we observe, which various sorts of empiricists put at the foundation of their theorizing. There may then be a problem for them with regard to terms that deal with things we cannot observe, like "gravity," "electrons," or "the wave structure of light." This raises the questions, Are the things we cannot observe actually real? And, are the things theories talk about real or imaginary or some third possibility? This has turned out to be an important issue in the philosophy of science as well as IR, where it has been debated by rationalists, constructivists, and others. Philosophers of the empiricist school of philosophy—a broad group that includes logical positivists and logical empiricists—have denied the importance of believing that unobservable things theories talk about must be "real." Other philosophers, known as "scientific realists," argue that science cannot be properly understood if the things the terms used in our best theories appear to refer to are not real. There are other positions, as well, as we will see.

Both scientific realism and empiricism seem to be supported by plausible arguments, and debate continues. Scientific realism is different from "common sense realism." While scientific realism is disputed, almost all philosophers accept common sense realism, the doctrine that there is a real world of material things, such as tables, chairs, dogs, and people, as well as immaterial things that are not debated by scientific theories, such as ideas, beliefs, emotions, dreams, and numbers. Scientific realism differs from common sense realism in that it asserts the existence of the things that are mentioned in scientific theories that are, in principle, unobservable and are rejected by various other serious scientific theories. Some of the objects that common sense realists accept are not observable in the scientific sense, but they are not ones that are postulated by some scientific theories and denied by others.

IR scholars have taken explicit positions on this question and have claimed that their positions make a difference for their theories. This is evident, for example, in the title of one of the constructivist Alexander Wendt's papers (coauthored with Ian Shapiro) namely, "The difference that Scientific Realism Makes" (Shapiro and Wendt 1992). Caution must be taken with terminology, which can be confusing. In IR, those who oppose *political realism* might support *scientific realism* (as is the case with Wendt), and those who support political realism might reject scientific realism (as is the case with Waltz). Moreover, scientific realism is only one sort of "realism" that philosophers talk about. There is also causal realism, common sense realism, critical realism, motivational realism, and others (see Chernoff 2002, 191–92; 2005, 214–15).

The unobservable entities that we call "theoretical entities" are not just things we have not yet observed, like a postulated bird species that we think must be the link between two known species or a postulated star far away that has not been seen by a telescope. Things like these could possibly be observed given the nature of our minds and sensory apparatus. What we call "theoretical entities" must be things that are postulated by theories and that cannot, even in principle, be observed. Our inability to observe gravity is not a result of any weakness of our eyes, ears, or available laboratory equipment. Gravity is something that is in principle, by its nature, impossible to observe directly. We only observe effects that we attribute to gravitational forces.

Some empiricists and pragmatists argue that observational laws and other components of theories are either true or false, but they hold that theories themselves should not be taken as either true or false. Rather, theories should be understood as tools or instruments that help people get certain types of jobs done. A good theory of physics will help us build houses and bridges and a good theory of astronomy will help us send rockets to Mars. But the theories are not themselves true or false. The empiricists and pragmatists in this group, like John Dewey (1948), are known as *instrumentalists*. For those theorists, a good theory is a tool that we use to our advantage to do things in the world. Different theories are useful for different tasks. Some elements of a theory are true and false, especially the general laws that deal with observable entities. But a theory may seek to explain the observational laws by proposing higher level laws that postulate unobservable, theoretical entities. We should not regard the higher level laws as true or false.

According to instrumentalists, the explanations scientific theories offer may fulfill our criteria for a good explanation. If they fulfill the criteria, then we should regard them as good explanations. But we should not also regard them as true. Good explanations and good theories are tools we use to get a job done. If we are building a house, we might have many tools in our toolbox, and we choose the appropriate ones to help us get the job done most efficiently. In the tool box we might have a ball peen hammer and a claw hammer. The claw hammer may be the most useful one for our immediate task. But that does not make it any more the "true hammer" than the ball peen hammer. For instrumentalists the same holds for explanations and theories. There is no reason to take the explanation as true or to conclude that the things the theory refers to exist.

One of the main arguments offered by logical positivists, logical empiricists, and others against accepting the reality of unobservable theoretical entities is that science became successful when it separated itself from the "unseen forces" of religion, magic, and the occult. These philosophers hold that modern science has been so successful a model for human knowledge because it adheres to what we can observe and does away with metaphysical entities, as far as possible. They say that we must separate genuine science from metaphysics, mythology, magic, and religion. Science deals with the observable world. It need not and should not regard as real anything that goes beyond our sensory experience.

Empiricists also argue that it is a basic principle of science and philosophy to seek the simplest among various possible explanations. If one set of entities or forces is enough to explain something, then we should not postulate anything more. This is a principle known as "Occam's razor." We might talk about unobservable entities as a way of helping us to organize our thinking into theories. But what we take to exist in reality should only be what we observe. The set of fundamental entities we are committed to accepting as real should be as small as possible. If we can explain the world in terms of observable things, then, by Occam's razor, unobservable entities should be rejected as part of the real world.

A third argument that empiricists offer against scientific realism has to do with the purposes of science, which they claim are to describe, explain, and possibly predict future events in the observable world. What needs to be described and explained is only the observable world. So our theories should help us do those things and those things only. Some empiricists argue that we can describe the actual world of observable events and processes just as well without invoking theoretical entities as real. And if we want to predict future events, we can do so just as well regarding theoretical entities as "possibly real" as we can by regarding them as "in fact real." Our goal is to account for the phenomena that we observe. Any theory that allows us to account for the phenomena will have some benefit for us. The theory has to be consistent with all the phenomena observed; that is, it must "save the phenomena." An instrumentalist might question a structural IR theorist like Waltz (1979) or Keohane (1984) about the role of international political structures. These structures seem less "real" than people or even nation-states. Some might object that these structural theorists should not attribute real causal force (or indeed any causal force) to "made-up" things like political structures.

They might object in particular that only "real" people (or "real" states) can have causal force in the social sciences.

Instrumentalists, like Waltz, might reply that we are perfectly justified in offering theoretical explanations using "made up" entities like "balances of power" or "international political structures." All scientific theories use theoretical terms. And we use the ideas associated with these terms to explain. We do not know that the theoretical entities are real. We may very well come up with a better theory in the future that discards them. But while we use theories that invoke them, we may attribute causal powers to them for the purpose of explanation. Instrumentalists would say that the best available explanation is not true; it is more useful than the alternatives. The only grounds we have for accepting a set of theoretical entities is that they are part of a theory that provides better explanations than the alternative theories.

Instrumentalists in IR, like Waltz, use the analogy with the natural sciences to support the use of possibly unreal entities, like balances of power or political social structures. Waltz claims theories that posit unobservable international political structures made up of states are better at explaining the observable behavior than theories that do not rely on those unobservable entities. Instrumentalists argue that in the natural sciences we accept many unobservable things, such as atoms, electrons, or gravitational force. But we accept the theories that posit them because those theories fulfill the criteria of theory choice, previously discussed, better than other theories. Once we accept a theory that posits them, we treat them as real and think of them as having causal powers. The only reason we believe in unobservable atoms is because the theories that talk about atoms are better at explaining what we observe.

A final example empiricists can cite to argue against scientific realists comes from one of the most important debates in modern science: the nature of light. Christian Huygens and his followers argued that light is propagated in waves, while Newton and his followers argued that it consists of very small particles. Each view was supported by specific behavior observed in the study of light. For more than a century it was not possible to determine what theory was superior and thus what the "true nature" of light was. Scientists for centuries were willing to use both views until a unified view should come along. A scientific realist could not in good conscience use both explanations at any time, which was a big limitation that would hinder scientific progress. The empiricist would argue that for a long part of the history of modern science the procedure most physicists accepted—using both the wave and corpuscular models—would be unacceptable to scientific realists because of incompatible conclusions they would have to draw about what entities exist. This is not a problem for instrumentalists and other empiricists.

Underdetermination of Theory by Data
One important empiricist-oriented criticism of the traditional account of science stems from the view that we cannot be sure that our best theory, no matter how well the data support it, is really the best theory humans can possibly devise.

With any finite number of available observations (and we always have only a finite number), there will always be more than one theory consistent with the observations. So the available data at any given moment are not sufficient to determine, in a way that eliminates all theories but one, which is the correct theory. This result, associated with the great French physicist and philosopher Pierre Duhem, is known as the principle of the *underdetermination of theory by data* (which we will call UD). This creates a problem for the scientific realist. Even if the data allow us to reject many theories, there will always be more than one that is consistent with all of the data.

Duhem argued against the standard view of science in several important ways. In addition to his argument for UD, he made a powerful case for *conventionalism* and for *holism*. The former notes that physics and other sciences make progress and exhibit growth of knowledge by accepting certain conventions of measurement. We might come up with a different set of physical laws if we believed that our standard measuring instruments changed size as we moved them to measure different distance intervals. We would then have to postulate certain forces that account for the changes of the measuring instruments' size. It is only because all physicists accept the *measure-stiplulation*, which says standard measurement instruments do not change size, that they can agree on which theory is the simplest and best.

On the question of holism, Duhem argued that we must evaluate all aspects of the knowledge we use to account for our observations in a field of study. Duhem wrote his major works before Einstein offered a theory of space-time that accepted non-Euclidean geometry. Even philosophers quite close to Duhem on many points, like fellow-conventionalist Poincaré, argued that physics would always accept Euclidean geometry because of its simplicity. Duhem understood that the simplicity criterion would be applied to the whole body of theory-plus-supporting mathematics. Duhem's argument for holism thus says that we should evaluate rational criteria on the entire body of beliefs we hold.

Duhem and his fellow physicists accepted (when he published his first major work on the subject in 1905) Euclidean geometry, not because it was simpler, but because the theory of space that makes use of it is the simplest of the available alternatives. If a theory should come along that uses non-Euclidean geometry but produces a simpler overall structure, which counterbalances the less simple non-Euclidean geometry, then we should choose that theory. Within a decade of Poincaré arguing this case, Einstein published a theory using non-Euclidean geometry that was simpler than any other account of all the known observations and, as Duhem expected, came to be universally accepted by the community of physicists. Duhem would insist that the criteria we use for theory evaluation-accurate predictions, simplicity, and the like- be applied to the whole of the body of knowledge we use to judge the truth of individual hypotheses and laws. We cannot test those laws under the pretense that every other assumption and belief we need to carry out the test is somehow known with certainty.

Radical Underdetermination

Some philosophers, notably Willard Van Orm and Quine, have taken Duhem's UD thesis and pushed it much further, formulating the radical underdetermination of theory by data. UD tells us that we can eliminate some theories given our finite set of data, but there will always be more than one (in fact, infinitely many unthought-of theories) that we cannot eliminate. The principle of radical under-determination (RU) goes further by stating that the data do not allow us, on grounds of logic, to eliminate or falsify any of the theories. On the standard view of science, when we find a contradiction between what our theory predicts and our observational results, the theory is falsified and we must modify or discard it. But Quine argues that we mistakenly believe that we must discard the theory because we mistakenly accept as certain the so-called analytic statements, especially the laws of logic; accepting these as unassailable is what forces us to regard the theory as falsified.

On Quine's view the accepted propositions are connected to one another by multiple and complex ties of confirmation and support. When a contradiction is discovered, the decision regarding which propositions are to be expelled is not given by any external rule of logic. Quine says that some of the propositions are more central to our beliefs than others, and we are less willing to give them up when a contradiction arises. Truths of logic and mathematics are connected to so many other beliefs that they would be placed at the center of the web. However, because for Quine there is no analytic-synthetic distinction, there is no hard-and-fast qualitative difference between truths of logic and other propositions. There is a difference in the degree to which we desire to hold on to them. But it is not a difference of kind. We give up propositions on the periphery that have fewer or less important connections to the others. However, logic does not prohibit us from rejecting some of the central propositions.

The primary implication of Quine's account of scientific knowledge for the criteria of theory choice regards the way we choose which statements should be removed from our body of accepted beliefs. Quine says that we do not have a hierarchical structure of statements built on a foundation of unquestionably true observations, analytical statements, rules of logic, and so forth. He thus does not endorse a foundationalist theory of knowledge. Our accepted statements comprise a network of interrelated statements. They include prescientific observations of the world around us, rules of logical inference, the results of scientific experiments, and theoretical statements from sciences. Some statements, like rules of logical inference, are near the center of the network and connected to many others, while some are further out toward the periphery and connected to few others. We choose what adjustments to make to our body of believed statements based on pragmatic considerations; our adjustments are the most convenient ones that help us accomplish activities in the world. When our existing theory has many anomalies we should replace it with the one that has the greatest significant similarities with the old theory. This is called the criterion of "methodological conservatism."

Quine thus argues for RU by rejecting both the analytic-synthetic distinction and foundational theories of knowledge. With regard to the analytic-synthetic distinction, Quine contends that there is no difference between the supposedly synthetic laws of the theory and the supposedly analytic laws of logic that force us to admit the contradiction. And his rejection of foundationalism allows him to say that, if we really want to maintain a particular theory in the face of apparently falsifying evidence, we can always make alterations elsewhere in our body of beliefs, including our beliefs about the laws of logic. As Quine puts it, we can always keep any proposition or theory "come what may." Quine concludes that the rejection of the analytic-synthetic distinction means that no matter what observations are made, we cannot follow Popper's recommended method of falsifying any theory through pure deductive logic alone. We always have the choice of rejecting some of our beliefs outside of the theory.

Critics of Quine have argued that philosophers have traditionally regarded the laws of logic as true and that Quine is unable to explain why they have. Because Quine rejects the analytic-synthetic distinction, he is unable to explain why they are true in terms of the concept of "analyticity." The questions that then arise for Quine are, What makes the laws of logic true, and what makes a theory true? Quine and his followers have to find a way to account for "truth" that differs from most other philosophers. They do so by building on the pragmatic theory of truth.

Three Theories of Truth

In order to see the way Quine's argument works we must look at competing accounts of what makes a statement true and what allows us to differentiate true statements from false ones. The most familiar account is the "correspondence theory of truth" which holds that a statement P (such as, "Monty is short") is true precisely when the conditions P talks about all are to be found in the real world (that is, precisely when it is in fact the case that Monty is short). So, the statement is true if what P says corresponds to the actual state of affairs in the real world. P is false if what it says does not correspond to real conditions in the world. This is the way we ordinarily think about the concept of "truth."

There are various difficulties involved in working out a full philosophical account of the correspondence theory of truth. To take just one objection, the explanation of what makes something true is that it fits with the facts of the world. But some hold that to say "it fits with the facts" is just another way of saying "it is true." Thus, on the correspondence theory, the statement "Monty is short" is explained to be true exactly if the statement "Monty is short" is true. This looks to be circular. There are other problems with explaining what the precise relationship is between the statement P and the fact that P is the case in the real world. Philosophers have argued that correspondence theories of truth are ultimately forced into metaphysical solutions that bring with them intractable problems.

Another problem often cited deals with how we might come to know a statement is true and the problem of "independent access" to the necessary knowledge. If we define a statement "Monty is short" as true in terms of its correspondence with the fact that Monty is short, then we must ask how it is that we can ever know that the statement "Monty is short" is true, since there is no *independent access* to any information about Monty's size that could lead us to be able to conclude or know that P is true? The relationship appears to be circular.

These difficulties have led some philosophers to propose a "coherence" theory of truth. According to the coherence theory, if a set of propositions (P, Q, R) are combined in our body of beliefs, then they must be logically consistent with one another. Once the set is created, new propositions may be added and counted as "true," if they do not contradict any of the propositions already accepted. A key difference between correspondence theories and coherence theories is that only for the latter would we say that the truth of a particular statement will exactly depend on the other statements we accept as true. There are problems with coherence theories as well, some centering on the high degree of relativism. What is true for Smith is not true for Jones. This is a particular problem because on the coherence theory of truth, the theory itself is true only if it coheres with other propositions that are accepted as true. That is, if Smith defends the coherence theory and Jones does not, Jones could continue to reject Smith's arguments for the coherence theory on the grounds that the coherence theory does not cohere with Jones's other beliefs. Some have attempted to ameliorate the extreme relativism by requiring that the set of propositions must be accepted by a community rather than by a single individual in order to be counted as true. But this approach creates various additional problems without avoiding relativism.

A third way to understand "truth" is along the lines of the pragmatic theory, developed by Charles Sanders Peirce—generally regarded as America's greatest philosopher. On this view, a statement is true if it helps people accomplish things in the world. The proof of a statement's truth is its "cash value" in aiding action. William James, John Dewey, and W. V. O. Quine, among others, follow Peirce in advocating a pragmatic theory of truth. They hold that the body of accepted propositions is "revisable" in the way Hempel argued that observation reports are revisable; just because they have at one point been accepted does not prevent us from rejecting them at some later point. Quine, for example, argues further that as we learn new facts we add them to our body of accepted beliefs as long as they do not contradict other beliefs. However, when a new observation contradicts our previously accepted propositions, then we face a choice of which to reject. We make that decision on pragmatic grounds. Logic does not force a specific solution on us. Rather, we decide which set of propositions to retain based on which allows us to accomplish more tasks in the real world.

Many philosophers go against Quine here by arguing that when contradictions arise among our beliefs, there are some propositions that we simply would never give up. In particular we would not give up truths of logic and mathematics because they are true simply in virtue of "relations among concepts" and the meanings of the terms involved in the statements. They are thus immune to falsification. We cannot go out and experience anything in the real world that will show us we were wrong to believe the analytic statement "all bachelors are unmarried" or "one plus two equals three." As long as we define our terms consistently, we cannot learn anything new that will require us to give up these statements.

Because Quine does not accept the analytic-synthetic distinction, he does not insist that we are required to hold on to the analytic statements in our body of believed statements, as we just noted in the discussion of radical underdetermination. Quine says that if we accept a theory T that tells us to expect outcome X in experiment E, but if experiment E is performed, and X does not occur, then we would be tempted to reject theory T. However, Quine says that this is not dictated by logic. Our claim that we have falsified theory T is based on the contradiction between T's expectation (in those circumstances) of X and the fact that X did not occur (under those circumstances). But there are many other propositions that are used in the inferences that allow us to connect the T's theoretical principles with the expectation X. And we are free to reject any of them. Quine thus says that our rejection of theory T is not grounded in unassailable and analytically true rules of logic. If we want to maintain the theory badly enough, we might make any number of other adjustments in the web of propositions accepted, including—if we were desperate enough to retain the theory—adjustments in the propositions that are ordinarily regarded as analytic.

Scientific Realism

Scientific realism, as noted, is the view that we should regard both our best scientific theories as containing true laws and the entities they mention, including theoretical entities, as real. On this view, good scientific theories are true, bad ones are false. They defend by noting that if a particular theory is true, then all of the statements in that theory must be true. And they also defend by arguing that a statement such as one that refers to theoretical entities can only be true if the things it refers to exist. Since some of the statements of our best theories refer to theoretically postulated unobservables, like gravitational forces, antimatter, or neutrinos, then those theoretical entities must exist.

Scientific realists hold that science presents us with theories that try to explain the world. Many of the explanations are causal explanations. Competing scientific theories offer different explanations and, in doing so, postulate different sorts of entities. We test the rival theories and, using the best available scientific methods, conclude that one of the explanations in a particular area of study is the best one. According to scientific realists, we may then infer that the explanation is true and we may infer that any entities that the explanation makes use of must exist. This view is called "inference to the best explanation."

Arguments for Scientific Realism

Scientific realists have offered many arguments to support their claims, sometimes invoking common sense to support them. The most well-known argument is the "miracle" argument. Scientists have sought to find the truth about the universe for many years. They have devised many theories. Over time the theories have improved and have come to explain more and more of the observable phenomena in the world with great mathematical precision. How could this happen, scientific realists ask, if the theoretical entities referred to did not really exist? It would be an extraordinary stroke of luck if our best theories refer to unobservables and then we observe things happening just as if those unobservables really existed. The success of science would simply be a miracle. It is too improbable that scientific progress can all be attributed to a "miracle." It is much more rational to believe that the best theories actually describe the world and that unobservable entities really do exist.

Another set of arguments for scientific realism also focuses on causation and common sense. In our ordinary nonscientific conversations we talk about causes all the time. We take for granted that events in the natural world are caused. We think of this as part of common sense. If causes exist in our ordinary experience of the world, then we should continue to find causes no matter how deeply we investigate why those phenomena occur. Scientific realists are much more closely tied to certain doctrines of causation than empiricists, some of whom do not want to talk about causation at all, viewing it as another unobserved "occult quality."

Some scientific realists argue that science, as instrumentalists acknowledge, has been very instrumentally successful. They use this fact against instrumentalists and empiricists. They note that we choose the theories that are best from an instrumental point of view. That is, the theory we prefer over its rivals will be the one that has the greatest instrumental value (though that may not be the main reason why we choose it). Over time the succession of theories that we accept gets better and better and each new theory has greater and greater instrumental value. This is a result in part of the methods scientists have developed. Scientific realist authors like Richard Boyd ask us to keep this in mind as we compare instrumentalism to other forms of empiricism and also to scientific realism. They then ask which of these various accounts of science offers the best explanation for how it is that our scientific methods can increasingly produce theories that are instrumentally successful. A theory that is instrumentally successful is one that yields true predictions. These authors then say that only scientific realism requires that the theories be true. What we see in science is that we start with true, or mostly true, observations about the world and, using scientific methods, produce new truths. Only scientific realism requires that the theories be true. Our observation that scientific theories, over time, become more instrumentally successful and produce true predictions can be explained only by one of the various accounts of science, namely scientific realism.

Empiricist Arguments Against Scientific Realism

Empiricists have responded to some of the major arguments of the scientific realists. Some of the important replies deal with the history of scientific theories that are accepted but later rejected. Consider Aristotle's theory of the physical world, which for centuries was universally accepted, though modified along the way. Those who studied Aristotle's system were entirely certain that the basic principles were correct and that the forces Aristotle postulated were real. But they turned out not to be. When the modern era began with the scientific revolutions of Galileo and Newton, people realized just how wrong Aristotelian theory was, and they were astounded by how powerful modern theories were—especially Newton's. For the next two and a half centuries almost all scientific observations added more certainty to the conviction that Newton had finally found the deepest truth about the physical world. People believed there were gravitational forces operating in the way described by Newton, that space consisted of absolute points of location, and so on. Eventually anomalies were observed and by the end of the nineteenth century there were serious doubts about Newton's theories. But before the doubts arose, Newton's theory dominated physics for two and a half centuries, during which scientists professed certainty in it.

At the beginning of the twentieth century Einstein's theories of special and general relativity were proposed; they soon replaced Newton's. Einstein's theories postulated different theoretical entities. For example, they rejected the idea that space has absolute points of location. Scientific realists were wrong about their beliefs in the entities that Aristotle postulated and later were wrong about those postulated by Newton. Therefore, physicists who accepted scientific realism had false beliefs. Empiricists say that these false beliefs were unnecessary. Investigators should not have taken Aristotle's or Newton's unobservable theoretical entities as real in the first place. They add that if such well-confirmed theories, which stood the test of time and scrutiny for centuries, turned out to be wrong, then it is highly probable that fifty, one hundred, or two hundred years from now scientists will have some radically different theory to replace Einstein's. Thus, by inductive reasoning, they would expect that it is highly probable—indeed, nearly certain—that Einstein's theory and the forces it postulates does not present us with the final truth about the physical universe.

To put it another way, if all of the past theories turned out to be wrong, no matter how overwhelming the evidence for them was at various times or how long they were believed to be true by the greatest scientific minds of the centuries they dominated, then we should conclude that the current theories in every field, no matter how strongly they have been corroborated, will eventually be shown to be false by superior theories devised some time in the future. This reasoning—called the "pessimistic induction on the history of science"—should, as just noted, lead us to believe that there is a very low probability that current theories will continue to be accepted indefinitely and thus a low probability that the entities postulated will turn out, in the long run, to be real. Empiricists fully acknowledge that, at the present time, Einstein's theory is the best we currently have to predict the future, to base engineering projects on, to build spacecraft that travel to their intended destinations, and more. Empiricists thus argue that we engage in less error by suspending beliefs about the entities, even while accepting Einstein's as the best available theory on which to base practical activities. They conclude that we should not accept as real the unobservable entities of any scientific theory.

A second important argument against scientific realism deals with the idea that there may be two competing theories, both of which are fully confirmed by all existing observations. There may even be two competing theories that would lead us to expect all of the same observable outcomes in any situation. The theories may still be different in that they account for the observable phenomena by using different laws (which in combination produce the same expected outcomes) and postulate a different set of unobservable entities. For the empiricist, and especially the instrumentalist, there may be various criteria applied to choose the best theory. Those criteria may have good rational bases, such as one theory is easier to apply than the other. But what if the other theory is the "true" theory? Such a question does not arise for the instrumentalist, for whom neither theory is "true." One is a better tool than the other for doing our job. However, for the scientific realist only one of the theories can be true and it is not clear how the scientific realist can be justified in believing that the chosen theory is, in fact, the true one.

Even if the two theories only deliver equivalent predictions about what we would expect to observe in the cases where actual observations are available, the problem for scientific realist would be just as great. At any given moment the scientific realist would say that our accepted theory is the true theory and the entities it postulates are real. So even if there are future observations that may distinguish one theory as better than the other, until those observations are made, the scientific realist has a dilemma about what to believe. The scientific realist might reply that we will have to perform the necessary experiments to see which of the two theories is correct and, once that is done, we will be able to eliminate all but one; at that time we will be warranted in believing the best theory to be true and the entities it postulates to be real. Proponents of the principle of underdetermination of theory by data and the radical underdetermination of theory by data, described in the previous section, would have grounds to challenge this argument.

Critical Realism

Critical realism is a form of philosophical realism that seeks to provide grounding in the social sciences for naturalism and for a notion of "causation." Critical realists accept the core views of scientific realism but go much further by adding a social element to the conception of scientific knowledge. Critical realism was developed in conjunction with Marxist theory but has taken on a separate identity over the past thirty years. Proponents specify three main pillars of the doctrine: ontological realism, epistemological relativism, and judgmental rationalism.

With regard to the first, ontological realism, critical realists agree with scientific realists that the terms we use in a theory that appear to refer to real objects do indeed refer to real objects. This applies to observable as well as unobservable theoretical objects. For a scientific realist, when a theory we accept uses a term that appears to refer to an observable object, we may infer that the object exists.

And when a theory we accept uses a term that appears to refer to an unobservable object, the object is real, though, of course, unobservable. So unobservable, theoretical entities are just as real as the objects we observe. Critical realists go even further and argue that the world contains much that we do not directly observe and that we do not know about.

Epistemological relativism is the doctrine that all beliefs are socially produced. Every society in every age has a set of guidelines and conditions that it imposes on what people believe. These change from one era to another and from one region of the world to another. There are no belief systems that transcend geography and history; every belief that anyone has ever accepted has been accepted under a particular set of geographical and historical conditions. The different sets of beliefs in different eras overlap. Reality forces that overlap. For example, reality conflicts with the belief that a person, by drinking enough alcohol, is able to walk in front of a speeding bus and continue unharmed. So it is unlikely that any society, let alone other societies that might have overlapping of beliefs, would include that belief because reality conflicts with it. Critical realists believe that there is a historical and geographical specificity to all beliefs, they reject "judgmental relativism"—the view that one set of beliefs is just as good as any other. Within any society, and historically, there are more and less well-justified beliefs.

Finally, critical realists endorse "judgmental rationality," which requires that theory and practice must be related to one another. The only way we can make sense of an action is to see it as making use of some idea of reality, which exists independently of any particular actor. So there is a social or collective aspect to reality that will be accepted by any particular actor in that society. Critical realists argue that these three elements are the key features of any natural or social science. [6]

Critical realists stress that in both the natural and social worlds, objects have real causal powers, even though the number and complexity of factors sometimes make it difficult for us to see the workings of those causal powers. These real powers exist and operate in the world whether we observe them or not; gravity is real even when we are not witnessing falling objects. Laws, like the law of universal gravitation, should be understood to state a tendency in the natural world, such as, "objects *tend to* attract one another with a force inversely proportional to the square of the distance between them." So critical realists vigorously reject empiricism, which they say confuses what we can observe with what is real. There is far more to reality than what we observe. Anyone who conflates the two is committing a fallacy, which they call "the epistemic fallacy." (Bhasker 1997, 36–38; Wight 2006, 28). Critical realists differ from scientific realists because, as critical realists see it, science is not purely objective in the sense that it is bound up in our social processes. And the world that science seeks to uncover has real powers that exist apart from science's inquiries.

The critical realist holds that there are layers of reality, with the observable world at one level and, at a deeper level, the unobserved causal mechanisms of which we can only have limited knowledge. The physical world can be treated experimentally in a way that the social world cannot. Both have very complex sets of factors that interact with one another. But in the natural world we can create artificial systems and isolate them from the workings and influences of other forces. Thus, experiments in the natural sciences allow us to create artificially "closed systems." In these experimental, closed systems it becomes more obvious that factor A consistently leads to factor B because we have removed other disturbances that might hinder us from seeing the connection. We can then take these artifices and draw well-founded conclusions about the open systems of nature. But we can only do this in the natural world, not in the social world. This is leads to the main difference between the natural sciences and the social sciences.

A closed system deals with a set of variables that interact only with one another. It is possible to identify those variables and then theorize about the influences that they have upon each other. In an open system there are far more variables than an investigator can identify. If we pick out the key variables and develop a theory based on them, there are always likely to be more factors that interact with them so that no matter how much we measure the interactions between the variables we have selected, there will always be factors outside of them that will influence the outcomes we are trying to understand. So a rigorous systematic theory that provides clear and relatively accurate expectations will be impossible. For a critical realist, reality consists of layer upon layer of causal forces. We may observe and explain one layer. But there are also deeper layers of real causal forces that, if understood, would help us account for the previous layers.

Critical realists believe that theories in the social science are always produced for a purpose, one of which should always be the improvement of the conditions for the people about which the theory is produced. Human beings have an inherent desire for, and right to, emancipation from oppression. Theories should strive to bring about human emancipation. This is a notable difference between the critical realist account of the social sciences and other accounts, including traditional scientific realism. One of the main distinctions is that critical realism, unlike other approaches, would take as a key criterion of theory choice that any acceptable theory in the social sciences should aid in human emancipation.

Causation and the Link between Policy and Theory

Causation

Before we leave the naturalist account of IR and social sciences, we should be as clear as possible about what "causation" is. We should consider how causation is supposed to work in various theories. Scientists who devise theories in astronomy, chemistry, and other physical sciences have typically regarded it as part of their task to explain not only what the regularities are but also how one type of event (the ball rolling off the edge of the table) leads to another event (the ball dropping to the floor). Different physical theories offer different causal explanations. Each invokes "scientific laws" that state what the regular behavior is.

Moreover, they assert that the law has held up in the past and will hold up in the future. The process of combustion is now explained by means of a process of oxidation, whereas medieval theories held it was the action of a substance called "phlogiston." Scientists have observed the same *law-like regularity* of fires igniting immediately after someone has struck a match. But now they offer a different causal explanation to account for the regularity. (Wendt 1995 offers a parallel IR example). Over time, one behavioral regularity may be replaced by another (as Newton's theory was replaced by Einstein's), likewise, one causal explanation may be replaced by another (as with phlogiston by oxidation).

In the social sciences theorists have also generally held that it is part of their task to provide causes, that is, to explain the forces and powers that show how high unemployment leads to social unrest or how a system of many great powers gives rise to more frequent major war than a system of two great powers.

It is helpful at this point to clarify the difference between "singular" and "general" statements. A singular statement like "Vladimir Putin is president of Russia" refers only to individuals, namely Putin and Russia, rather than to any categories or classes of things. General statements like "all objects with mass exert gravitational force on one another" or "all tyrants seek to expand power" refer to classes of things. The latter statement, for example, refers to everything in the reference class without exception, that is, all tyrants. The statements, "most tyrants seek to expand power" or "80 percent of tyrants seek to expand their power," refer only to some members of the class. The first sort of generalization is a "universal generalization" and those of the latter sort are "probabilistic generalizations." Laws in the natural sciences have traditionally been formed as universal generalizations.

What is involved in making a causal claim? Take the example of the regular connection between watching someone strike a matchstick against the matchbook and the subsequent igniting of a fire on the match head. We see this happen over and over again. Why does it happen? One answer is that it is merely a coincidence. It has just happened that fire has started on the match head right after someone has struck the match.

One problematic consequence of regarding the conjunctions of the two events as mere coincidence is that there would then be no good reason to believe the next time the matchstick is struck it will ignite. This means that there would be no basis for any prediction, which creates a problem if we would like the theory's generalizations to help us formulate policies. Without some belief in the necessity, even of a probabilistic sort, of the cause bringing about the effect, there is no reason to believe that the pattern observed in the past will continue into the future. So we would be willing to let small children play with matches, since we would have no reason to think there is any more danger that the match would ignite than we would have to believe that a basketball would ignite.

All that we ever observe with our eyes is that the first event is followed by the second event. If we think only about our observations, we have no basis for any other kind of connection between the two events. We see only that there is a "constant conjunction" between them; that is, they happen in the same sequence all the time. If, beyond the mere coincidence there is a deeper connection, then it is something that we do not directly observe.

Any claim that we might think of as a "law of nature" involves a deeper, unobservable relationship, which connects cause and effect. These connections are called "nomic" regularities (from the Greek word "nomos" for law). For empiricist philosophers, our knowledge of the world comes primarily from our senses. But our senses allow us to observe only the constant conjunction of the events and not any "necessity" in the cause bringing about the effect. David Hume, the eighteenth-century Scots thinker—the most important philosopher to write on the subject of causation—concluded that what we call "necessity" in a case like this is something that we humans imagine and impose on the basic observation of the two distinct events, after we experience the constant conjunction between them. According to Hume, we learn about causal relationships by experience. Hume goes further and says that all knowledge claims we make about the empirical world "seem to be founded on the relation of cause and effect" (Hume 1977, 61–62).

Hume maintains that knowledge must either come from abstract reasoning (like logic or mathematics, which he calls "relations among ideas") or from experience of the senses (probable knowledge of the empirical world). He accepted that logic and mathematics can produce genuine knowledge, even certainty. Most contemporaries of Hume believed that science could also produce certain knowledge. They believed this, in part, because of the astounding power of Newton's theories of mechanics and optics, which were, by the mid-eighteenth century, long accepted and seemed certain beyond any possible refutation. Hume radically parted company with his contemporaries and argued, to their surprise, that physics was not capable of logical or mathematical certainty. Indeed, he showed that physics was founded on a view of "scientific law" and "causation" that did not stand up to strict standards of philosophical scrutiny.

Hume argued forcefully that, in the domain of empirical reality (as opposed to abstract reasoning), we cannot know what the future will be like. We can be certain tomorrow that one plus two will equal three, since it is a matter of relations among ideas. But we cannot know that Newton's laws will continue to hold true tomorrow. Hume argued that our beliefs about what will (or will probably) happen in the future can be explained less by logic than by peculiarities of human psychology. If we had no knowledge of fire or of matches, we would not know anything about the causes of a match lighting, even if we saw someone strike the match on the matchbook. We only come to know anything about causation or about "causal powers," as Hume correctly notes, by repetition and constant conjunction.

Suppose we see someone who simultaneously stamps her left foot on the ground, whistles "Take the A Train" and strikes the matchbook with the match. If this is our first observation of matches, we would not know which of those events (or indeed if it was any one or some combination of them) was causally related to the match igniting. Over time we see other people whistle, stamp feet, and strike matches separately and see them do so in different combinations and different circumstances (we might even conduct experiments). We then begin to see that it is the striking that is constantly conjoined with the match igniting and then reason that the striking is the cause. After we see repeated instances of match striking followed by match igniting, our psychological disposition leads us to expect the lighting after the striking. According to Hume, our minds' habit of producing the expectation of igniting provides the only "reality" to the "necessary connection" between the two events.

Independence and Contingency of Cause and Effect

To understand contingency we need to think about different types of statements. "Mr. Benny is married" is true if "Mr. Benny has a spouse" is true. We cannot imagine one being true and the other being false, unless we change the meanings of the terms. So there is a *necessary connection* between the two statements. "Mr. Benny is married" and "Mr. Benny is the world's greatest comic" are not necessarily related. If Mr. Benny had suffered vocal chord injuries as a child, he would never have become a radio comic. There might have been an injury. It was luck that there was not. The fact that he was never seriously injured is not a necessary truth but rather a *contingent* truth. So Mr. Benny's escaping any any vocal chord injuries in his youth is causally related to his becoming a great comic. Further, we can think about the concept of "Mr. Benny avoiding a bad injury" and "Mr. Benny becoming a comic" as quite separate. They are *independent events*. We cannot think about Mr. Benny getting married without thinking about Mr. Benny having a spouse. Most philosophers regard causal relationships as connecting two independent events in a contingent way.

Causal Overdetermination

Some have tried to define "causality" by saying that if one event causes another the first has to be present, or is necessary, for the second to occur. ("Y would not have happened but for X having happened." Or, "without X, Y would not have occurred.") For these people, X is a cause of Y if X is a *necessary condition* of Y. *Counterfactual conditional* statements are often taken to be helpful in understanding causation. The statement "if the brakes had worked, the collision would not have occurred" is a conditional statement (that is, an "if-then" statement), since the "if" clause expresses something other than what actually happened. We imagine what would have happened if X had not taken place; if Y had not subsequently happened, then we are led to say that X caused Y.

Consider the example of a police investigation of an automobile accident at a sharp curve in a road. It turns out the driver was under the influence of drugs, was driving at twice the safe speed limit, and the car had a severed brake cable. What was the cause of the accident? Was it the severed brake cable? The investigation concludes that because of the high rate of travel the car, the driver would have been unable to make the turn. A severed brake line would have caused the accident at slow speeds. The investigation notes also that drivers who have ingested similar drug doses are unable to make sharp turns of that sort even going the legal speed limit.

If "necessary condition" is the defining feature of causation, then none of the conditions (drug consumption, severed cable, excessive speed) caused the crash, because if we take away any one of them, the collision would still have occurred. While all of the conditions are causally relevant, none of them was necessary for the accident because of the presence of the others. In this case the effect, the accident, was *causally overdetermined* by antecedent conditions. The conditions were causally relevant, but none was a necessary condition. Thus the "necessary condition" analysis of the concept of "causation" is undermined by examples in which the effect was a result of "causal overdetermination."

Others have taken a different tack, saying that if the first event is enough to guarantee the occurrence of the second, then it is a cause. For them, "X is a cause of Y" is true if X is a *sufficient condition* for Y. Again, this turns out to be an inadequate account of "causation" because when we think of a house fire, a carelessly discarded cigarette may have been the cause; but a carelessly discarded cigarette does not in every case lead to a house burning down. So sufficiency alone cannot be used to define "causation." There are similar problems with the attempts to define "causation" by combining necessary and sufficient conditions, as there are problems that stem from multiple and distinct paths to the effect.

Multiple Paths and Conjunctive Paths

The example of the motoring collision shows that the effect can be arrived at by various distinct alternative paths. If only one of the causes would have been present, the effect (the collision) would have occurred. There are also complexes of causal conditions that may be necessary to bring about effects. Sometimes these different and independent factors all occur together, and only when they occur together (perhaps even in a specific sequence in time) will the effect occur. This is the norm in the social sciences; rarely do we have acceptable *monocausal* (single-factor) explanations for important phenomena. Sometimes a combination of conditions is needed to bring about the effect. Only when the conjunction of factors occurs does the effect occur. There also may be separate *alternative* factors or sets of factors working in conjunction with one another that can bring about the effect. And often the complexes are part of alternative paths so that Y occurs when the factors present are either A and B; B and C; A, C, and D; or E.

Types of Causes

Part of the philosophical task of analyzing the concept of "causation" involves probing how people use the term. Most terms, as they are used in common parlance, have many meanings. And often they are used carelessly. As the careless uses become more frequent, the term may take on a second, third, or fourth meaning. When we try to strip away the careless uses, we still find that there are several different senses of "causation." Aristotle identified four meanings: formal, efficient, material, and final. One of the most important IR theorists, Kenneth Waltz, has emphasized two different meanings: precipitating and permissive. Waltz argues that both are genuine meanings of the term. Therefore, IR theorists should try to identify and understand both types of causes. The idea is not new. Thucydides describes the Corinthians as telling the Spartans that those who permit evil to occur are more the cause of it than those who precipitate it (Thucydides 1996, 39 [L69])

A precipitating cause is an event that triggers the effect and is close to it in time. But the precipitating cause would typically not lead to the effect in substantially different circumstances. Many other conditions play a causal role. They are properly understood to be "causes," albeit, "permissive causes"—that is, conditions without which the precipitating event would not have brought about the effect. Some of the permissive causes might be long-term conditions, like interwar economic hardship in Germany as a cause of World War II, or even essential elements of the state system, such as the anarchical relationship of states within the system. A proper causal analysis of war or of World War II, for example, would, in Waltz's view, have to include both types of causes.

Probabilistic Causation and Laws

This chapter began with a qualification about the social sciences providing only probabilistic knowledge. We should then ask whether this qualification clashes with the general assumption of this chapter, that IR and the social sciences can be studied and understood along the lines of the natural sciences. We must consider the following objection according to which, if the most important generalizations are statements of probability, then perhaps there is some fundamental and insurmountable obstacle to thinking about the social sciences as parallel to the natural sciences. Thus perhaps the social world as merely probabilistic, is so essentially different from the natural world that we cannot produce respectable scientific-style theories. The answer lies in noting that many, if not most, "respectable" natural sciences also use nomic generalizations that are purely probabilistic; these include, for example, genetics, quantum theory, epidemiology, plate tectonics, and meteorology.

Almost everything theorists say about how the world works in international politics or any other area of the social sciences is phrased in terms of probabilities rather than universal truths. The social sciences like the natural sciences are *empirical sciences* that deal with the world of experience and observation. Mathematics and logic, in contrast, are *formal sciences* that probe the relationships between concepts that are in the human mind. True statements in the logic and mathematics can be known with certainty. For example, we know with certainty that any statement that is true cannot also be false (logic), or that the sum of the squares of the sides of a right triangle equals the square of the hypotenuse (mathematics).

In the natural sciences our theories may always, upon further examination, turn out to be wrong. But if they are right, then, in at least some fields, they appear to be universally true: we would expect that at sea level water will always—100 percent of the time—freeze at zero degrees centigrade (chemistry) or that falling objects near earth will always—100 percent of the time—accelerate at a rate of thirty-two feet per second squared (physics). In the social sciences, just like in the natural sciences, as we get more evidence and devise new alternative theories, we may begin to see that our accepted theories are wrong. But even if they are right, then the social sciences (and some natural sciences) give us only probabilistic truths, like "democracies are very unlikely to go to war against one another" or "an increase in the number of failed states in the system will probably lead to more international terrorism in the system". Philosophers have raised questions about possible differences in the nature of singular versus general probabilistic statements; these will not be addressed here (see Levi 1965).

There may be some conceptual difficulties with the idea of "probabilistic causation," but they affect IR as well as respectable natural sciences. For instance, it is quite common in medicine or epidemiology to talk about exposure to asbestos as a cause of cancer. But not every worker exposed to asbestos for a specified period will develop cancer. Such exposure is not a *sufficient condition*. If it doubles the subject's chances of developing cancer, epidemiologists will typically say it is a cause of cancer. Physics deals in probabilistic generalizations, too, at the quantum level. One can talk about the distribution of subatomic particles only in terms of their probabilities. This is not just a limitation on the quality of instruments or on the development of the theory at present; the theory states that the probabilistic characters of the generalizations are inherent in theories about that particular aspect of the physical universe. Thus even when terms like "probably" or "likely" are not explicitly used in social science generalizations, we should understand them as qualified in that way. The fact that we usually talk about "probabilistic generalizations" rather than "universal generalizations" in the social sciences does not separate them from the natural sciences.

Conclusion

The traditional view of science has some clear implications for what makes a good theory and thus for criteria of theory choice. Similarly, many of the critics of the traditional view have some alternative criteria. However, most accounts of science largely agree about what makes a good theory, though some put a higher priority on certain criteria than others do. For example, the many different accounts of what constitutes "good science" would all agree that Newtonian mechanics was a great advancement over earlier theories. But there are areas of difference that we have outlined. The traditional notion of science was challenged in the 1920s by logical positivists, soon thereafter by logical empiricists, and over the past half century by a variety of philosophers who offered even more radical critiques. This chapter has drawn conclusions about how these different philosophical accounts of science would evaluate competing theories. The chapter highlights criteria emphasized by each philosophical account.

The greatest overlap among different philosophical accounts of science would be on the "simplicity" criterion, which is especially emphasized by empiricists who also value explanatory breadth and other criteria. Most philosophers of science would prefer a simpler theory to a more complex theory. There are, however, some scientific realists and especially critical realists who have downplayed the importance of simplicity (Dessler 1989; Wight 2007).

If we were to lay out all of the criteria of theory choice accepted by each of the schools in the philosophy of science, there would be much overlap, but there would still be distinct combinations in every case; no two schools would include and prioritize all of the same criteria in the same way. Because of these differences, when we have a specific set of evidence (whether we are looking at theories in natural or social sciences), we would likely draw different conclusions about which theory is best, depending on which philosophical account of science (and thus which specific set of criteria of theory choice) we accept. Most of the time our choice of a philosophical metatheory will lead us to lean toward or away from one or more theories. But the final decision on the best theory at any given moment in the history of a discipline or field will depend on the metatheory one accepts along with the set of observations available to the investigator and range of competing theories.[7]

Table 3.2 lists the philosophical principles and doctrines of the traditional view and some of the challengers. Table 3.2 identifies at least one philosopher who has defended that position, and it lists at least one important criterion of scientific theory choice that arises from that view of science. The last column of the theory indicates how each principle tends to advance or undermine one or more of the theories from Chapter 2 (drawing on C1–C4). The table suggests one or two particular theories that each criterion would incline an IR theorist to be more

Table 3.2 Doctrine, criterion, and effect on evaluation of theories

Doctrine or challenge to doctrine	Major supporting philosopher	Key criterion of theory choice	IR theory evaluation*
Empiricism	Carnap, Russell	Simplicity	(+) Realism
Corroboration	Hempel	Range, corroborating cases	(+) Realism
Instrumentalism	Dewey	Predictive success	(−) Constructivism (+) Liberalism
Methodical falsification	Popper	Falsifiability	(−) Realism
Methodology of scientific research programs	Lakatos	New facts/fecundity, constancy of hard core	(−) Realism (+) Liberalism
Incommensurability	Kuhn	Mainly descriptive	
Value neutrality	Russell	Avoid moral propositions	(+) Realism (−) Constructivism
Moral element	Gramsci, Marx	Justice, goodness	(+) Constructivism (−) Realism
Scientific realism	Boyd, Putnam	True causal relations	(+) Realism (+) Liberalism
Critical realism	Harre, Bhaskar	Human emancipation	(+) Constructivism (−) Realism

* (+) indicates a positive effect on a theory; (−) indicates a negative effect on a theory.

likely to either accept or reject. This is only intended as a very rough guide and draws on some of the literature in IR theory. A complete argument for why Lakatosians, for example, would reject neorealism would depend specifically on the database they have available.[8]

CHAPTER 4

Reflectivist Opposition to the Scientific Approach:
Critical Theory, Poststructuralism, and Interpretive Constructivism

The previous chapter laid out some of the basic features of the natural sciences and some of the principles of methodology and some criteria for theory choice that have allowed scientists to develop better theories over time. Because these principles have led the natural sciences, like astronomy, chemistry, or physics, to such great successes, it seemed reasonable to many people to try to use these methods in an analogous way to guide the social sciences as well. Chapter 3 showed how they have been adapted for use in the social sciences. This chapter considers three important ways in which philosophers of social science and IR theorists have argued that the natural science analogy does not apply and why IR, in their view, should be regarded as something radically different from any of the natural sciences. The three are interpretive constructivism, poststructuralism, and Frankfurt School Critical Theory. Each is distinct from the others, but there are some points of overlap in the principles they espouse and, in some instances, in the sources of intellectual inspiration.

The naturalist approach of Chapters 2 and 3 modeled the study of the social world on the methods of the natural sciences. In stark contrast, all three of the reflectivist theories say that the study of language provides a better model and a source of theoretical grounding. And all three reflectivist theories share the "critical theory" idea that theories of the social world are not merely neutral descriptions of the way social actors (individuals, organizations, corporations, banks, states, etc.) behave but are also "critical" in the sense that they understand one of the functions of social theory to be a thorough critique of the societies in which the theory are produced. Wendt refers to these anti-naturalist theories as "critical" theories. Keohane and Martin use (1995) the term "reflectivist theories."[1]

Reflectivist theories encompass a number of different strands of academic thought stemming from philosophy, linguistics, literary theory, history, and social theory. The main thinkers in interpretive constructivism include Wilhelm Dilthey, Ludwig Witgenstein, and R. G. Collingwood. The most prominent contemporary scholars who apply it to IR are Nicholas Onuf and Freiderich Kratochwil. Poststructuralism is generally associated with French thinkers like Michel Foucault, Jacques Lacan, and Jacques Derrida. Prominent exponents of poststructuralism in IR today include Rick Ashley and R. B. J. Walker. And the main sources for the Frankfurt School Critical Theory are Theodor Adorno, Max Horkheimer, and, more recently, Juergen Habermas. In contemporary IR they include Andrew Linklater and Richard Wyn Jones. This chapter will look at how the founding ideas in each approach conflict with naturalist social science and the how IR theorists have made use of these reflectivist theories. For the most part interpretive constructivists and postmodern poststructuralists have taken their key ideas from linguistics, literary theory, and the philosophy of language. Critical Theorists of the Frankfort School and their followers have taken their inspiration from social theories, including Marxism.

All three reflectivist theories argue that the nature of the subject matter of IR and the social sciences is so different from that of the natural sciences that a completely different sort of method is needed. This implies that the nature of social science theories are different from those of the natural sciences, which in turn implies that we need different ways to choose between competing theories. This chapter will consider several ways in which reflectivist theories dispute the principles and presuppositions of traditional social sciences that are based on naturalism, rationalism, and materialism.

If the subject matter of the social sciences is so different from that of the natural sciences, then just *how* does it differ? And in what ways must the theories be of a different sort than theories of the natural sciences? Different authors have advanced different answers. This chapter begins by charting some of the ground that the reflectivist theories have in common, especially the interpreted nature of social "facts," the reflexivity of theory, and the role of constitutive relations. It then considers the ways in which traditional naturalist theories of IR are criticized by interpretive constructivism, poststructuralism, and Critical Theory.

Common Ground for Reflectivist Theories: Interpretation, Reflexivity, and Constitutive Relations

Facts and the Interpretation of Facts

One reason reflectivist theorists give for arguing that the analogy between the social sciences and the natural sciences must be rejected is that the social sciences always involve *interpretation* while the natural sciences do not. The natural sciences are based on scientists' ability to gather objective facts. Scientists use these facts to generate ideas for theories and, once the theories are proposed, they use the facts to test and compare theories. Some critics say that in the social sciences, unlike in the natural sciences, the "facts" that are used to stimulate, test, and compare theories are fundamentally different and are not objective at all. They say that in order for an event to be used in a systematic theory in the social sciences, we must be able to describe it, which requires interpretation. That is, whenever something happens in the social world there are many ways to interpret and describe it. Authors who hold this view are often called "interpretivists." *Interpretive theorists thus oppose the claim of objectivity in the scientific approach.*

Consider an example. We would say that the act of murdering someone is different from saving someone's life. We might witness a scene on a street and we would want to know which of the two it is. Suppose that we hear a gunshot and see person A fall to the ground; we then witness someone else, person B, rush up to person A, pull out a knife, and plunge it into A. We cannot tell from what we have just seen whether B is (or is an accomplice of) the shooter trying to make sure A is definitely dead, or whether B is an innocent passerby with surgical training who is trying save A's life by extracting the bullet. What we have available to observe is not sufficient for us to know with high confidence whether B is a killer or a lifesaver. The observable physical actions in the two cases might be exactly identical. The interpretivist would say that which conclusion we should draw depends upon the context and B's intent. It is not a matter of simply observing the physical action.

If we had had the opportunity to follow B for weeks before the incident, we would have information about the context that would allow us to produce a better interpretation of the event. For example, if we had seen B walk into a hospital every morning, put on a white coat, enter an emergency room, and plunge medical instruments into the bodies of hospital patients (and a few days later see the patients walk out of the hospital), we would have confidence that B was trying to save A's life. If, on the other hand, we had followed B and seen her walk up to shooting victims in streets, plunge a knife into them, and see the victims expire, we would have confidence in concluding that B's recent action was trying to kill A.

As we saw in Chapter 1, when North Korea revealed in 2002 that it possessed nuclear weapons, President Bush issued an order to keep the revelation a secret. Someone might describe that act as a selfless and courageous political sacrifice, since President Bush would be risking much future criticism when the story becomes public. They might say that President Bush understands that only one major world problem at a time can be solved and, in the autumn of 2002, he was in the midst of applying as much pressure as possible on Iraqi President Saddam Hussein to force him to step down. Another theorist might describe the event as a cynical and self-serving deception perpetrated on the U.S. Senate and the American public by President Bush, which aimed to conceal the true relative degrees of threat of different countries in order to push ahead the invasion of Iraq for political gain. On this interpretation, President Bush and his top advisors would be seen as desiring war in 2003 to get reelected in 2004; since war with North Korea was virtually impossible, Iraq would be the best target. The Bush advisers might have calculated that the American public would never support a war against Iraq if it knew that North Korea is in fact building nuclear weapons and, in contrast, Iraq is almost certainly not. At most it might have chemical or possibly biological weapons. The deception, these scholars might say, was so that the public would continue to insist that Iraq posed a greater threat to the United States than any other state. Was the decision to hide North Korea's announcement an act of courage or a cynical manipulation of public opinion to aid reelection? Some say Bush was advancing U.S. national interest. Others say Bush deceived the United States for his own gain. Which act was performed?

Whether we interpret President Bush's act as one of wisdom and courage to advance U.S. national security or as one of self-advancement and manipulation of the electorate to enhance his chances of reelection depends upon what we observe President Bush to have done in earlier cases—and later cases, as time passes. Of course, each of these other acts may be interpreted in more than one way. But there are some possible interpretations that are highly implausible. For example, neither the action of person A with the knife nor that of President Bush in 2002 can plausibly be interpreted as an attempt at a musical recital. We will consider this circularity next.

At this point we can see that reflectivist theorists who take the interpretive approach would reject any attempt to draw a parallel in the social sciences with the natural sciences on at least several of the standard features. One would be NS1 from Table 3.1 stating that the senses provide a solid basis for identifying facts. Interpretivists hold that facts are identified by constructed interpretations and there might be many good interpretations. Interpretivists would also reject NS2 and NS3 in the social sciences, since the lack of clear, uninterpreted facts would make it impossible to identify regularities among the facts and to quantify the regularities. The claim that there are no uninterpreted facts in the social sciences would also undercut the argument for applying NS6 to the social sciences. If there are no truly "observational terms" then there can be no clear distinction between observational and theoretical terms.

Hermeneutics and Interpretation

The problem of interpretation, and the possibility of a kind of circularity that scholars must confront, was developed by authors who called it "hermeneutics." The interpretive questions were initially faced by scholars seeking to understand Holy Scripture. But we will see how the same ideas have been applied to IR. Through much of the history of Christianity, theologians following in the tradition of Augustine understood the Bible to be a set of allegories. Centuries after this view gained dominance, Protestant theologians began to assert that the Bible should be understood literally. Who is right?

Scholars then had to pose the question, how should we interpret a text? It became one of the important questions in Western scholarship. Scholars also asked whether different readers would understand a text like the Bible in the same way. A traditional view, dating at least back to Plato, is that language is precise enough and human reason is powerful enough to ensure that different readers will understand a text as it was meant by the author. But scholars in the hermeneutic tradition have challenged this view, arguing that every individual has a unique set of experiences. People will always interpret new experiences, including what they hear and read, though their own framework of prior experiences and learning. And individuals in different cultures are even more prone to interpret the same text in different ways.

The Bible was written by human beings and copied by hand by other human beings generation after generation. Mistakes have certainly been made along the way. After centuries of copies, how do we know if the text in front of us is correct or incorrect? The Old Testament was written in Ancient Hebrew and the New Testament in Koine Greek. So those who do not read the original language must also consider errors in the translations. The field of hermeneutics began as a way of studying scriptural texts to determine authenticity. After the Reformation, it took on a new role as Catholics and Protestants disputed theology.

If a biblical scholar encounters an error, suchh as a misspelling, she can still understand the passage. You probably had no trouble understanding the previous sentence, even though "suchh" was a misspelling. If you were hand-copying that sentence, you would see it as an error and correct it. However, if there had been many such errors, then the copyist might not be sure what the sentence meant and how it should be copied. And different copyists might well come to different conclusions about what the author truly meant and about how it should be written as they produce new copies. And if this book had been a hand-copied text, then the copyist who makes the next generation of copies would have to make a decision about whether or not to correct the error (copying "suchh" as "such").

In interpreting the works of great philosophers, we presume that part of their greatness was their ability to produce coherent arguments. The arguments are often written in complex language that cannot be straightforwardly interpreted (or translated into another language). What do we do when we find two passages in the works of a great philosopher that appear to be contradictory? Should we try to find out what the author could have meant by the contradictory statements that would render them noncontradictory? Should we assume that every apparent contradiction is simply a flaw in the philosopher's argument? There are no obvious answers. Most historians of philosophy believe that at least some apparent contradictions are most likely inadequate representations of what the author meant, although they accept that occasionally great philosophers err by contradicting themselves. Here again we can only hope to find the true meaning of a philosophical treatise not only by interpreting the whole work sentence by sentence, but also by understanding the whole argument and seeing that some of the statements might contradict others in the argument. Only then can some of the apparent contradictions be discovered and possibly resolved.[2]

The Hermeneutic Circle

We cannot understand any given sentence without understanding the words in it. Hence the possibility of interpreting a text requires that we understand the words in each sentence. But the sentences cannot be understood without our understanding the whole, since words have different meanings in different contexts. So it appears at first glance that if there is such circularity, then there is no "starting place" for interpretation. If so, then any attempt at interpretation would be impossible. However, many scholars hold that there are solutions for the dilemma of the "hermeneutic circle" and for some cases where we run into the problem of inaccurate copies or translations. One sort of solution is to focus on the way we can get a "somewhat inaccurate," "incomplete," or "partial" interpretation, and then improve it little by little. The idea of a "partial interpretation" is an important one in finding a solution. Once a vague understanding is achieved, then gradual refinements are possible in increments. According to this process, we can go back and forth between the whole sentence and the individual words to gain an accurate interpretation.

Another important question of meaning is, whose meaning do we seek? When we seek the correct meaning of a text, is the right answer what that text meant to its author, what it meant to the intended audience, or what it means to us? When we try to interpret a literary work written thousands of years ago, we must face the fact that the author's cultural context and central challenges of society are vastly different from our own. What may be important in the author's ideas, for us, may be different from what would have been most important for her audience in her own era.

When we seek to understand a text each of us comes to it with a particular set of beliefs that interpretivists call "presuppositions," which shape how we understand it. The presuppositions arise out of the particular culture and the particular historical moment in which we live. One scholar brings to a text one set of presuppositions while another scholar in another culture and in another century brings a different set. According to hermeneuticists, we not only seek to understand the text itself but we must also seek to identify our presuppositions, analyze them, and adjust our interpretations of the text accordingly.

In the late eighteenth and early nineteenth century Freidrich Schleiermacher extended the scope of hermeneutic study beyond scripture and beyond literature to all human activities that are intentional, symbolic, or creative. In the late nineteenth century Wilhelm Dilthey argued along similar lines claiming that hermeneutic principles should be applicable to other artifacts of human intention, whether it is sculpting a figure, painting a landscape, writing a philosophical treatise, composing a symphony, or deciding whether to invade a neighboring state. These are all human activities that have purposes, intentions, and meanings. For this reason he held that hermeneutics should be the foundation of all social science. According to scholars in the hermeneutic tradition, human knowledge is always incomplete; the parts of it must be understood to gain an understanding of the whole, but the whole must be understood to interpret the parts, and there are ideas we bring to our study of the problem that might need adjustment. After they are completed, others will have to take up the challenge of trying to decide what they mean. And those others might disagree about their meaning. So how do we decide who is right?

Dilthey found, moreover, that the way we find objectivity in the natural sciences is fundamentally different from the way we find it in the social sciences. In the natural sciences, individual humans make observations of the world, for example, measuring the time it takes a ball to fall from a tabletop to the floor. We then have to extract our own unique characteristics out of the experience so that the observation can be entered into the overall body of scientific statements. In the social sciences we find objectivity in a different way. When we study why President Bush kept secret North Korea's nuclear weapons declaration in 2002, we are making observations as individual humans. But we do not try to take subjective elements out of the picture to create objectivity; rather, we try to "get into" the subjectivity of President Bush and his key advisors to gain an understanding of their actions.

Followers of the hermeneutic tradition in the twentieth century such as Martin Heidegger and Hans-Georg Gadamer have argued that seeking meaning and producing interpretations of the actions of others is one of the essential features of what it means to be human. The circularity is compounded in their view because the person doing the interpreting must interpret her own actions and behavior, which inescapably includes the act of interpreting. Some have argued that the only way to understand an author's text or a political leader's behavior is to try to get to know as much as humanly possible about that person. That is the work of an interpreter or scholar. Reflectivist theorists thus disagree with the application of a foundationalist theory of knowledge (which was connected to NS1, Chapter 3) to the social sciences, since knowledge is developed in a circular and not linear way.

IR Theory and the Circularity of Interpretation

The idea of the "hermeutic circle" has been applied to the social sciences and IR. Let us consider the U.S.-North Korea case. An interpretive scholar would seek to understand the case by looking for an interpretation of President Bush's behavior that fits with all the "facts." If we interpret many of President Bush's foreign policy decisions as attempts to advance U.S. national security interests regardless of the effects on his own personal standing, then the 2002 North Korea decision is more plausibly interpreted as such an action. However, if we interpret Bush's behavior as president, and perhaps even in the years before becoming president, as calculated political maneuvers to advance his personal political fortunes at the expense of the public good, then we would interpret the 2002 decision as a self-serving deception. Was it a courageous and selfless act or was it a calculated political maneuver for personal or partisan gain? What the nature of the act was, and how we properly describe it, depends on our framework for interpretation.

Hermeneuticist authors would say that we need to use the full collection of interpretations to come up with the best interpretation of President Bush's 2002 decision for secrecy. Our choice of how to interpret that act will be part of the framework that we have available for interpreting the other acts we observed. There is, then, circularity. We need the other interpretations to interpret the 2002 secrecy, and we need an interpretation of the 2002 event to interpret the other events in the framework.

Another way to see the circularity involved in describing social action is to note that social contexts always have sets of rules, written or unwritten. Consider social actions where there are clearly written rules, like games and sports. In a game of chess the pawn is permitted to move one or two spaces forward on that piece's first move and one space forward on later moves. If Gracie moves her pawn diagonally so that it is next to (and "threatens") Montmorency's king, the action is not counted as a "move," much less a "check", because it violates the rules of chess. We cannot correctly describe what she has done as a "move" because we have to take into account the rules and the context.

Players learn that the rules of chess require that the only permissible moves of the pawn are forward at most two spaces on the first move and one space thereafter. Diagonal or other moves are not permitted. The context includes the fact that in all recorded chess matches of the past (and there are thousands in chess books), only moves of the pawn in accordance with these rules are recorded as official moves. We would interpret the player's decision to shift her pawn diagonally either as "not playing chess" or as "cheating." If all past chess players shifted their pawns at points diagonally, then we would call Gracie's diagonal move a chess "move." The physical action of moving the chess piece is identical to the physical movement of moving the bishop from the same beginning space to the same ending space (in another match). But the diagonal move of the bishop, unlike the pawn, is within the rules of chess and therefore constitutes a chess "move."

The rule also has to be part of the motivation for the player to relocate the chess piece. For example, suppose that Gracie is about to make her move but gets up from the chess board instead to get a drink of water and accidentally bumps the board in a way that causes only the pawn to move to a legal space. We would not classify that action as a chess "move." The opposing player, Montmorency, would allow Gracie to shift the pawn back to its original place and move again. The action has to be in accord with the rules, but the rules must also be part of what *motivates* the player to make that particular move. That is, the intention of the player is relevant to whether what physically happened is a chess "move." Since we do not have "direct access" to anyone else's thoughts or motives, we have to interpret the other actions. We thus find ourselves in the hermeneutic circle by having to examine other actions to try to determine if cheating is a plausible, or perhaps the most plausible, interpretation in those cases.

Interpretivists would argue that our study of the social world is not only very far from the way that we study the natural world, but it is really very much like the way we study language. When we study language we discover the rules of semantics, grammar, and syntax constitute words, phrases, and sentences. These rules allow us to interpret and understand people speaking or writing in English or another language. But the rules do not explain why they said what they said nor does the study of language help us predict what they will say in the future. Certainly no one would expect any such predictive ability from the study of language. The best we can do in studying the social world is to try to *understand* the behavior of leaders and states after the fact, and that can be best done by trying to devise a set of rules that will allow us to interpret the meanings of their actions. So interpretivists would say that the study of IR can provide a set of rules of grammar or syntax that can allow us to interpret actions most effectively. The study of IR thus helps us understand the meanings of actions that cannot be well understood without the sort of careful study that produces interpretive frameworks. But our study does not give us scientific-style *explanations*. Still less does it justify *predictions*. Reflectivist theorists thus reject the idea of extending to the social sciences principle NS9 (from Chapter 3) stating that theories, at least when specific conditions of their application are known, must be able to generate meaningful predictions.

In the 1960s and 1970s Gadamer argued that the goal of objectivity in the social sciences is misconceived. We undertake the study of North Korea or China from our particular historical, cultural, and geographic position. No amount of study will allow us to erase this. We inherit the events of 1648, 1939, and 2002 and cannot understand the world without our experience of the effects of Westphalia, World War II, and North Korea's nuclear policy. We are part of a circle because we inherit the effects of those events; we then go back with that heritage and try to understand the events as if their aftereffects had not yet occurred. This *historical circle* imposes many restrictions on our knowledge that form the limits of what we are able to see; they form our "horizon of understanding."

People in previous generations had their horizons defined by their understanding of distant cultures and people. The best we can do is to try to understand the horizons of previous generations and bring our horizons in line with them—thus creating a "fusion of horizons." Some of the recent scholars in this tradition have moved away from the idea that we must learn everything possible. They claim that authors' intentions can never be recaptured or known with certainty, so the project is futile. Others argue that, as we seek to understand a text, we must find what the text means *to us*. This is all we are capable of discovering and is all that can really matter to us, since the author's actual intention is unknowable and irrelevant. Authors, especially poststructuralist authors discussed later, take interpretivism to entail that language does not provide us with a relationship of a sign (like the word "stone") to something outside of us (such as a stone by the side of the road) or even to something in our minds (like the idea of a stone). These poststructuralists hold that language provides us only with relationships between one sign and other signs. There is "nothing beyond the text" itself.

Causes and Reasons

One major difference between naturalists and reflectivist theorists is the *role they give to "causation" in the social world*. Scientific thinking and theorizing have been regarded as tremendously powerful in practical terms and tremendously successful as an intellectual endeavor, and one of its most central features is "causation." While different philosophers have defined "causation" in various ways, they all accept that one event or event-type is said to bring about the occurrence of a separate and independent event or event-type. We might say the chess player shaking the table that the chessboard sits on caused the white king to fall to the floor. The shaking of the table is a clearly identifiable action. The chess pieces are small, upright, and not normally affixed to the board. The shaking of the table is followed in time immediately by the white king tipping over, falling off of the table, and landing on the ground. We have reason to believe the general statement, "whenever tables are shaken with sufficient force, small upright untethered objects on them will tumble over and fall to the ground."

Contrast the shaking example to that of a chess match in progress in which one player pushes her pawn forward one space. What would philosophers say about causation in this case? Would they say that the player's pushing the pawn forward one space caused the chess move? No; they would say that her pushing the piece *was* the move. In this case there are not two distinct things, the "pushing of the chess piece" and the "move." The pushing of the pawn constituted the move. If there had been no game in progress, the action of placing the piece one square forward would not have been a chess move. Because of the rules that created the context for the player's action and because of the player's intention, the shifting of the piece *constituted* the chess move.

Virtually all of the reflectivist theorists considered in this chapter emphasize the crucial importance of drawing a sharp distinction between one event *causing* another, where the two can be described independently of one another, and one event description *constituting*, at least in part, another event. The shifting of the chess piece forward constitutes the chess move. We cannot describe the move the chess player made without reference to the shifting of the piece from one square to another. In a causal relationship, we can always describe the two events and imagine either event occurring without the other. There is then a crucial difference for reflectivist theorists between *constitutive* and *causal* relationships. Reflectivists would object to extending NS4 from Chapter 3 (see Table 3.1), which is the core idea in the natural sciences of "causation," to be taken as a core idea in the social sciences, as well.[3]

Reflexivity

A *second important difference* between traditional naturalism and recent reflectivist theories in the social sciences *deals with "reflexivity."* The notion of reflexivity separates IR and the social sciences from the natural sciences by emphasizing that IR theory requires that people study the actions of people. That is, human beings are both studying and being studied. The problem that emerges is that if new beliefs are developed by the people doing the studying (the theorists) then when their results are published, the people who are being studied (the leaders) might read those results, learn from them, and consequently change their behavior. This could invalidate the work that was just published because of self-defeating prophesies. There is a similar effect with self-fulfilling prophesies.

Many scholars agree that the study of IR is reflexive in the sense that the theories they develop might change the subject matter they are studying by affecting the decisions leaders make. Consider two examples from American foreign policy: the creation of the League of Nations and U.S. Middle East policy during the 1973 Yom Kippur War. Reflexivists argue that President Wilson's actions after World War I were affected by his having studied the writings of Immanuel Kant. Wilson followed most of Kant's precepts involving an international federation of democratic states developed in Kant's famous essay on "Perpetual Peace." Wilson's belief in the Kantian theory of democracy and peace and of institutions helped to motivate Wilson to go to war against autocratic Germany and then to create the real world institutions of the interwar period. Similarly, reflectivists argue that President Nixon's belief in realism's "balance of power politics" led to the sort of Middle East settlement Nixon and Kissinger constructed after the 1973 Yom Kippur War.[4]

There are self-fulfilling and self-defeating prophesies that result from people theorizing about the behavior of people. Let us consider two hypothetical examples. Suppose it is widely believed that small states who border larger states should not develop nuclear weapons because the larger neighbor is likely to feel so threatened by those weapons that it will invade the smaller state to prevent it from producing an operational nuclear force. Now suppose that, as a result of this belief, small states fear the invasion-triggering consequences of moving toward developing a nuclear weapon and avoid doing so. A team of scholars examines various states that have developed nuclear weapons and compares them to states that have not. It then studies the reasons for these actions. It finds a widespread belief that developing nuclear weapons invites preventive attack (defined in Chapter 1) by larger neighbors and predicts that nonnuclear weapons states will remain nonnuclear. But it also reveals that, in fact, large states virtually never engage in preventive war and even less often do they attack a state because of a belief that it was developing nuclear weapons (perhaps citing Israel's attack on Osirak as the only case in history). One result of this might be that leaders who learn of the study will conclude that the larger nuclear-armed states, no matter what they threaten, are not actually likely to attack the weaker states that acquire nuclear weapons. Once leaders come to believe the new study, they would be more likely to build nuclear weapons. This would be a self-defeating prophesy.

There are also self-fulfilling prophesies. Realist theories are sometimes cited as having these effects. If all leaders choose to believe that realism is the most adequate theory, then they will act on the basis of zero-sum calculations; they will expect others to do the same. As a result, wars will occur. Critics charge that when leaders believe realist theories, they act in more war-prone ways and thus prove the theories right. Liberals argue that international institutions can create conditions to overcome some of the features of anarchy that are most responsible for allowing wars to begin. If leaders accept realist theories, they will be on higher alert and will be more likely to respond by using force. This would be true even when there are international institutions that have the purpose of securing the borders and other national interests of member states. If they accept the realist theories, then the realist prediction of continued outbursts of violence will be a result of the leaders' acceptance of realism. The peace-prone, liberal-leaning leaders would presumably rely on international institutions, believing that they have the ability to avoid war, in many instances where realist-leaning leaders would dismiss the ability of the institutions to safeguard their borders and security. The actions of the realist-leaning leaders, based on their beliefs, would undermine the ability of institutions to perform their peace-promoting functions. These effects of theories on the behavior of leaders and states define what is meant by the term "reflexivity."

Critics of the naturalist approach argue that there is nothing comparable to this reflexive effect in the natural sciences. When an astronomer studies a nearby galaxy, the publication of the results will not lead the nearby galaxy to act in some new and different way. As was noted in Chapter 3 (see Table 3.1), two of the hallmarks of the natural sciences are NS7 and NS8—that is, the study of nature reveals patterns that occur whether or not they are being studied, and that the patterns would be observed to be the same if studied by different investigators. Reflexivist IR theorists who criticize naturalism argue that this essential feature of the natural sciences does not apply as we study social action in IR. Thus they argue that some new framework for developing and evaluating theories is needed. All three sorts of reflectivist theorists considered in this chapter—interpretive constructivists, postmodern poststructuralists, and Frankfurt School-inspired Critical Theorists—are reflexivists in this sense. They reject the notion that NS7 or NS8 could properly be applied to the social sciences.

Interpretive Constructivism

Constructivists include some authors squarely in the poststructuralist postmodern camp and some in, or very close to, the naturalist camp. For the most part, interpretive constructivists are in the first group and conventional constructivists are in the second group. Conventional or American constructivism, discussed in Chapter 2, is often argued to be a middle ground between the traditional social science IR approach of naturalism, rationalism, and materialism, on the one hand, and poststructuralisms's radical rejection of any parallel with the natural sciences, on the other hand (see Adler 1997). We now turn to interpretive constructivists who, along with poststructuralists and other postmoderns, reject most of what is considered central to the naturalist approach to the social sciences, including some of what conventional constructivists advocate.

Constructivists disagree with rationalists on a number of key points. Three closely related points will be considered in the next three subsections. One is that the identities of agents or actors in world politics are not fixed and are not the same in all regions and time periods in the way that rationalists (especially neorealists and neoliberals) presume. The formation of identities influences the ordering of preferences. Second, agents in international politics are not truly separable from the structure in which they develop. Each changes the other as processes unfold. While we might analyze agents and structures as separate, each cogenerates the other. They are thus mutually constituted. Third, constructivists are highly critical of the rationalist conception of "anarchy," especially of the view that only one sort of anarchy is possible.

Identities

Constructivists thoroughly reject the rationalist understanding of the identity of agents, which is very important because the identity of an actor affects the actor's preferences and goals. For example, an actor whose identity includes being a judge will seek justice while an actor whose identity includes being a businessperson will seek profit. What the agents in the international system (states, leaders, banks, etc.) seek will, in turn, affect what choices they make. Let us turn to the first point: the constructivist's claim that identities are not fixed.

The rationalist view of "identity" is the one that is most familiar to us. A realist might explain an action like Britain's defense of Poland in 1939 as a result of Britain recognizing that Nazi Germany had already taken over Austria and Czechoslovakia, violated international agreements, and could not be trusted to honor any promises it made. Britain was a great power with interests all over the world; it recognized that its power would be threatened by Germany controlling most of the European continent.

Traditional naturalist approaches to IR would include debate over whether this argument is entirely correct. But all parties to the debate would acknowledge that in 1939 the UK was a nation-state; that it saw itself at that time as a great power; and that nation-states act in certain regular ways, which might be related to national interests and threats like territorial expansion of other rival great powers. While these seem very straightforward to us, constructivists and poststructuralists question how we should understand these claims (see Chapter 2). These reflectivist theorists argue that *what a state is* turns out to be the result of historical accidents. The UK is a nation-state and acted as one in 1939 because people in the UK happened to believe they were part of a great power state. People in London also believed that they were Londoners, people in Scotland that they were Scots, and people in Yorkshire that they were Yorkshiremen. But they all believed themselves to be British strongly enough so that they would join the armed services and fight the Nazis. What led them to support the war and to fight was their awareness of being British, which was a large part of the psychology of who they were. At much earlier points in history that part of the self-identity of people who lived in that region might have been weaker or nonexistent.

Constructivists hold that there is nothing automatic about the way most people in the world see themselves as part of one nation-state or another. People could think of their primary group identity in different ways, and long ago, they did. Even today there are people in some places where most of the inhabitants do not primarily identify with the state, such as Kashmiris in India, Kurds in Iraq, and many clan members in Somalia. Fifteen years ago we learned that most people in Yugoslavia thought of themselves as members of their various republics more than they thought of themselves as Yugoslavs.

Constructivists and poststructuralists emphasize that state A exists only because people in state A believe that A exists, and because people in other states believe that state A exists, which leads them to formally "recognize" state A. If no other state in the world recognized A's existence, then A would not, in a legal sense, exist as a sovereign, independent state. When Slovenia and Croatia declared their independence from Yugoslavia, there was a possibility that no other state in the world would recognize them as independent states. This might well have happened because almost all major states agreed that borders should not be changed unless it was by the consent of all parties, such as happened when Czechs and Slovaks agreed to a peaceful dissolution of Czechoslovakia. The states of the world then reasoned (and still do) that if they did not stand together to avoid border changes, chaos might result, since there were scores of groups around the world who claimed, based on historical events, that the current borders were unjust and should be redrawn. (The Confederate States of America declared independence, but were not recognized by others and were subsequently forced to remain in the Union.) Had Germany not recognized Croatia, then Croatia and the other Yugoslav republics most likely would never have come into existence as independent states and would instead have merged back into Yugoslavia. Germany, however, in a controversial move, chose to proceed with recognition. Once the most powerful and influential state in Europe chose to recognize Croatia, then it was difficult for other states not to follow suit.

As noted, constructivists argue that the subjective identity-formation is important and must be part of our theory of IR. Identities cannot be assumed to have a fixed character. A good IR theory must have an account of what states' preferences are and how they come by them, and rationalist theories do not generally provide them. Waltz, for example, says that states that do not start out with a preference for security and power are either eliminated from the system because they are overrun by those who do, or they learn that they must adopt those preferences in order to survive.

Identities and interests are developed by what we do. Our "doing" creates our sense of identity. We can do things to reinforce our own identity as aggressive. Over time we might start to do things that are less aggressive, if the proper incentives are in place, and performing these less aggressive actions will, in fact, change our identity. At any given time we have specific ideas about who we are and who we are dealing with in our world. These ideas influence how we interact with others. If we think of ourselves as weak actors in a world of strong neighbors, we will give in to their demands more easily. Similarly, how we interact with others (aggressively or peacefully) influences how we understand our own identity (as weak or strong, aggressive or peaceful) and how we understand the identities of our neighbors and the nature of the world around us.

Identities are affected by what the agent "does." But the constitutive nature of that action—what it is—also depends on the social structure. A clear example in IR would be Germany's deployment of troops abroad in Southern Europe. How we interpret Germany's action might differ over time; we see the different meanings at different times. Germany ordered troops to be deployed to the Balkans during World War II and then again sixty years later. The two decisions were interpreted in radically differently ways. During World War II German forces were seen as the principal agents of ethnic violence in Europe. Today German troops in the Balkans are part of a cooperative effort to prevent ethnic violence from recurring in the former Yugoslavia. In the 1940s German entry into the Balkans was abhorrent to France and the UK, while the German deployments are now encouraged by them because Germany, as the largest economy in Europe, has the resources to help lighten the burden for France, the UK and their neighbors, many of whom are working to bring stability to Southeastern Europe.

Agents, Structures, and Cogeneration/Mutual Constitution

Critics of naturalism and rationalism have focused on the relationship between agents and structures in social sciences like IR. We tend to regard something as vast and system-wide as World War I or World War II as truly epochal events that can be described by reference to the international system and the changes the war brought. They are very large events. Let us contrast them with small, physical actions. The physical actions of a person, even someone like Wilson or Churchill, are typically quite small. Their actions might include talking in front of news reporters or television cameras or signing a piece of paper. Even the sum of all of Churchill's official actions during World War II is very small compared to the physical activity of a world war. The actions of a bomber crew carrying out an attack are also relatively small, as they include flipping switches, holding controls, and talking to other crew members. How can such minor actions play a role in creating enormous effects like world wars that lead to millions or tens of millions of deaths, massive destruction, and the redrawing of state borders? The answer given by structural theories or constructivists in IR is that they are *mediated by* social structures like the state or the international system of states. In addition to the many structural constructivist theories of Wendt and others, there are constructivists theories that focus on the actions of individuals and states, on the one hand, and theories that try to combine these unit-level theories with systems theories, on the other hand (see Katzenstein 1996).

Is a structure made up of a collection of individuals? If so, then the individuals must exist before the structure can exist. They would have primary status and the structure might possibly be "reduced to" the individuals. A kitchen cabinet might hold a collection of canned food. The food available there is the physical sum of the food that can be found in the individual cans contained in the cabinet. The total is the sum of the parts. Is a social structure such as a national legislature, a nation-state, or an international system similarly equal to the sum of the parts that comprise it? That is, are these social structures simply the same things as the collection of things in them, like human beings, buildings, and armies? The answer that most scholars have given is "no." They would say that, in the world of social relations, a structure is more than a collection of individuals.

The U.S. Senate, for example, is a structure. It contains one hundred men and women, but is not simply the collection of those one hundred people. Senators are duly elected. But the status of "being duly elected" is not a physical trait, like "containing cans of food." Structures are complexes made up of relationships and thus are quite different from a collection of material things. Most scholars are more likely to say that a structure is made up of relationships, which are not themselves physical things. If Washington, DC had been bombed during World War II, the senators could have been moved to the basement of a farmhouse in Iowa and could have functioned in a fully normal way, even though the U.S. capitol and the Senate buildings were completely destroyed. U.S. senators are people who have physical and mental aspects, but the U.S. Senate is not a physical thing. The U.S. Senate, the British Parliament, and the Russian Duma are among the many structures that play roles in putting into action some of the decisions of particular individuals, which, on occasion, can produce massive world transformations and global conflagrations like World War I and World War II. So the small physical actions of individuals produce the immense results of world wars by means of the mediation of social structures. But we might still ask, how do agents and structures interact? Is it like the problem philosophers face when trying to explain how the human mind can interact with physical bodies?

Constructivists try to solve the problem of interaction between agent and structure, as noted, by depicting them as "cogenerated." They argue that social relationships are "opaque" rather than "transparent." Let us consider three hypothetical cases. First, suppose that President George W. Bush had traveled to Texas for his first weekend in office as president of the United States rather than staying in Washington. This diverges from what he, in fact, did. Even though it never happened, we can easily imagine it, and we can easily answer some questions about this hypothetical event. For example, would he have worn the same clothes? Probably not. And we can answer the question, would that person be the same person as the President Bush who, in fact, served as president from 2001–2005 and then began a second term? There is no difficulty in answering "yes."

Second, let us suppose that George H. W. Bush married someone other than Barbara Pierce. Let us imagine it was Barbara's sister, Martha, and imagine further that they had five children, including a son whom they named "George Walker Bush," who had the same upbringing as the real-world George Walker Bush. Suppose that son, in a disputed 2000 election on a ticket with Dick Cheney, becomes the forty-third president of the United States. Would *that* George Walker Bush be the same person who took office in 2001? The answer to this question is not as clear, since he would have had a similar upbringing but still some slightly different DNA. This is harder than the question about the Bush who hypothetically traveled to Texas in January 2001. But, despite the fact that this hypothetical President George W. Bush would have a slightly different genetic inheritance from the real-world President George W. Bush (since the hypothetical George W. Bush's mother is the Martha, not Barbara), most of us would be inclined to think the answer is also "yes." Some of us might answer "no."

Third, suppose that all four of President George W. Bush's grandparents had chosen to move to a rural village in Uganda to become missionaries, spent their entire lives there, raised their children there, learned the local language, and chose to speak it exclusively. Suppose further that George H. W. Bush and Barbara Pierce had met there, gotten married and produced six children, including a son whom they named "George Walker Bush." We might imagine that Uganda-George H. W. and Uganda-Barbara Bush loved the area and the simplicity of life so much that they chose to provide their children only with the education that local village children receive at the mission school. Suppose then that Uganda-George W. Bush, a non-English speaker, chose to live out his life in that village. Would we say that *that* George W. Bush is the same person who is now president?

The answer would seem to be "no," even though this third hypothetical George W. Bush would have the same genetic makeup as the real-world President George W. Bush. The reason we would answer negatively is that all of the *social relationships* in rural Uganda in which he was involved are so vastly different from those of the real-world George W. Bush. Those relationships were a big part of making him who he is. The Uganda-George W. Bush would be so different from the man who was born in Connecticut, attended ivy league universities, started oil companies, sat on corporate boards, bought a share of a major league baseball team, and then became governor of Texas and president of the United States. The point is that what makes up the individual we call "President George W. Bush" is not just his physical traits, which would be more or less the same in this third case (since the Uganda-George W. Bush would have the same DNA as the real-world President Bush). What makes President George W. Bush the specific person he is derives not only genetically from his parents and grandparents, that is, his DNA structure, but from the complex set of social relationships in which he is involved.

If there are no people or animals in the world, then obviously there can be no social relationships. However, as the Uganda example suggests, the social relationships are an essential part of making the individuals who they are. This seems to be a dilemma. Which came first—the individual or the social structure? Most critics of rationalism have answered that agents and structures each have a part in making the other what it is. They are, as we have seen, "mutually constituted" or "cogenerated."

Anarchy and the Structure of the International System

Structures and Relationships

Let us remember that in Chapter 2 we saw the difference between characteristics of individuals and relationships between individuals. When we say "Britain is an island" we are talking about the characteristics or properties of a single thing. When we say "Britain is larger than Iceland," we are talking about a relationship between Britain and Iceland. Relationships always require reference to two or more things. We noted in Chapter 2 that when we say, "Britain was powerful in the nineteenth century," we do not appear to be comparing Britain to anything else, since the sentence mentions only Britain. But when we think for a moment about what "power" means, it is clear that it is a relationship. Political scientists have offered many definitions of "power." One common way to define it is to say that power is the ability of one party to influence the behavior of another by getting it to do something it would not otherwise do. This definition makes sense only if we are referring to more than one party. The statement "Britain is rainy" does not express a relationship. If Britain were the only nation-state in Europe or in the world (for example, if the plague had wiped out everyone in all other states but had left Britain unscathed), we could still correctly say that Britain is rainy. But it would be meaningless to say that Britain was powerful, since there would be no other states whose actions Britain could influence to any degree. Power is a relationship.

A *structure* may be understood as a set of relationships. The structure of the European international system in Europe in 1900, or that of the global system today, is a set of relationships. Power relationships among states are one example and are the relationships that realists would say are the most important ones in defining the system. The set of alliances that exist today constitute another set of relationships. There are states inside the United States (like Alaska or Georgia) and inside Germany (like Schleswig-Holstein or Hesse), but they are not truly sovereign because there are hierarchical bodies (the federal governments in Washington and Berlin) that have authority over them.

Although there are no such hierarchical bodies with authority over the nation-states in the world today, we can at least imagine them. If there were such a body, then there would be another set of relationships of great importance. There are institutions like the World Trade Organization, International Monetary Fund, or the UN; they do not constitute a world government, but they represent a significant set of relationships between states. This absence of a world government creates another set of relationships among the nation-states, namely equality of authority. No state or nonstate body has the right to tell a sovereign state what to do. The absence of a hierarchical world government is, of course, exactly what we mean by the term "anarchy." So anarchy in our world defines another important set of relationships: the relationships of legal equality. Liberals acknowledge that the international system is anarchical and say that the power relationships and the institutional relationships are all significant in affecting world politics. Realists, in contrast, emphasize the importance of the power relationships and the anarchical nature of our system, arguing that these best enable us to explain the behavior of any international system. Realists also usually argue that "anarchy" is a fixed concept and that our system could not be organized in any other way. Must anarchy look the way realists depict it?

Varieties of Anarchy

The idea of "anarchy" is central to realist and neorealist theories of IR. It is cited as one of the chief factors that allow wars to occur again and again. On the realist view, states expand their territory as far as they are able until another state forcibly prevents them from going any further. Constructivists and reflectivist theorists generally argue that anarchy need not take the Hobbesian form of a jungle where each state-actor tries to destroy the others and only allows the others to survive insofar as it lacks the capabilities to destroy them. Constructivists say that this is only one of various ways to understand anarchy in the international system.

Hobbes had a major impact on the development of the realist tradition (as noted in Chapter 2). In IR Hobbes is known for his description of the *state of nature*, a hypothetical world in which there are no rules or social norms of any sort to regulate human activity. Hobbes said that in such a world people would steal from one another and commit violence against one another to get what they want. Like various other social and political philosophers, he said that such actions would not be immoral since there is no society in the state of nature. Furthermore, even the strongest individuals in this environment would be vulnerable to attack, as their goods could be taken when they are ill or asleep. Life would be so miserable under such conditions that it would be rational for all individuals, even the strongest, to give some of their autonomy to a sovereign power if that sovereign would use the authority over them to rule in a way that alleviates their misery. People would be able to begin to cooperate with one another only once a sovereign power is created. The cultivation of land or development of business and commerce are possible only when people leave the state of nature, because these developments require individuals to have confidence that others will respect their property and honor promises and contracts. All parties benefit from moving out of the state of nature into a society in which agriculture and commerce are possible. So conditions must be created where it becomes reasonable to entertain such expectations.

According to Hobbes, the relationship of nation-states to one another in the international system closely parallels the relationships of individual people in the state of nature. But there is a big difference when it comes to moving out of the anarchical state of nature. According to Hobbes, states, unlike individuals, will not all gain by surrendering autonomy to a sovereign power and therefore will not voluntarily do so. That is, since the strongest actors in the international system do not gain by giving up some of their autonomy to a sovereign, they will not rationally choose to give it up. A world government will, then, never be legitimate and anarchy will never be overcome. So the standard realist view of anarchy in the international system is that states take advantage of one another whenever possible. They form alliances frequently and honor them only for as long as they believe the alliances will bring them some advantage. And anarchy will never be eradicated because there are always some powerful actors who see their interests as hampered by giving power over to a sovereign authority.

In Chapter 3, the views of the "English School" were briefly presented. Our look at some of the philosophical ideas that underlie interpretive constructivists' critiques of rationalism requires that we have a clear picture of those views. Let us suppose we know three students at different universities: Immanuel, John, and Thomas. They have different attitudes toward their classmates. Immanuel is a very caring and sympathetic person. He helps his classmates with their studies. Sometimes he even overlooks his own needs to do his best to see that his classmates succeed. No one forces him to behave in this way; it is his preference. His goal is to see that everyone does well and he gets satisfaction from knowing that others in his class are succeeding. We might also imagine all students at Immanuel's school coming to adopt the same attitude.

John has a different attitude. He wants to do well. He knows that if he attends all his classes, takes good notes and studies hard he will pass. But he firmly believes that if he also works with other diligent students, exchanges lecture notes with them, meets with them in study sessions, and shares ideas about what questions the professors are most likely to ask on the exams, then all of them, including John himself, will learn more and perform better on the exams. But again, no one forces him to cooperate with others in this way. His goal is to achieve the highest grade he possibly can and he believes that cooperation will best lead to that result. We might also imagine all students at John's school adopting the same approach.

Thomas, like John, wants to do the best he can in the course. Unlike Immanuel, he is not concerned with the welfare of the others. And unlike Immanuel and John, he believes that he will do best by working on his own and against the other students. In his view he should try to steal notes from the others, hide important library books so that others will not have access to them, and so on. In short, Thomas believes that he will do best by exerting effort both to advance his own knowledge and to undermine the success of his classmates. Again, no one is forcing him to act in this way. He believes that it is the most effective way to get what he wants. And again, we can imagine that all of the other students think like John in this regard.

These three cases are, of course, parallel to the sorts of conflict and cooperation we would find in the international systems envisioned by Immanuel Kant, John Locke, and Thomas Hobbes, respectively. We can imagine different international systems in which states share these orientations. From these hypothetical examples, constructivists draw two important conclusions. The first is that there is nothing inherent in the definition or concept of "anarchy" that requires us to believe that the international system must *inevitably* have evolved in the way it has. It might have evolved in a way that would have looked more Lockean or Kantian. And there is nothing to prevent it from evolving more in those directions in the future. The definition of "anarchy" does not entail anything about ferocious competition or about the necessary evolution of a Hobbesian system. The second conclusion they draw is that the actual world is, in fact, not truly Hobbesian. It is certainly dangerous and could be vastly more cooperative than it is. But a truly and thoroughly Hobbesian world would be far more competitive and dangerous than our world; would not include completely unarmed states (Iceland, Luxembourg, Costa Rica, San Marino, and many others); would not have militarily weak yet prosperous states next to large and militarily powerful states (like Canada next to the United States); and would not have the many cooperative institutions we find in our world, from the World Trade Organization and World Bank to the European Union.

Liberals typically take the existing structure of anarchy as given and use it as a starting point to develop theories about how to change the international system to promote greater cooperation. They do not generally deal with the possibility of ridding the system of anarchy. Nor do they deal with the question of whether the system of anarchy *could have been* other than it is—that is, could have been more Kantian. Most contemporary liberals work to develop substantive theories of international politics rather than metatheories. One way of describing the core of social constructivism would be to say that the outcomes are not determined by the nature of things; that is, even given the nature of things, outcomes could have turned out otherwise than they did (Hacking 1999, 6). Constructivists stress that the violent, self-help form of anarchy, which is taken as a fixed feature of the international system of states, is a construct and is not given by nature—not even "social nature." It could have evolved in a much different way. Poststructuralists agree but take the analysis a step further and argue that states themselves are constructed and that they could, and indeed should, fade away.

While almost all IR theorists hold that there is "something constructivist" about the politics of the international system, neorealists are the most resistant since they maintain not only that the system is anarchical but also that anarchy exercises an extremely powerful influence on states in the system, which cannot effectively be overcome. They also dispute that there is a "nature of things" in the social world.

Constructivists are quick to point out that the more a social practice is followed, the more enduring it becomes. *Reinforcement* of social practices occurs whenever those practices are followed. The sociologist would explain why this happens by noting that when we observe the practices in action, the observation brings them to our attention and makes us more conscious of them. The more we observe those practices, the more deeply ingrained they become in our consciousness. Production and "reproduction" of the practices perpetuate them and in this way makes them more likely to endure into the future. The practice of power politics by states, for example, reinforces power politics in the international system. Nevertheless, power politics does not enter the system because of some inevitable force of (social) nature. Institutions and norms of behavior like the practice of "power politics" could come to be less used; and the less they are used in the short term, the less they will endure in the long term. Constructivists conclude that the less power politics is followed, the less need there will be to follow it in the future. Because of the long period of reinforcement, transformation of the semi-Hobbesian system into something more cooperative, according to constructivists, is possible, but would be difficult. And now is a good time to try to move toward such a transformation because of the great changes already under way in the international system—such as the disappearance of both the Soviet Union and the conflictual, bipolar structure of power, as well as the simultaneous rise and economic liberalization of China, which might make it both a less determined foe of the West and less a rival to the United States.

Can a Realist at the Substantive Level be an Interpretive Constructivist at the Metatheory Level?

Chapter 2 presented conventional constructivism as many of its proponents do, namely as a substantive theory of IR with cause-and-effect principles about why things happen in world politics.[5] This chapter presents constructivism, in the form of interpretive constructivism, as a metatheory of IR. This book has emphasized that a particular metatheory will not necessarily entail one particular substantive theory, especially in the absence of a set of empirical beliefs or evidence about the real world. This raises the question, is it possible to adopt interpretive constructivism as a metatheory and realism as a substantive theory? Are these two different dimensions (in the way that the dimension of male/female is simply a different dimension from that of blue-eyed/non-blue-eyed)? It seems possible to combine constructivism with liberalism, since there is a lot of overlap of the principles that actual liberal and constructivist IR theorists accept, as Chapter 2 showed. Is it then possible to combine a constructivist metatheory with a realist substantive theory? Various authors have answered that it is possible to combine them in this way.

A realist-oriented constructivist would hold, as a constructivist, that the world is made up of socially constructed institutions and, as a realist, that all social structures have in common the fact that they have one or another distribution of power among the units. The norms and rules of the system are bound up with those institutions. As constructivists they would admit that the institutions might have been different today from what they are if certain accidents of history had worked out differently and if people, who have free will, had made different choices from those they made. Without necessarily intending to produce such a system, people freely made choices that led to a system where power politics are practiced. In every international system some, but not all, states are great powers that get their way at the expense of the weak.

The fullest form of realism is inherently rationalist, since it takes as fixed the anarchical structure of states and the state system, as well as the preferences of states. It regards anarchy as inherent and not something states can overcome. However, we can imagine a nearly realist view that uses a constructivist metatheory. It would hold that the structures of the state and the state system have a sociological dimension. Those structures are what states make of them. But the constructivist-realist would say that the system that states have constructed and have been living with since at least 1648 is a "realist power-politics" institutional structure. Such a theorist could argue that the world is the way it is, not because of fixed, given structures, but because we have created the structures. This theorist would argue against the liberal-leaning constructivists discussed in Chapter 3, such as Wendt and Adler, and argue that mostly realist national leaders over the past 350 years have constructed the best attainable world.

One brand of constructivist-realist might even argue that the world of power politics is better than a Kantian system of perpetual peace. This theorist might, as

Table 4.1 Rationalism-constructivism distinction as separate from substantive distinctions

	Substantive realism	Substantive liberalism/idealism
Constructivist foundations	E. H. Carr, Morgenthau	Wendt, Katzenstein, Lebow
Rationalist foundations	Mearsheimer, Walt	Keohane, Nye, Martin

a constructivist, admit that the system of semi-Hobbesian anarchy *could* be transformed in the future but might add that it is better to work to continue with (reproduce) the existing relationships. On this view constructivism is not opposed to realism and is aligned substantively with liberalism. The distinction between the metatheories of rationalism and constructivism is simply unrelated to the distinction between the substantive theories of realism, liberalism, Marxism, etc. The two distinctions are as unrelated as the distinction between male/female and the distinction between blue-eyed/non-blue-eyed people. One pair of traits is not connected with the other. We are just as likely to encounter a blue-eyed man as a blue-eyed woman.

A metatheory, with its particular criteria of theory choice, will incline an investigator to prefer one theory over the rivals, but a clear choice is only possible when the criteria are applied in the context of the empirical evidence available. There is no inherent reason why one of the foundational-philosophical positions is locked into supporting one particular substantive theory over others. The foundational theory we adopt might make it unlikely we will accept substantive theory A or B. But it does not guarantee that we accept C or that we accept D. Which of the various substantive theories (A, B, C, or D) we accept will depend on our metatheory along with the empirical observations we have made.

Postmodernism—Poststructuralism

Postmodernism is a broad-ranging set of views that seeks to overturn rather than modify many traditional ways of looking at the world.[6] Poststructuralism is a more specific family of theories that are radically opposed to rationalism, naturalism, and the scientific approach to the social sciences. While poststructuralism overlaps a good deal with interpretive constructivism it goes much further in its critique of modern social science, the ways almost all scholars have tried to understand society, and especially the ways scholars themselves function within the institutional structure of academia.

Postmodern poststructuralism has been most fully developed in France in the last half-century by philosophers like Michel Foucault, Jacques Derrida, and Jean-François Lyotard, and the psychologist Jacques Lacan. Others who have had influence include the American philosopher Richard Rorty, the Canadian philosopher Charles Taylor, and the Sardinian political theorist Antonio Gramsci (also influential on contemporary followers of the Frankfurt School). In the world of philosophy, postmodernism is associated with an emphasis on the role of language in shaping society and with its rejection of many of the central ideas in the history of modern philosophy. This section will look at postmodernism and poststructuralism and thus begins with a brief look at what constitutes "modernism" and "structuralism."

Modernism

Most scholars use the term "modern world" to refer to developments dating to the early seventeenth century. In the realm of international politics the modern system is regarded as having begun in 1648 with the Treaty of Westphalia, which concluded the Thirty Years' War. In the intellectual world it is said to have begun about the same time, especially with the work in science of Galileo and in philosophy of René Descartes. Descartes, one of the great rationalist thinkers, sought a firm and unshakable foundation for knowledge. He realized that many things people commonly accept might be false and, at the very least, could be doubted. What if everything people accept as knowledge was false? Is there anything that was beyond doubt? Descartes set out to doubt everything that he could possibly doubt and then see what was left. He found the one thing that he could not doubt is that he doubts. So if he is sure that he doubts, then he is sure that he is thinking, since doubt is a form of thought. And if he is sure that he is thinking, then he must exist. This is the basis of his most famous inference, "I think, therefore, I am." By the use of reason alone, and without any appeal to the observable world around him, Descartes claimed to prove his existence.

Descartes and the great rationalists who followed him, Benedict de Spinoza and G. W. F. Leibniz, sought to solve philosophical problems by the use of reason. Not coincidentally, Descartes and Leibniz developed some of the most important mathematical tools we have today, coordinate geometry and calculus, respectively. It is helpful to remember their great mathematical achievements at this juncture in order to provide us with insight into their intellectual orientation, since mathematics, more than any other intellectual enquiry, holds firm to the belief in *universal, objective, and timeless truths*. There are many things about mathematics we do not know; there are many unsolved problems. But what we do know in mathematics we know by means of correct proof, and no matter how much conditions change over time, we never have the experience of a correct proof being falsified. The worst that can happen is that some flaw is found in a proof. But if there was a flaw, then what we took to be a theorem or truth of mathematics was never proved true. Our belief about it may change but its status as true never changes.

The explosion of mathematical developments in the seventeenth and eighteenth centuries provided great hope that all problems could be solved if only enough intellectual power and energy could be focused on them. The laws of the physical world were deciphered by Newton. Modern democracy, the American form of government, and the French republic were created during the Enlightenment and are results of Enlightenment philosophy. This conception of knowledge dominated from the early seventeenth century until the mid-twentieth century with only sporadic challenges. Postmodernism in most of the academic world can be understood as a refusal to accept the notions of "objective knowledge" and "universal truth" and as an attempt to challenge the optimistic belief that there are, even in principle, solutions to all our problems.

Structuralism

In the early twentieth century, as hermeneutics was taking hold in European social science, Ferdinand de Saussure developed ideas in linguistics that held sway among scholars for many years. Saussure's structural linguistics was so influential in the social sciences that the famous anthropologist Claude Lévi-Strauss said of Saussure's work: "[it] cannot help but play the same renovating role for the social sciences that nuclear physics, for example, played for the exact sciences" (Culler 1986, 109).[7]

Saussure had a major influence on the following generations in linguistics and related fields. Foucault and various others were inspired by many of Saussure's principles but took them further and ultimately used the adaptations and extrapolations against Saussure. Several key principles of Saussure should be noted. One is that, because Saussure regarded the study of linguistics in the nineteenth century to be in shambles, he wanted to place it on a much more methodologically rigorous and scientific footing in order to make it worthy of scientific respectability.

Saussure also noted that in linguistics, the object of study, language, is completely constructed by human beings, often in rather arbitrary ways. But at the same time, in order to approach it scientifically, linguists must use language to formalize and express the observed "facts" about languages and the general principles. The reasoned abstractions that are part of the field of linguistics also constitute the language that is the object of study. For this reason Saussure believed that linguistics was a unique and special field.

Saussure rejected the common-sense view accepted also by earlier thinkers that every word has (or even most words have) a unique concept attached to it. Translation from one language to another is relatively unproblematic according to the common-sense view. Saussure saw two reasons why this view is incorrect. One is that our concepts shift their content over time and the symbols used to designate them shift in different ways. For example, at one time in English the word "cattle" referred to any property, then to livestock, and later to the particular animal it now designates. A second reason for rejecting the common-sense view of meaning and translation is that the words in one language might not "line up" with those of another. The difference between a "stream" and a "river" in English is a matter of size. This does not line up with the difference between the terms "fleuve" and "rieviè" in French, which have to do with whether or not the water flows into the sea. Saussure showed that languages divide up our world and our experiences of the world in different ways.

With respect to the way words function as a part of the structure of the language, we note that in English we also need terms for size to differentiate streams and rivers. And in French we need terms for the sea if we are to understand either of the French terms and how they differ. Thus on Saussure's view, words gain meaning only *by virtue of their place in a system of symbols* that constitute the language. Saussure's structuralism included the idea that "the linguistic system consists of different levels of structure; at each level one can identify elements that contrast with one another and combine with other elements to form higher-level units, and the principles of structure at each level are fundamentally the same" (Culler 1986, 61). Saussure's view of linguistics is known as *structuralism* and held sway for most of the first half of the twentieth century.

While Saussure changed linguistics, he did not completely reject what had come before. He retained the idea of language as a relatively neutral tool that relates a word (in the form of a mental imprint of the written marks on paper or the spoken sound) to a mental image or idea. This was a traditional element of linguistics. Later authors challenged it by arguing that it was based on an unacceptable view of human psychology.[8]

Modernism, Postmodernism, and Poststructuralism

Postmodern and poststructural theorists in particular reject the claim that the human mind is able to solve virtually all problems by the application of reason, which they associate with the rise of the conception of "instrumental rationality," and think in clear and sharp dichotomies that philosophers have worked to clarify, such as fact-fiction, true-false, subject-object, public-private and fact-value. They reject the idea that human knowledge of the social world can produce certainties about the world, can produce objective facts, can produce claims that are universally valid (since there is no external validation for claims about knowledge), and can build up a set of true beliefs by using a foundation of more basic propositions that cannot be doubted. Further, in criticizing the modern rationalist ideas of knowledge, they emphasize the role that language plays. Poststructuralists provide an extensive analysis of how language is used to shape society. They argue that language is not a neutral tool that we use to communicate realities external to us—the subjects—but is a social activity that in part constitutes the social world. Some poststructuralists also see an economic component to modernity and associate the rise of the modern world with the dominance of capitalism.

Postmodern poststructuralist theories draw on the Dilthey's and Gadamer's hermeneutic work on the nature of interpretation, and they draw on Ludwig Wittgenstein's views on the social role of language. Finally, in rejecting the rationalist-Enlightenment conception of knowledge itself and, specifically, knowledge of society, poststructuralists argue that identities are formed by means of discourse and interactions. Poststructuralists conceive of societies as structured largely by their *dominant discourses*, which produce stories or *narratives* about what is and what is not desirable, legitimate, and acceptable. Whichever narrative in fact has come to be dominant and shapes a society was able to acquire that status only by a series of accidents; there was nothing inevitable about it.

As Jean-François Lyotard says, poststructural authors generally distrust "metanarratives," which purport to give us some deeper truth beyond the dominant narrative of the society. These stories deal with the moral and political obligations of humans as moral agents rather than as historical, culturally bound, and even culturally defined beings. The metanarrative story provides a grounding for particular allegiances and loyalties, but without the historical dimension of the narrative the metanarratives are always suspect to the poststructuralist.

Language and Discourse

Poststructural theorists have developed many novel arguments, but they also draw heavily on philosophers and others who are not entirely "postmodern" in their outlook. One source of inspiration to poststructuralists has been Kuhn's attack, discussed in Chapter 3, on the rationality and the theoretical-neutrality that scientists believe their theories possess. Wittgenstein is often cited as an influence on the poststructuralist account of language. For example, Lacan follows Wittgenstein in holding that to learn a language is to learn a set of rules, which brings the learner into a specific view of the world, namely, the world created by those rules. This is because using the words and sentences of the language have effects in the real world; use of the language allows a person to do things. Wittgenstein's later work shows that language does not merely reflect a preexisting reality surrounding us but it also creates the reality in which we live. Thus a *third major difference* between rationalist and reflectivist theorists, especially poststructuralists, is the *emphasis on how we analyze language.*

As we know, in the early twentieth century, logical positivism thrived. It was part and parcel of a broader movement in English and German language philosophy that focused squarely on the analysis of language and the importance of precision in the use of language. These "analytic philosophers" sought to reduce the confusion that arises in philosophy (and science) by developing more precise ways to communicate. Better answers will be possible to key questions if those questions are formulated in more precise ways. These philosophers not only worked to improve the precision of ordinary language but also created artificial and "formal" mathematical languages for this purpose. Many philosophers at this time sought to explain how language tells us about reality.

Wittgenstein began writing at a time when physics had just undergone a revolution and logical positivism was in its heyday in philosophy. In physics, not only had Einstein presented his revolutionary theory but quantum theory had also been discovered, which advanced our understanding of the atom by breaking it down into smaller parts. In philosophy there was a kindred movement by major figures like Bertrand Russell, who developed the doctrine of "logical atomism." According to that doctrine we can understand truth and reality by means of an analytic method that systematically breaks down our key concepts into fundamental components. What was going on in physics seemed to work in concert with what was going on in philosophy. However, Wittgenstein's arguments about language went in the opposite direction. He said that we cannot understand the way in which language conveys meaning by breaking language and thought into smaller units. Rather, language works in a holistic way. Words gain their full meaning by their uses in sentences and specific contexts. Engaging in communication through language is a basic human activity, which shapes our understanding of reality. The attempt to understand how language conveys meaning is itself a social process and, as such, is subject to a similar analysis. However, there is a fundamental difficulty—a circularity—involved in using language to investigate social reality because the use of language is part of, and in fact constitutes, our social reality.

Wittgenstein focused his intellect on the philosophy of knowledge, language, science, and mathematics. He did not develop a critique of society or a theory of social and political oppression, exploitation, emancipation, or liberation. While some poststructural IR theorists have drawn from his work, many have taken more of their direction from explicitly political authors, such as Adorno, Horkheimer, Foucault, and Gramsci. The remainder of this section focuses on French poststructuralism. The next section turns to Critical Theory.

Poststructuralism and Foucault

The historian and philosopher Michel Foucault developed intellectually at a time when structuralism in linguistics, hermeneutics in philosophy, and Marxism in political theory were very popular in French academia. Foucault developed sharp critiques of these dominant views and of the Enlightenment conception of "knowledge" that serves as their foundation. His work along with that of Jacques Lacan, set in motion the poststructuralist movement.

Foucault was inspired by Saussure's structural linguistics but regarded it as too willing to accept the Enlightenment idea of scientific enquiry and the notion that the field of study could be separated from the act of studying it. Saussure made it clear that he was treating language as a separate entity that could be studied in a detached and objective way. Foucault and poststructuralists strongly opposed this claim. But Saussure was also aware of the way in which reasoning involved in scientific linguistic analysis also constitutes the object of study, namely the structured language. Foucault accepted this notion and expanded it to all of the social or human sciences.

Knowledge and Truth

We ordinarily think of "knowledge" as something mental, intellectual, and possibly attainable even by someone raised by wolves with no human contact. French poststructuralism, in contrast, conceives of "knowledge" as something inherently and thoroughly social and as essential to power. To be more specific, according to the standard view, knowledge is a relationship between a person (or any sort of agent possessing mental faculties) and an "object of knowledge," such as a knowable fact, theory, or principle. We think of a person being able to attain knowledge irrespective of who else exists in the society. We could say, "If there were only one person in the world, she could spend all her time studying nature, literature, mathematics, and develop a great deal of knowledge." There is no logical problem with such a statement. In contrast, we cannot think of a lone person (like a lone nation-state) in the world as either powerful or powerless (as noted in the first section of this chapter).

Foucault and his followers reject a sharp separation of knowledge and power. They see knowledge as something that always exists within a society and is used either to support or oppose the existing power-relationships within that society.

Poststructuralists have argued that knowledge is indeed a form of power within a society, which can be used for advancing the goals of that society. This is a central principle of postmodern theorists.

Foucault, like other postmodern theorists, opposed the traditional idea that human rationality has a specific character and can be used to solve problems in the way that Enlightenment thinkers claimed. Foucault's analysis of "rationalism" began with a history of irrationality, that is, "madness." He sought to understand what was accepted as "rational" by studying its limits and learning what things people at different times defined as insane or mad, that is, as "not rational." Foucault shows that over time there have been changes in what behavior leads society to judge someone as insane, how society views those judged to be insane, and how society treats those so judged. At one point in Western civilization the mad were considered divinely inspired, treated preferentially, and accorded certain benefits. Later they were viewed as possessed by malignant spirits and treated by confinement. Later still, they were regarded as sick and treated with drugs. Foucault thus showed that the boundary of what is rational and what is not has evolved and that there is no single, enduring conception of "rationality" that endures over time.

The definition of "madness" and what we know about people who are mad, like virtually all knowledge, is culture-bound. Knowledge in every society is produced to be used for a purpose. And those who produce and acquire knowledge exercise a form of power. Foucault viewed power and knowledge as so closely bound together that he used the expression "power/knowledge."

Our understanding of Foucault's connection between knowledge and power is aided by recalling the discussion of "identity" earlier in this chapter. Foucault agrees that individuals do not have a transparent "essence" or "nature" that would be the same no matter which culture and set of norms were in place as they grew up. George W. Bush, as we saw, would clearly not be the "same person" if his parents had each grown up in Uganda, met there, married there, and raised their children there, teaching them only the local language. The fundamental character of each individual is shaped by the society—just as the society is shaped by the choices and behavior of the individuals in it.

For Foucault, knowledge is tied to power. But it is not merely a matter of the powerful exerting their will over the weak; the weak participate, too. Foucault's approach is to understand how power in society is made up both by the actions of those who rule and also by the acquiescence of those ruled. It is a complex and interactive process and is the focus of much of Foucault's historical work.[9]

Archaeology and Genealogy

Foucault argued that we only come to understand something by carefully studying how it came to be, which, following Nietzsche, he termed its "genealogy." That is, in order to understand a society we must learn how it arose. Foucault, as a social historian, did precisely this with Western society. He produced detailed historical works on such social issues as the changing definitions and treatment of criminals, sexual deviants, and madness.

The basis for Foucault's position was his effort to uncover the hidden assumptions shared by all people of a particular civilization—those assumptions that change only after being accepted for decades or centuries and after a difficult struggle to repudiate them. Foucault saw his historical, genealogical work as digging into the grounds on which other societies stood in order to find the presuppositions of those societies. He regarded this to be a form of intellectual archaeology. For centuries all educated people, regardless of their "ideology," believed that the Earth was the center of the universe. It took an extraordinary individual and a long struggle to bring about a change in this view. The Earth as the center of the universe was part of the background framework of knowledge and belief for everyone in those societies. The place of the human race in the cosmos that went along with this view was a presupposition of these societies.

When we study the history of philosophy, language, or art, or the history of a state like the United States, Iraq, or China, we are typically presented with one way to represent that history. And we always find that that history highlights certain actors and events, interprets those events in particular ways, and ignores or marginalizes other actors and events. Poststructuralists argue that there are always other, competing ways to represent it, and there are no objective grounds for dismissing the alternatives or even for privileging the standard interpretation over the alternatives. For Foucault a genealogy is a critical examination of the way in which scholars portray the standard origins or history of the subject and of the different ways that people have portrayed it over time. A genealogy is intended to uncover aspects of the subject that other accounts of its origins exclude. On this view there is not just one alternative to the accepted history, there are many.

As Foucault developed his view of society, he came to call the framework of society its "discourse." The term "language" had always been understood as something neutral. Foucault believed that the way communication takes place within each society is far from neutral in that it shapes a society and has a significant political element. Foucault thus preferred to use the term "discourse" to refer specifically to the political slant that is a feature of any communication within society. Each society then has its characteristic discourse, and the structure of that discourse makes it possible to express some ideas but impossible to express certain other, incompatible ideas.

Foucault developed a "discourse theory" to be employed as a primary tool in social analyses. The very possibility of any political action comes from a set of social relationships; and those relationships are structured by the existing discourse at any given time.

To cite a simplistic example, some languages have no term for what in Chinese would amount to "giving face." The notion of "face" in the West has little relevance to core social interactions, where having the respect of others or a good image in others' minds is important. In English we use the Chinese concept of "saving face," which we translate merely as the avoidance of humiliation and the gaining of respect. But the translation does not fully capture what Chinese mean by "saving face." In Chinese, the concept of "face" is not only connected to humiliation and respect but also has a meaning closer to having social dignity.

One reason why there is no direct translation of "face" and "saving face," and especially "giving face," is that the concept of "face" is so much more central to Chinese society. That centrality, and the meaning that goes along with it, cannot be translated fully.

A second example that perhaps comes closer to Foucault's precise meaning in this context is the debate over how "torture" is to be defined by the United States. The Geneva Conventions ban the use of torture and the United States was found to be violating the ban. Rather than comply with the long-held definition of "torture" in the Geneva Conventions, the Bush administration chose to propose a new law with a new definition of "torture." Different groups within the United States argued for different formulations. Some wanted to retain the established and internationally recognized Geneva Conventions' definition; others argued for different threshold levels of intensity. This is a classic example of competing discourses. Once a new definition is set, it then becomes, in a literal way, difficult to talk about certain detention and interrogation practices as "torture," because the dominant group has defined those methods of interrogation as non-torture. The discourse of a society could exclude discussion of those practices as torture.[10] This illustrates how, for Foucault, discourse is a social practice that characterizes the framework of beliefs of a society. Foucault concludes that discourse or language cannot be seen as a neutral set of symbols that connect our minds and intellects to a separate, external reality. Discourse is a social practice and it creates our understanding of our world.

Foucault argued that there was a great deal of discontinuity between discourses across societies, over time within a single society, and in different disciplines within societies at any given time. The discourses do not neatly fit together and do not form any "progression." One area of enquiry may have a very different history, for example, it may be much older than another. And the dominant discourse today is not likely to be one that evolved smoothly from the previous dominant discourse in that area. One discourse is succeeded by another through a power struggle whose outcome is decided by power relationships, not by rational criteria of "theory choice." The newer discourse is neither objectively broader nor more comprehensive nor more accurate than the previous one, because there is no external standard by which we can make the claim of "more comprehensive" or "more accurate." While Foucault's work has strong parallels to Kuhn's simultaneous work on paradigms and paradigm shifts in the natural science, which is a part of specifically Western culture, Foucault's analysis was broader because it looked at whole cultures.

Different groups favor different discourses and stories about the society. The discourses compete for dominance or hegemony. One of them will gain acceptance, though it will continually be challenged—over time the challenges can produce gradual changes in it. The dominant discourse shapes what questions we can pose and limits the range of meaningful answers that we may offer. Various scientific, material, and economic factors play a role in what becomes the hegemonic discourse. There is always one class that rules society and does so largely by means of its hegemonic discourse. Among the groups competing, the government has special power in shaping the dominant discourse.

To return to the question of "truth," is the claim that the insane are a danger to society a true one? In medieval Europe it was false, according to Foucault. The insane were regarded as having a special gift from the Creator that led society to permit them to roam free. The discourse of mad persons was part of the overall struggle for discourse dominance. In a later period the claim was true, according to Foucault, since the insane were a danger and confined. Their discourse was judged unfit to participate in the struggle for dominance. In a later period we, as social scientists, seek to understand the struggle for dominance. However, any such attempt to analyze the politically loaded discourse of a society is still a form of politically loaded discourse. Our attempt at interpretation is then always subject to further interpretation. For Foucault and poststructuralists, there is no final phase.

Foucault was interested in the puzzle of how humans can study humans. The quest for universality in truth can never succeed because the idea of "truth" varies from society to society and from time to time. But he believed that within the confines of the time and place we inhabit, we must try our best to understand the precise limitations of our past attempts to define "truth" and "knowledge." This process will help us advance the quest for knowledge as far as possible in our own time. With this point in mind, it should be clearer why poststructuralists objected to Saussure's determination to make linguistics into a "science" and to clarify the basic concepts of the discipline. Saussure treated the subject matter in a detached and scientific way, as if objective observation and hypothesis were possible. For Foucault and poststructuralists, it is an illusion to think that linguistic or other human endeavors can be understood objectively.

The interpretations are illuminating and valuable because they help to uncover the presuppositions and techniques of subjugation. Derrida is also very clear that the real world is "constituted" like a text. All we can do is interpret it and then interpret the interpretation with techniques he advocates. We cannot know it through any direct access. He agrees with Foucault and other poststructuralists that the process does not produce any final answers or final truths.

IR Theory as a Part of the Real World—Reflexivity and Moral Obligation

Postmodern and poststructural theorists regard the academic world as a part of the real world. And they regard the struggle over discourse in the academic world as part of the struggle for hegemony within a society. They argue that language shapes and forms our social world and grants a privileged status and power to some social and political groups. It creates some possible solutions and cuts off others. Thus they investigate the discourse not only of political and economic leaders and organizations, but also scholars and IR theorists. Poststructuralists are extremely interested in how academics convey their theories, what sort of language they use, and how the theories might legitimize various approaches to problems in the real world. A *fourth difference* between traditional natural IR scholars and poststructuralists is the latter's *emphasis on reflexivity*. While traditional naturalist scholars pursue scientific-style IR and regard the object of their study as the real world of international politics, poststructuralists regard the object of their study as both the world of power politics and the academic world of theories that legitimize power politics.

Consider the example of political realism. Poststructuralists say that realism's focus on the state as the only significant actor is not a way of describing the reality that objectively exists outside of the individuals proposing the theory (as realists claim it is) because there is no such distinct reality. Rather, it is a way of reinforcing the importance and centrality of the state in the future, which serves the interests of current states.

In their study of IR theory many of the poststructuralists take the genealogical approach advocated by Foucault. They follow Foucault in replacing the traditional Enlightenment question of knowledge, "What is it possible for us to know?" with the question, "How were our questions produced?" They use this approach to show that the field of IR has centers of power capable of shaping the sort of discourse that is deemed acceptable. The dominant theories, they argue, have become dominant precisely in order to support the political power structure.

Poststructuralists argue that societies create a feeling of separation between "us" and "them." But this, like everything else in society, is manufactured by the dominant discourse. So the perceptions we have of "difference" are a creation of humans through the manipulation of discourse by the most powerful interests. There is an "us" and "them" separation between "our society" and "theirs" and also within our society. The division between "us" and "them" is a fundamentally artificial one, according to poststructuralist postmoderns. They build on Lacan's claim, developed in his studies as a psychiatrist, that our own sense of identity as individual humans is not entirely inborn. It is something we learn at approximately the age of six months. Until that time a child is "a body in bits and pieces" and entirely "de-centered."

Once we realize that very young children mediate their own physical desires through what they believe are the wishes of "others," namely their parents, we see that the desire is not something arising purely subjectively from the child ; it thus becomes "intersubjective." The child's perceived attitude of the parent can even affect whether the child acts on bodily demands, like hunger. This analysis supports the conclusion of the example of Uganda-born George W. Bush, which showed that individual agents arise out of their social structure and they are not discreet beings unrelated to it.

Poststructuralists argue that the "us" of members of the dominant academic discourse seek to marginalize poststructuralists as "them." Poststructuralists tend to conclude that they themselves, as poststructuralists, are a genuinely dissident group in the real world (because the academic world is real) suffering oppression at the hands of the powerful. In journal articles and conferences they raise the question of which strategies will be effective to gain sway in academia in a way similar to their discussions of strategies to support other dissident groups who seek emancipation in the nonacademic world. Some authors (see Ashley and Walker 1990) have studied how mainstream IR theorists have used certain sorts of language to marginalize poststructuralism and thereby failed to engage the criticisms. These mainstream scholars try to use the dismissive language of poststructuralism's critics as a tool against those critics.

When it comes to the influence of the most powerful academics, poststructural IR theorists ask why a small privileged group of certain texts have been selected out of the vast array of texts written in the past 2,500 years. Why have scholars interpreted them in the particular ways they have? Why have works by Machiavelli and Hobbes been taken to be "timeless classics"? Those texts are interpreted as emphasizing power and as legitimizing violence perpetrated by states. Why have the texts of pacifist authors not been esteemed classics? Why have the texts that have been elevated to "classics status" not been subjected to debate about various interpretations, as they should have been? Poststructuralists have disputed the particular way in which Machiavelli and Hobbes have been interpreted, especially the way they are seen as legitimizing violence. Some prominent poststructuralists have questioned whether those interpretations are justifiable and have offered alternative interpretations (see Walker 1989).

Poststructuralists say that IR theorists have studied only the Western state system—a system where states have historically been the dominant actors and where they use force to settle disputes. The lack of attention to other systems, like that of precolonial India or that of the North American Indians, implies that they are not important enough to consider (Crawford 2002). Only by thinking about what alternative arrangements of institutions might look like will it be possible to transform the existing system to something better. A "better" system, according to poststructuralists, is a system that creates a greater potential for human emancipation (Walker 1988, 3). Poststructuralists hold, like many other reflectivists, that all theory serves political purposes. Thus *a fifth difference* between traditional rationalist IR scholars and interpretivists is that the latter hold that theorists *must be focused on choosing to acquire knowledge and produce theories that serve moral purposes.*

The ethical requirements of theory are very important to postmodern authors. Their attacks on the international state system argue that the rights of the individual are overlooked. The rules and norms that have developed over time give primary rights to states. If a state is acting unjustly toward its people, then the norms of the system are to leave that state alone unless its violence crosses a border. But as long as it is contained within its borders, then the dominant theories that underpin our current legal set of rights would tell leaders of other countries that they need not do anything. Poststructuralists regard this as an abdication of their moral responsibility to help victims of state abuse.

IR and Historical Reality

Poststructuralists hold that our construction of theory and our construction of reality all serve political purposes. Some purported past events are real (Boswell's first meeting with Dr. Johnson, Stanley's first meeting with Dr. Livingston) and some are not (Holmes's first meeting with Dr. Watson). According to poststructuralists, what makes some real is that we weave them into the dominant discourse or narrative of the origins of our subject. So our view that they are real does not arise from the fact that the event happened in the real world, because poststructuralists hold that there is no objective reality of the events beyond the presence of those events in our memory, provided they fit into a coherent narrative (Campbell 1998, 36, 54). Our belief in these "real" events then typically serves political purposes. They help to promote or justify certain loyalties and actions.

For example, the belief that the American colonies were taxed by the British crown without adequate representation in London helped to legitimize the violent rebellion that led to the creation of the United States. The Nazi's mass, systematic killing of millions of Jews helps justify the legitimacy of the existence of a Jewish state. Compare the belief that the United States should not be involved in Iraq or the Middle East in the wake of the terrorist attacks on September 11, 2001, because there were no Arabs involved in the terrorist attacks on the United States. (A recent report by the Pew Foundation found that a majority of people in every Muslim state hold this belief.) These beliefs become facts if they are woven into a discourse that becomes dominant (Pipes 2006).

Sovereignty

Poststructuralists generally reject the claim that anything has a basic, inherent character or "essence." Social entities and relationships like states and state systems are whatever the dominant discourses ascribe to them and they can change over time. The boundaries are not clear and sharp. They reject the standard rationalist accounts of IR theory based on a system of sovereign states coexisting in an anarchical system and reacting in regular or predictable ways, understandable by means of the essential nature of "sovereignty." For realists these include arming themselves, watching out for threats, and forming alliances.

Authors like Ashley, Weber, and Micheal Shapiro have offered interesting poststructural critiques of the way recent IR theorists understand "sovereignty." Ashley argues that many of the concepts we use in social theory are vague and lack clear boundaries but are treated as if they were clear and unproblematic. This is especially true, according to Ashley, when we move from theory to real-world applications. The concepts are made to appear "natural," inevitable, or a result of something in the nature of the social world. Ashley argues that both "sovereignty" and the "state" are notable examples, since they are very messy concepts but treated by theorists as unproblematic. Cynthia Weber (1995) has subsequently undertaken a genealogical study of "sovereignty" in which she concludes that the concept has changed over time in significant ways.

Poststructuralists are consistently critical of the existing structure of the state and the system of states. Even humanitarian activities like the delivery of food and medical supplies or military intervention to halt human rights abuses or ethnic cleansing, when carried out by the state or by institutions created and run by states, stifle human emancipation. Poststructuralists like Shapiro, David

Campbell, and Jenny Edkins have argued that the way we envision such aid being delivered gives more power to states and organizations supported by states. The way aid is delivered causes the people in camps to have their political voices ignored and their human dignity stripped away. They are treated as means rather than ends; each refugee is a full moral agent and these programs do not treat them as such.

Campbell has used the poststructuralist analysis of "us/them" in social theory and argued that the state system is a creation, or construct, that uses violence to "constitute" the states. There is an "us/them" norm in politics that helps to create states. Campbell does not view the ethnic cleansing in Kosovo as a violation of the usual norms of politics we find in the modern world but rather as an application and extension of the "us/them" norm that states use to justify the use of force. He accuses the NATO bombing campaign of serving as a way of trying to "constitute" NATO as an important and legitimate actor in world politics. Edkins had made a similar point about NATO, arguing that after the demise of the Soviet Union the NATO alliance, which for so long had a clear purpose and identity, has lost both. It has sought to create a new identity and purpose for itself as the protector of human rights in Europe. But it went about establishing this identity by claiming to halt ethnic cleansing in the Balkans through a bombing campaign. Violence was used to establish an identity. Edkins adds that in this important respect it was like Nazi Germany whose identity was established through violent bombings and invasions of Czechoslovakia, Poland, and other states.

Poststructuralist authors see the acceptance of the idea of "sovereignty" as a way to create a power-enhancing division between "us" and "them." It separates those inside the territorial boundary from those outside it. But it also separates the sovereign power—those with authority—from those slaves, resident aliens, or citizens who are not part of the decision-making hierarchy. It is a way of managing the rivalry and competition among discourses within the society. However, according to poststructuralists, even the discourse of those excluded is a discourse or system of meanings through symbols. Neither the dominant nor the weaker discourses have any greater claim to be true than the others. This is why many critics of poststructuralism (and many of its adherents, as well) claim that poststructuralism is, ultimately, a skeptical position. That is, it does not allow that there is anything even remotely resembling our ordinary idea of "truth" in the world. There is no reality behind the struggle for dominance among the discourses. Poststructuralists' and postmoderns' refusal to accept anything that looks like our ordinary ideas of "truth" or "objective reality" leads some to use the term "postmodern condition."

Poststructuralists in IR often point out that one of the chief goals of their approach is to bring to light the hidden presuppositions of a dominant discourse and the artificial or accidental nature of something that we take as bedrock truth. Actions like delivering food and medical aid to victims of natural disasters and failed states or military intervention to stop human rights abuses and atrocities are generally considered altruistic. However, as just noted, a number of poststructuralist IR theorists have seized on some aspect of the relationship between violence, sovereignty, and identity to advance the power/knowledge claim that these "humanitarian" acts all rest on the same self-interested use of violence to support a dominant discourse.

Narratives, Models, and Analogies

Suppose that in September 2002 we hear three different political leaders talk about the conflict with Iraq. Each of the three begins with a different image. The first argues as follows:

> International violence is a virus that can spread from one subject to another. To prevent a virus from spreading, the infected subject must be carefully isolated from the rest of the population. International violence like any virus can be contained only if the proper course is taken. Otherwise, it will continue to spread further. Saddam Hussein has repeatedly committed violence against others. When public health leaders face a viral outbreak they follow a policy of quarantine and isolation. We must, then, isolate Saddam Hussein so that the virus of violence cannot spread. The best solution now (in 2002) is to show the world that he is a pariah. The world must cut him off from all normal relations, especially trade and finance. Only by such isolation can he be prevented from continuing to acquire the dangerous weapons that will allow him to gain the influence to spread his violence.

In this analogy a war-prone state is compared to a virus; the states of the system are compared to the various people in a society who interact with one another. The solution to the public health problem is to isolate the infected individual(s). In applying the analogy to IR, the solution requires isolating Saddam Hussein, but, we should note, it does not necessarily entail going to war.

A second political leader offers a different comparison:

> The international system should remain in balance. Violence erupts when there is an imbalance among major powers and alliances. Only when the system is in balance will it function smoothly. The configurations of international power must be in balance just like any natural or created system. The laws of the physical universe are in perfect balance. We can see this by observing the planets in our solar system, which have centrifugal forces on them pushing them away from one another and from the sun. But they are also subject to centripetal and gravitation forces pulling them together. The system remains in perfect balance because any one set of forces exerted on the planets is precisely counterbalanced by the various opposing forces. We can see this also in human activity, for example, in making a mechanical watch, which is composed of springs and gears. When the forces operating on the inner works of the watch are in perfect balance, the watch will run smoothly and keep good time. When they are out of balance, it will go awry. The system of international relationships works well when great powers and their alliances are in balance with one another. However, today (referring to the time of the debate, 2002) Iraq is gaining influence by its pursuit of chemical and biological weapons—and perhaps nuclear weapons. The United States, the UK and

other responsible Western states should work to restore balance in the Middle East by offering military aid to the various rival states in the region who oppose Saddam Hussein.

Here the analogy is between the international system of states and physical laws of the universe, as exemplified by the movements of the planets in the solar system. The prescribed action is not invasion but the development of military alliances with states in the region. The different analogy leads to a different policy toward Iraq.

Many Western leaders have followed this balancing strategy in the Middle East. Let us return to an earlier example. President Nixon and Secretary of State Kissinger worked to bring about a peaceful disengagement of Israeli forces after the 1973 Yom Kippur War. Israel had been attacked on its most sacred holiday and suffered extensive losses in the early stages. After frustrating delays, President Nixon finally succeeded in demanding aid to Israel against his reluctant cabinet and resistant executive branch. That is, clearly Israel was, and Egypt was not, America's ally in that war. However, when Israel was on the verge of crushing the Egyptian Third Army in the Sinai, President Nixon and Henry Kissinger viewed the weakening of Egypt as sure to bring about an imbalance in the Middle East. Even though that imbalance would be to the advantage of America's ally, Israel, the imbalance itself was more dangerous, in their view, than the threat posed by the Egyptian army remaining intact.

Another example is the Reagan administration's support of Iraq in the 1980s. When President Reagan saw Iran as becoming too powerful after the fall of the Shah and Iran's surprisingly strong showing against Iraq in the Iran-Iraq war, Reagan worked to help Iraq in the war, especially by providing intelligence to Saddam Hussein on the movement of Iranian troops (see Crile 2003, 274–76). President Reagan was not ideologically aligned with either side, and so he was not in favor of either Iran or Iraq gaining too much power over the other. Indeed, he worked with Iran to finance the U.S.-sponsored insurgency war against the government of Nicaragua.[11] Neither Nixon nor Reagan put U.S. forces into combat in the Middle East. Their balancing strategy required that they work to strengthen the side that was becoming weaker. In general, for a leader who believes in the importance of balances, the solution to growing imbalances is to aid the weaker side. Finally, a third speaker offers the following analysis:

> International violence is a cancer that can only be dealt with by cutting it out. If it is not removed, it will invariably spread. The regime of Saddam Hussein in Iraq is a cancer on the body of the international system and, like any cancer, the only treatment that can keep the system healthy is to remove Saddam Hussein in as surgically precise a way as possible. We must attack and defeat Iraq while at the same time reassuring the rest of the Arab world that the target is only the violent and rogue regime of Saddam Hussein.

The speaker draws a comparison between war and cancer. A malignancy typically starts in a specific location and, if left untreated, spreads until it produces a fatal result. The public's ordinary understanding of cancer treatment, which the analogy draws on, is that the best option is early detection of the malignancy and complete surgical removal. Some cancers spread slowly and some quickly but all spread if not treated. If a warlike leader such as Saddam Hussein were a cancer, then the right solution in Iraq in 2002 would be the use of force to remove his regime. Unlike the first two analogies, the third leads to a recommendation for war.

Each of the speakers uses a story or narrative that makes use of an analogy to help us understand war and ultimately formulate a policy. Why use analogies? They are often used in explanations by comparing something that we do not understand well, Y, to something that we understand much better, X. Some of the relationships within Y are known and some are unknown. Because X is better understood, we will say that more of the relationships within X are known. By showing that some of the known relationships within Y are similar to some of the known relationships within X, the speaker then argues that some of the unknown relations within Y must be like the other known relationships within X.

In the example of the three analogies, each speaker takes something from the physical world that, while complex, is relatively well understood—at least compared to the cause-and-effect relationships of war and peace. Each speaker then uses a natural science phenomenon to offer a prescription or recommendation for dealing with the consistently violent Saddam Hussein. Each different speaker, by using a different analogy, makes a very different point about how to deal with Iraq. As we can see, it makes a lot of difference which analogy we regard as the best one, because each leads to a different recommendation: isolation, versus aid to regional rivals, versus war. There is a great deal riding on the choice of which analogy we choose. So how do we choose?

Poststructuralists take a distinctive position on this question. They generally subscribe to the principle of the radical underdetermination of theory by data (RU). To see their position clearly, let us first recall the principle of the underdetermination of theory by data (UD), as described in Chapter 3, which states that when we consider several theories and have a set of observations on which we choose the best theory, we have to admit that there is no objectively identifiable advantage of one theory over the others. Radical Underdetermination (RU) goes beyond UD by saying that no matter how many observations we have and how much better they make theory T2 look as compared to theory T1, we can always retain T1 if we like, because we can always make (perhaps awkward, but logically permissible) adjustments elsewhere in the set of statements we accept as true in order to remove the contradictions theory T1 brings with it. We can always adjust our beliefs to accommodate whichever theory we prefer.

But poststructuralists go further even than RU here, because their idea of "different narratives" shows how they reject the idea that we can even conceive of truly objective or universal truths about human behavior. What scholars can do is tell a story that describes and explains actions in the way that ancient Greek or Norse mythology explain why things are the way they are. In many stories the gods take advantage of weaker mortals, and stronger gods even take advantage of weaker gods, which could justify stronger city-states dominating weaker ones.

Poststructuralists and interpretive constructivists are interested in the stories that we, as social scientists, tell about how the narratives are formed. Kratochwil, for example, makes very clear that reality serves our understanding not because it is real but because it is a *metaphor* in IR theory. He says, "perplexities [are] created by the extensions of metaphors . . . that originally made sense [and which] allowed us to orient ourselves" until the subject matter was extended (Kratochwil 2007, 47). We use metaphors to aid our understanding. But the purposes are always limited and, as we expand the subject matter we are examining, other metaphors may be more appropriate.

In sum, most philosophers and virtually all non-philosophers have held the standard view that includes all of the following (modernist and structuralist) statements.

1. Language among humans is a neutral tool that is used to communicate emotions, ideas, theories and, significantly, objective facts about the natural world (e.g., "There are four trees in the garden") and the social world (e.g., "There were more marriages in Los Angeles County this year than last").
2. The sentence, "There were more marriages in Los Angeles County this year than last" is true precisely if, in the real world, there were more marriages in Los Angeles County this year than last; if there were not more, then the sentence is false.
3. There is an objective fact that the sentence reports either truly or falsely.
4. Theorists can collect these facts, categorize them into groups, and formulate generalizations.
5. The generalizations themselves may be either true or false (e.g., "People are marrying later and later in life over time") and may be causal claims (e.g., "Good jobs require more education over time, and the need for more education causes people to marry later in life").
6. As science proceeds, the theories get better. On the standard view this means that the descriptive scientific generalization over time comes closer to the objective facts of the world, and the causal principles become more comprehensive and more accurate, coming closer over time to expressing true universal generalizations.

These six beliefs have formed a part of the normal view of the world by all normal adults in Western societies over the past several hundred years. While they are ordinarily accepted, philosophers have come to question most of them. Poststructuralists like Foucault, however, reject all six of the statements. For them society has discourses, that is, systems of ideas, that are taken as expressing truths and as producing knowledge. These truths and knowledge operate in the realms of science, politics, and ordinary life. The discourses are discontinuous with one another. They create limits on what we can think, believe, and express, but they also create the opportunities we have to think, believe, and express. The discourses are not about an external world of objective things and facts. The discourses create the reality that we take to be objective. They are constitutive rather than objectively descriptive. Both objective fact and universal generalizations, which are generally accepted in the natural and social sciences, are illusions. The various discourses within society struggle against one another. Poststructuralists say that the dominant discourses at any given time result from the previous history of struggles. The outcomes of those struggles are not predetermined. They could have turned out differently. So the discourses we have inherited at any given moment define for us what is true. But it is certainly not objective and certainly not universal. The dominant discourses are local in both place and time.

Critical Theory and the Frankfurt School

Principles of Critical Theory

The school of thought known as Critical Theory was developed in Germany between the two world wars and preceded major works in poststructuralism. The leading thinkers in this movement were Theodor Adorno and Max Horkheimer. Other significant figures were Herbert Marcuse, Otto Kirchheimer, and Walter Benjamin. They were Marxists and highly critical of both modern European society and traditional social theories that sought to explain it. During World War II these men dispersed but some later returned to Frankfurt. They were inspired by Freud's notion of the "self" and "consciousness" and especially by Marx's analysis of class conflict, the exploitation of workers, and the dynamics of capitalist economic systems. But in some ways they took these ideas even further. Critical Theorists in Germany, along with other Marxists like Gramsci, placed the highest value on the goal of *human emancipation*. In their view, whatever else theory does, it must work toward that goal.

Kant had argued in the eighteenth century on behalf of human emancipation but conceived of emancipation as a set of circumstances under which people would be free to pursue their own interests and especially their own rationality and moral perfection. Certain conditions are needed for this to be fully possible; in particular, the just laws found in a republic are best suited to create them. But war can still interrupt them. Hence Kant argued for the obligation to create an international system where peace would reign. The notion of human emancipation in Marxism and the Critical Theory was quite different.

The Critical Theorists are sometimes considered to be in the poststructural or postmodern camp because of their sharp critique of some elements of modernity. However, they are, more often than not, separated from that group because Critical Theorists generally tried to revise or push further many of the Enlightenment views of how society may be studied and changed. Critical Theorists are close to poststructuralists on several points, including rejecting as oversimplified the idea that the proper use of *instrumental rationality* could solve all problems connected with society and human affairs. Critical Theorists hold that Enlightenment thinkers accepted the idea of instrumental rationality without considering the moral consequences. Critical Theorists and poststructuralists agree that, in the past few centuries, the use of instrumental rationality had produced two major outcomes: modern science and the modern economic system. Both were used to undermine human emancipation. Science had largely been a tool of the state, and modern economics was capitalist. They blamed instrumental rationality for justifying various economic and political forms by which the ruling class dominated the ruled.

As noted, Critical Theory was intended to offer a critique of both society and the traditional theories about society. Critical Theory holds that traditional theories lack any self-critical element and, whether intended or not, they legitimate the unjust social and political orders in which they are developed. A sociological theory that says, for example, "every social institution arises and endures simply because there is a function it serves in that particular society" is justifying and legitimating all such institutions. The theory should, instead, be taking the society to task for allowing the institution, if it is an unjust one, such as slavery.

The problem for Critical Theorists was that instrumental rationality was presented as a purely neutral tool that could be used by a value-neutral social science to solve problems in whatever way its users wished. It could then, presumably, be used for morally good purposes. Critical Theorists have a double objection to this view of instrumental rationality. One is that "all theory is *for* someone and *for* some purpose, as the oft-quoted Canadian Marxist Robert Cox has said (Cox 1981, 128). Critical Theorists argue that instrumental rationality is not value-neutral but is itself a carrier of a value in that traditional social scientists *place a high value* on instrumental rationality. Traditionalists might admit that they do value it but could go on to say that it is not a moral value, but rather an intellectual and, thus, morally neutral value, like the value of a valid proof in geometry. We think a valid proof is better than an invalid one. But there are no moral or political implications that follow from our accepting that sort of value. Such values are sometimes called "epistemic values" to make it clear that they are values we endorse in the pursuit of knowledge (see Chapter 2 and Chapter 3). Critical Theorists do not accept this reply by traditionalists. Critical Theorists hold that the modern world has created a capitalist economic order and a liberal free-trade system that provides benefits to some groups and exploits others by using and embracing instrumental rationality. They hold that the claim that instrumental rationality is value-neutral for society is a deception.

How critical of modern society is Critical Theory? The major thinkers, Adorno and Horkheimer, were quite critical. They cited the many forces working against the emancipation of the individual in modern society. Horkheimer, and especially Adorno, felt that the creative forces were powerful and could, if properly guided, bring about transformation. However, within a decade or so they came to see modern society as so severely controlled that even the creative, progressive forces were not likely to bring about enough of a change. Their coauthored 1944 book, *Dialectic of Enlightenment*, expresses very little hope for the possibility of transforming society. For Marxist economic forces would be the most influential in a society and the industrial workers would be the group pushing for change in the political and economic structure of society. Adorno, who placed a high value on the power of artistic and cultural leaders, initially saw culture and the arts as having the creativity and capacity to transform society in a progressive way. But by the mid-1940s he had lost much of his hope. He came to see culture as having been turned into another consumer commodity and the production of art as having been turned into another industry and becoming a part of the world of modern capitalism. In the process it boiled away the creative core of the cultural forces.

Hegemonic Discourse and Gramsci

As noted earlier, poststructuralists emphasize language and discourse. Critical Theory accepts this analysis, at least up to a point. Foucault, the poststructuralist, followed Wittgenstein in seeing the social world as fundamentally composed of discourse. The views of the Italian Marxist Antonio Gramsci were closely aligned with those of Critical Theorists. Gramsci combined the importance of discourse with the Marxist idea that there is class conflict and domination. Gramsci used the term "hegemony," which was popular among Marxists in a new way—to describe the winner among those competing to influence the discourse of the society. Hegemonic discourse exercises influence on people's ideas and perceptions and has historically done so in a way that reaffirms the privileged position of the hegemonic forces in society.

When we consider the cases of U.S. foreign policy we see that the government's language of public discourse (essentially identical to the media's) leaves room for some policy options and excludes others. The use of force is part of the public discourse in the cases of North Korea and Iraq but not China. (Recall that soon after taking office in 2001 President Bush suggested that the United States would militarily support Taiwan in the event of a war with China. He was apparently unaware that this was not part of the public discourse on China, and his administration immediately began to issue corrections to his statement.) The framework that emerges from the dominant discourse of a society filters into the "everyday consciousness" of the masses, according to Gramsci (1994, 1334).

It is helpful to see how the emphasis on discourse arose in a more practical way in Gramsci, who desired not only to develop a sound theory but also to bring about social change. Gramsci, as a devoted Marxist, was branded an enemy of the state in fascist Italy and, consequently, spent many years in prison. He argued that a Marxist society has to come about but said that it had not done so and will not do so in the way envisioned by Marx. The political successes of socialism up to that point had not resulted from popular uprisings in the most advanced industrial societies, as Marx had forecast. One resulted from a coup d'état in Russia and the other resulted from a twenty-year-long civil war in poor, agrarian China. And both socialist regimes maintained power largely by force.

Why did socialism arise in different ways than Marx predicted, and why was force needed to maintain it? Gramsci considered the loyalty and affection of the masses as a key factor. It is this loyalty that should be the basis of the rise of socialism. But it was not happening under current, mid-twentieth-century circumstances. So the circumstances, and especially the principle loyalties of the masses, must be changed. The loyalties of people are primarily to their families and their countries. Marxists need to learn how to transfer those loyalties to the goals of human equality and social progress. People's minds had to be changed. How could this be accomplished? Gramsci's answer was that it would require a change in society's dominant discourse. So there must be a struggle over that discourse. When the proper discourse dominates, then people will accept the benefits of a more egalitarian social and economic order. Our choice of a way to view the world is inherently a political one (Gramsci 1987, 61).

One of the chief goals of theorizing is to bring about human emancipation. Like poststructuralists, most Critical Theorists make this claim in one way or another. Gramsci placed much emphasis on it. Many believe that by identifying the presuppositions of a society we can begin to liberate ourselves from an unjustified or uncritical acceptance of them. In their view this process is a form of human emancipation in that it allows us to free ourselves from having to base our actions on an unwilling acceptance of those views.

Contemporary Critical IR Theory

Contemporary Critical Theory in IR makes clear what the goals of a social theory must be and argues that any principles must have the consent of all of the individuals to whom they apply (Devetak 1996b, 71). When a norm loses legitimacy something has to come in its place. That next step, in their view, is settled by applying Habermas's notion of "discourse ethics," which, because it embodies democratic values, is universal and is imbued with moral content. Discourse ethics, in turn, depends on Habermas's theory of communicative action (Rengger 2001, 98). Critical Theory in IR then has an obligation to work for a more democratic world in which the individuals participate in authorizing the institutions that affect them.

One of the most important contemporary Critical Theorists in IR is Andrew Linklater. On his view what is important about how Critical Theory applies to IR is that it tells us that knowledge always reflects preexisting social conditions and interests; greater freedom in the world is possible because of the error of believing that the rules that govern international politics are unchangeable; some of the weaknesses of Marxism can be overcome by applying critical ideas of social learning, which help to create an emancipatory historical sociology; and Critical Theory judges social arrangements by their capacity to engage in open dialogue among those with different interests. It envisages new forms of political community.[12]

The changes that must be made to advance human emancipation, according to Critical IR Theorists, include the transcending of the entire modern international system. Linklater argues that this is the only way in which human emancipation can be realized. There have been various claims in recent years that, because of globalization, the state system, which is at the center of the realist analysis of world politics, is in decline. States, these observers say, are becoming less important in world affairs as borders are made irrelevant by the rise of technology, as democracy spreads around the globe, and as the world capitalist system comes to dominate the world economy since it makes trade freer than ever; it has brought into that system states that had long been separated from it, such as the former communist states that comprised the Eastern bloc; it has even come to incorporate currently communist states, like China and Vietnam. Cultural dominance of Western styles and American pop culture are erasing the differences between societies around the world. The major role that banks, non-governmental organizations, and even terrorist organizations are said to be playing is rendering borders less important.

The Relationship between Metatheory and Substantive IR Theory

When we think about the difference between the foundational theories of constructivism and rationalism it is not immediately obvious why any of them should connect any more with one traditional substantive theory than another. And some scholars have begun to comment on this (see Jørgensen 2001; Barkin 2003; Jackson and Nexon 2004). There are obviously rationalist-realists and rationalist-liberals. And there are also scholars who are constructivists at both the substantive and metatheoretical levels. But can there be a position that is constructivist at the metatheoretical level and realist at the substantive level? If so, is it possible that there could be foundational-constructivist realists?

Constructivism as a substantive theory is fairly close to liberalism. Those who adopt the foundational/philosophical view of constructivism tend to agree with liberals on many substantive principles and, under proper circumstances, on many policy questions. Similarly, many Critical Theorist and poststructuralists often spent part or all of their careers as Marxists, such as Foucault and Gramsci. But there is nothing inherent in the philosophical position that forces a constructivist to be liberal-leaning, and there is nothing inherent in poststructuralism that forces one to be Marxist-leaning. Critical Theory is very much derived from Marxism, but a number of adherents have put some distance between their views and those of Marx. It will illuminate the relationship between substantive and metatheories to note some examples of those who did not fit the molds. With regard to the liberal-constructivist connection, a recent paper by Barkin (2003) contends that one could be a substantive realist and also a philosophical constructivist. In the case of Marxism and poststructuralism, Wittgenstein's theory of language fits closely with that foundational view, but Wittgenstein endorsed no political ideology along the lines of Marxism and he offered no views on IR.

We should reiterate the point made at the end of the second section of this chapter, that, given most sorts of empirical evidence one is likely to have, the criteria of evaluation that a foundational theory will stress and those that it will delegitimize might have a systematic effect in supporting one particular sort of theory be it Marxist, Liberal, Realist, or other. But there is no inherent reason why one of the foundational-philosophical positions is locked into supporting one of the substantive theories in particular. The foundational theory we adopt might make it unlikely that we will accept substantive theory A or B. But it will probably not guarantee that we accept C or that we accept D. Which of the various substantive

Table 4.2 Nine reflectivist principles and reflectivist theories

	Interpretive constructivism	Poststructuralism	Critical Theory	Naturalism / Rationalism
1. Language creates reality and truth.	Yes	Yes	No	No
2. All knowledge is local and historically contingent.	Yes	Yes	No	No
3. Knowledge and power produce each other.	No	Yes	Yes	No
4. Instrumental reason is misconceived and dangerous.	Yes	Yes	Yes	No
5. Human emancipation is the moral imperative and chief goal of theory.	No	No	Yes	No
6. Knowledge always reflects social conditions and serves someone's interests.	Yes	Yes	Yes	No
7. Impossibility of universal principles in social theory	Yes	Yes	No	No
8. Reflexivity and self-fulfilling/defeating prophesy	Yes	Yes	Yes	No
9. Moral content	Yes	Yes	Yes	Some

theories (A, B, C, D) we accept will depend on our metatheory along with the empirical observations we have made.

Conclusion

We have seen different ways of studying IR. In the previous chapter we looked at the broadly scientific or naturalist ways. In this chapter we have looked at the antiscientific conception of social theory and various criticisms of the naturalist approach. The first section showed the way the common interpretive character of theories leads reflexivists to reject the analogy of the natural sciences with the social sciences; reflexivists deny that NS1-9 from Table 3.1 can be applied to social theories. The next three sections showed how the three types of reflectivist theories each formulated its arguments. The next chapter will look at some of the naturalist replies to reflectivist theories. But for now we note that the scientific approach takes the material world as a central part of what we study when we study IR while the antiscientific approach regards the world of IR and social interactions as made up of discourse—this allows us only to develop interpretations, which themselves are subject to further interpretation.

Structuralists, starting with Saussure, tried to understand language in a scientific way, carrying out the study at some distance from the object of their study. Poststructuralists denied that this distancing is possible, though they accepted or adapted other principles of Saussure's. For them the world ultimately boils down to discourses. The discourses that have evolved and have been handed down to our world (today or at any other time) are in no way "natural" or unavoidable; they are the result of many interpretive acts that worked to the benefit of one set of people and against the interests of other sets. As Derrida puts it, the real world is constituted like a text in that all we can do is interpret it and then interpret the interpretations; we cannot know it through any direct access. This view contrasts with Critical Theory and especially with conventional constructivism, discussed in Chapter 2. The latter looks at the constructed institutions and actors that we have at a given point in time, accepts their existence for as long as they operate, and then seeks to theorize about them as real entities.

One way to see the difference is to think about some of the empirical hypotheses that IR scholars examine. Let us consider an element of the Iraq war decision. One rationale, R3, says "a democracy would lead to a more peaceful relationship between the West and Iraq." This rationale was derived both from the liberal democratic peace principle and from neorealism's view of cooperation with the United States. Suppose a liberal scholar says, "democracies are much more peaceful than nondemocracies." We then ask, Is it possible to find out, based on historical experience, if this statement is true or false? And would knowing whether it is true or false help to guide our actions? Naturalists and rationalists would answer "yes" to both. Poststructuralists will say "no" to both, arguing that the powerful interests and states (indirectly) create the reality that we use to evaluate true or false, to serve their interests.

Interpretive constructivism sees the world of human affairs as entirely created in the minds of people who live in each society. The relationship between the people and the institutions and structures of their society is interactive. Each helps to constitute the other. And they see the study of the social sphere, including IR, as a search for meanings rather than a search for causal connections.

Reflectivist theorists discussed in this chapter tell us that all knowledge is simply a set of beliefs or presuppositions that do not rest on any foundations; any body of knowledge provides only one of many possible perspectives; there is no underlying reality that ties together the different perspectives. The familiar allegory of the three blind people and the elephant may be somewhat useful. For those who might not be familiar with it: we imagine three individuals who are fully competent but who lack sight. Each encounters an elephant for the first time. Each touches a different part of the elephant and goes home to report what the creature is like. The first touches its trunk and describes it as tall and slender with a snake-like shape. The second touches its ear and describes it as wide and flat and floppy. The third touches its leg and describes it as thick and solid and powerful. Of course we can imagine that a sighted person could look at the elephant and describe it as we know it—as having those features and much more.

For reflectivist theorists, and especially for poststructuralist thinkers, the pursuit of knowledge is much like the blind persons' pursuit of the nature of the elephant, with three major exceptions. First is that we have to suppose the idea of a sighted person, to contrast to the blind person, is unimaginable. There is just no social theory concept analogous to that of a sighted person seeing the elephant and coming up with a perception of it that goes far beyond the perceptions and accounts of the blind. Second, there is no elephant. That is, there is no independently existing entity that unifies the various different perceptions held by the different people who come at the object of study from different perspectives. The perceptions, or interpretations, are all that exist. The third difference is that, not only is there no elephant but we are mistaken to think there are three persons touching the elephant, at least in the usual sense of "persons." In the allegory we begin with these people. We have a fixed concept of them as human beings, as rational, as blind, and as able to describe to their friends at home what the creature is like as they perceive it. However, poststructuralists and interpretive constructivists would say that the three people do not have these "essential features" that we ordinarily attribute to people; their interaction with the elephant helps to constitute their identity; it helps to make them who they are. The allegory allows us to ignore the fact that the pursuit of knowledge in the real world is, poststructuralists would say, always for some purpose and always benefits some particular group.

Among the reflectivist theorists discussed in this chapter, poststructuralists most completely reject the Enlightenment idea of the pursuit of knowledge of the social world. The concept of objective and value-neutral social theory that can help us solve practical problems is radically misconstrued. Poststructuralists are adamant that knowledge is not objective. Rather all knowledge is situated in a particular place and at a particular time. Had the subject matter been studied at other times and places, what is "known" would appear in a different way. Knowledge is imbedded in the dominant discourses of the society. Thus knowledge is bound up with power; so the power relationships affect what counts as power; and power relationships affect what counts as knowledge. The pursuit of knowledge and the development of theories always have a particular purpose for a particular person or group, which the allegory overlooks.

Critical Theorists reject the traditional approach to social science theory for a number of reasons. They reject the idea that any theory can be value-neutral. A theory of society can never simply describe things as they are because doing so will reinforce the current conditions. Theory can only properly be used to critique traditional (supposedly value-neutral) forms of theorizing and to critique society itself. Critical Theorists openly advocate a moral order where humans are emancipated from exploitation and oppression. They attack the traditional study of social science for its reliance on "instrumental reason," which traditional theory takes to be a value-neutral tool of great power. Critical Theorists object; ascribing to it such power is to assign to it a high value. They add that it is, furthermore, a morally loaded value (rather than an epistemic value), because it has been used specifically to support a liberal free-trade order that has winners and losers.

The final chapter will consider what we need to do in order to see if any of these attacks on traditional theory have merit. Must we give up traditional theory and accept interpretive constructivism, poststructuralism, and Critical Theory?

CHAPTER 5

Conclusion: Contending Approaches to the Study of International Relations

C hapter 1 showed that we need to answer various theoretical questions in order to be able to make effective foreign policy choices in cases like relations with Iraq, North Korea, and China. Chapter 2 showed the different theories that would influence the policies a policy maker would choose in those cases. Chapter 3 laid out the naturalist view that IR and the social world can be studied in a way that is descriptively objective, ethically neutral, and capable of producing reliable predictions. Chapter 4 presented reflectivists' opposition to naturalist claims that scholars can study IR in a way that has such scientific attributes. This chapter offers some guidelines about how to solve the disputes and some possible naturalist replies to the arguments of Chapter 4. In particular, it sketches a *conventionalist* metatheory.[1] It is ultimately up to the reader to explore the various issues surrounding this question and to come to her or his own conclusions about which methods are best for which purposes.

The Difficulty with Using Logical Positivism as an Example of Rationalism or Empiricism

As we have examined the question of whether the social sciences can be objective, ethically neutral, and predictive, we have seen that the strongest "yes" answer comes from logical positivists of the 1920s and 1930s, and the strongest "no" answer from poststructuralists of the 1960s. But there were criticisms of logical positivism before poststructuralists attacked it. Analytic philosophy itself produced many trenchant criticisms, starting with Karl Popper and Ludwig Wittgenstein in the 1930s. By the 1960s even the leading proponents of the school acknowledged that logical positivism, in its various formulations, was not a tenable doctrine. Rudolf Carnap and the other main figures in the movement either modified their views, often adopting logical empiricism, or they focused their energies on other problems. They did not continue to promote logical positivism. So refutations of logical positivism are not new.

In contemporary IR we occasionally find scholars who claim to discredit empiricism or naturalism generally by "discovering" flaws in logical positivism. Because logical positivism is but one form of empiricism and naturalism, and there are many others, this critical argument against empiricism commits the "fallacy of the straw man." That fallacy occurs when someone argues against a doctrine by (1) examining a version of that doctrine that is far from the strongest version of it and far from the one best able to withstand scrutiny, (2) showing flaws in that version of the doctrine, and (3) concluding that the doctrine is false.[2]

In the theory of knowledge there are more persuasive forms of empiricism than logical positivism, and in the philosophy of the social sciences there are much more persuasive forms of naturalism than logical positivism. As just noted, in order to avoid the fallacy of the straw man, and thus to make a persuasive case against a general philosophical approach like naturalism, a critic must characterize the position in the strongest available form(s). The doctrine of logical positivism was rejected half a century ago by analytic philosophers and even by its chief proponents; it is far from the strongest version of naturalism. *The errors of logical positivism do not provide evidence that empiricism or naturalism are mistaken.*

Theory of Knowledge and What the World Consists of

There is an interesting imbalance in the IR literature between work focused on empirical and theoretical studies, which are mostly done by naturalist/rationalists, and work focused on metatheory and the philosophy of science, which is mostly done by anti-naturalist critics of traditional naturalist theories. Mainstream authors rarely engage in debates about which theory of knowledge (epistemology) or metatheory they should accept or how they should respond to questions about assumptions concerning the existence of certain sorts of entities (ontology), where the entities include different sorts of actors (like individual leaders, states, corporations, banks, political parties, and terrorist organizations) and different sorts of structures (like international systems, legal structures, regimes, and international organizations).

The best traditional IR scholars offer sophisticated philosophical arguments, which in no way rely on the 1920s-style logical positivist principles just cited. They do not even have to rely on foundationalist views of knowledge. For example, they could draw on pragmatist theories of knowledge like those by Peirce, Dewey, James, or even Rorty. Reflectivist theorists often argue against traditional naturalist methodology because foundational theories of knowledge are, in their view, unacceptable. But neither IR theorists nor philosophers of science claim that they need a foundationalist view of knowledge. Since we do not need to choose between foundationalism and non-naturalism, any argument that insists we must do so is guilty of the fallacy of the false dichotomy.[3] And any argument that treats foundationalist views as the best naturalist theory is guilty of the fallacy of the straw man. *Naturalism does not require a foundationalist theory of knowledge.*

Methodological Pluralism

Tracing Long-Term and Short-Term Consequences

The introduction to this book characterized a theory of IR as a set of principles that tell us how the world works. A theory tells us what actions lead to what consequences. When we talk of actions C leading to consequences E, we would be interested in the consequences that follow in a week or in twenty years. In the case of Iraq, in March 2003 policy makers were worried about what might happen in the next three to six months, while in the case of China they are largely concerned about the consequences over a period of decades. Many scholars would say that one sort of theory is needed to answer questions about short-term effects and a different sort to answer questions about long-term effects.

Suppose we want to know how China might react if a U.S. aircraft enters Chinese airspace. We might need to know about the composition of the Chinese leadership, the personality traits of those leaders, the issues that were discussed at recent Sino-American meetings, and how productive those meetings were. We might then try to compile a systematic set of generalizations about how these individuals react to certain sorts of conflicts. However, someone could argue that the long-term consequences are not just the sum of a series of short-term action-reaction cycles but rather the results of shifts in the material capabilities of the United States, China, and the other major actors in world politics. A policy maker might say that a macro-level structural realist theory is the best available theory to look at long-term relations. But she might say that very different factors will guide us to the most successful theories (which may be more micro-level theories or perhaps "decision-making theories") to predict short-term effects.

Social scientists operate on the belief that if there is an underlying structure to the social world, then there must be consistency among the theories that are applied to a specific domain or level of generality. So it is not reasonable to argue that liberalism explains World War I and realism explains World War II, unless there is a further explanation for why there was such a difference. IR theorists investigate different sorts of questions in different domains (empirical versus moral) and different methods and theories would be appropriate for them (as questions 1–7 in the next subsection show).

"Inside" and "Outside" Methods of Study

The introduction to this book noted the broad distinction between "inside" interpretivist and "outside" naturalist approaches to IR. According to the outside approach, we can study IR by searching for general, lawlike regular patterns of behavior and causal relationships that parallel those that natural scientists seek in studying the natural world. But according to the inside approach, because causal connections are not a major feature of the social world, we should focus on the study of meanings and meaning systems. For example, we must try to discern what meanings actors attach to the actions of others by trying to "get inside" the actors' thought processes. Outside approaches, discussed in Chapters 1–3, are typical of traditional theorists. Inside approaches, discussed in Chapter 4, are interpretive and often normative.

Scholars typically present these two approaches as mutually exclusive alternatives and suggest that we must determine which one is correct and join that camp. Sometimes the choice is said to rest on a decision about "ontology." For example, if we learn that the nature of the social world is not really like the nature of the natural world, and thus cannot really claim there are causal relationships, then we must become interpretivists. A naturalist might argue that this interpretive, or inside, claim is wrong in a number of ways. The first is that "causality" does properly apply to the social world. A second error stems from the fact that we have to get our ontology from the best theory and not exclusively from a set of abstract philosophical conditions (though some abstract criteria are important, such as avoiding inconsistencies within theories). A third error is that the inside and outside approaches are not necessarily mutually exclusive.

The first point draws on the standard view of the concept of "cause" in Western science and philosophy. The interpretivist argument against social causation holds that our basic notion of "cause" must involve two genuinely independent events that bear a contingent relationship to one another, such as lightening striking the tree and the tree bursting into flames. The argument also states that we never encounter events in the social world that are truly independent. Additionally, the events in the social world are constitutively and not causally related. Thus, it is a misleading extension of our Western notion of causality, which is so integral to theorizing in the natural sciences, to apply it to the social world.

Naturalists have several possible responses. They might begin by rejecting the first premise and arguing that the concept "causality" in Western science is itself an extension of social causation. The earliest Greek philosophers took the example of human action and reaction and extended it to nature. Thus our natural science notion of "causality" is historically derived from the social sphere.[4] The second reply emphasizes that we have no direct access to the underlying nature of social reality. We can only infer it from empirical observations. Thus naturalists and empiricists reject the idea that we should determine our ontology first (perhaps by reading interpretivists, reflectivists, or other philosophical works on ontology) and then reject theories that are inconsistent with it. Rather, empiricists and naturalists say that we determine our ontology only *after* we have accepted a theory. If we seek a theory of physics, we do not decide that quarks, neutrinos, or other subatomic particles exist based on some purely abstract reasoning and then find a theory of physics that is consistent with that ontology. Rather, empiricists and naturalists hold that we have a set of observations (which would typically use very sophisticated equipment in that field), and then we consider various possible theories that explain those observations. Each theory in physics, as in any field, assumes the existence of certain kinds of things—that is, each theory has a set of "ontological commitments." The theory that explains the observations best (based on criteria discussed in Chapter 3) is the theory that we, as physicists, accept. We *then* accept the ontological commitments of that theory. Reflectivists who are scientific realists and critical realists (Chapter 3) warn against the empiricists' faulty reasoning, which they call the "epistemic fallacy," in which empiricists argue that if we cannot know something exists, we conclude that it does not exist. But we note that critical realists and some scientific realists commit what we might call the "ontological fallacy" of holding that we have access to the real objects of scientific theories (just as we have access to the ordinary, prescientific objects of everyday experience) *prior to* our scientific theorizing (see Chernoff 2008b).

Scientific realists and critical realists are right in pointing out that we cannot know something does not exist simply because we cannot prove that it does exist. But those who suggest further that all empiricists who commit the epistemic fallacy are themselves committing a further fallacy—the false dichotomy. They are claiming that we either accept empiricism or accept that there are real but unobservable objects with causal powers in the world, which scientific theories try to describe, that give rise to the appearances that underlie our basic observations. These are not the only two possibilities. To illustrate, consider the work of Bas Van Fraassen (1980, 2002), one of the most influential empiricists, who has developed a position known as "constructive empiricism." Whether one accepts his account or not, the fact that he has developed a cogent approach that does not fit into the two categories is a clear demonstration that there are no conceptual grounds to insist that there are only those two philosophical possibilities. He agrees with other empiricists that we cannot conclude that unobservable things like neutrons exist simply because they are part of our best theories. One of the main reasons we cannot conclude that they exist is the "pessimistic induction on the history of science," the fact that, in the past, our best theories have eventually proven false. But Van Fraassen does not say we are thereby justified in concluding that unobservable, theoretical entities such as neutrinos do not exist. He argues that we have to admit that neutrinos may or may not exist, and we will never know which. We choose the best theory from those available based on our criteria of theory choice. And we accept a theory that uses the term "neutrino" for one sort of unobservable, theoretical entity if and only if it is the best available theory. But it does not follow that the theoretical entities really exist.

It is true that we need some sort of ontology to pose the questions. We must start with an ontology of things that play a role in our basic empirical observations. But the ontological commitments of the questions are typically much less problematic or controversial than the ontologies of the theories needed to answer them. For example, if we ask in physics, why did this cloud form in the cloud chamber? we are committed only to the existence of cloud chambers, certain gasses, and clouds. The subatomic theory that explains the observations best is far more complex and involves debatable, controversial, unobservable entities, such as electrons or neutrinos. Or in IR, if we ask, why did the United States and UK invade Iraq? we are already committed to a set of entities but not controversial ones, namely, the United States, UK, and Iraq as examples of nation-states, and the existence of armies and invasions. These are not philosophically problematic and are much less controversial than the theoretical entities postulated by some IR theories, such as "international power structures," "international regimes," and "balances of power."

The third reply that naturalists might offer is that the inside and outside approaches may be compatible. To see how this is possible, we should note that IR theorists ask a wide variety of questions, such as the following:

1. Do autocratic governments start more wars than democratic states?
2. Are unipolar systems more stable than bipolar systems?
3. Was the North Korean missile test over Japanese territory in August 1998 intended as a warning signal to Japan?
4. What did Leonid Brezhnev mean by "correlation of forces"?
5. Is the use of nuclear weapons ever justified?
6. Is detention of enemy combatants without due process immoral?
7. Do wealthy developed states have an obligation to help poor states?

The appropriate methods for each of these questions differ. Some of these questions (1–2) are clearly best answered by "outside" methods that would include an examination of many cases and an attempt to find associations among variables; some (3–4) are most effectively answered by means of "inside" interpretive methods; and others (5–7) are best answered by the analysis of concepts and the application of moral theory.

There is, moreover, no single, overarching super-theory of IR or that all observations must fit into, though there are some specific logical forms of reasoning that are applicable to all. Because the social world is complex and multi-faceted, even a study of a possible war between the United States and North Korea produces questions that, though related, sometimes require very different kinds of methods and approaches. Wendt notes that rationalist and constructivist theories need not be seen as entirely opposed; each seeks to answer a different set of questions, neither set of which is "more important" than the other (Wendt 1999, 34). For some questions, naturalist outside methods are most likely to yield clear answers. For other questions, typically those that do not require predictions, interpretivist inside methods would be best. The demand that we choose once and for all between inside and outside is another false dichotomy. Moreover, a look at different sorts of policy needs, for example, long-term versus short-term, show that one sort of theory might be most efficient for one while another sort of theory, perhaps more at the macro- or micro-level, might be most effective for other policy questions. Thus, *a plurality of methods is best, given the many different sorts of inquiry in which IR theorists engage.*

Moral Issues

One of the key debates between naturalists and anti-naturalists is whether we can pursue theories of IR without already having moral commitments that give the theories a moral tint. Naturalists argue that social science theory can and should proceed without moral dimension. It is only possible to make progress in an intellectual discipline if moral values and empirical description and explanation are clearly separated. IR theorists should be able to employ "instrumental reasoning" to provide theories that tell us how the world works, that is, what actions lead to what responses. It is up to policy makers to decide which goals to pursue. Once those goals are chosen, the empirical theories can be applied to help the policy maker achieve the goals most efficiently.

We have discussed arguments against a strict separation between "facts" and "values." Some philosophers argue that there are no purely factual statements and no purely evaluative statements. Every statement of fact has some evaluative element and every statement of value has some descriptive or factual element. However, even if there is no absolute barrier between factual and evaluative statements, it might be enough for naturalists to make their case by distinguishing the proportion of factual or evaluative content of statements. They might admit that IR will not progress as fast as physics because there is some "leakage" of facts to values and vice versa. The statement "Kim Jong-il is the son of Kim Il-sung" is much more factual and much less evaluative than "Kim Jong-il is a ruthless tyrant." The problem that philosophers try to solve by the fact-value distinction might be solved by focusing on the difference between primarily factual statements, which have very limited moral content and primarily evaluative statements, which might also include some nonmoral content. So if we stick to primarily factual statements as much as possible, perhaps the progress can still be substantial.

This sort of response works for some of the arguments against a "value-free" social science but not the more radical poststructuralist arguments. Poststructuralists do not usually see theory as an effective way of promoting action. For the reflectivist theorists who do see theory as a springboard for promoting effective action, there may be a dilemma, since they all seem to deny the possibility of prediction. Theories that see the purpose of theory as motivating action and at the same time deny predictive capacity for social theory might face serious problems, as the next section shows. Some deny that there is a hard-and-fast fact-value distinction. *Nevertheless, on all accounts, there are differences between primarily factual statements and primarily evaluative statements.*

Prediction and the Cost of Giving it Up

Naturalist Arguments Against Prediction:
Three Sources of Prediction Skepticism

Even naturalists can argue that while the social sciences are like natural science theories in many ways, they are not capable of generating reliable predictions.

Three reasons cited by various authors are, first, that the social sciences are more complex than the natural sciences and there are more forces operating—too many to isolate and evaluate in a way that allows reliable prediction. We cannot set up a situation of, say, three great powers entering a conflict based on a specific set of conditions and observe the outcome. In contrast, we can create experimental situations in chemistry or physics. Experiments in the natural sciences allow us to create closed systems simple enough for the necessary calculations. The experimental conditions model the real world closely enough to allow us to make predictions based on the parallels. A second argument holds that in the natural sciences we have superficial regularities, and we also have deeper laws that explain the superficial ones. The deeper laws give us reliable predictions, while the superficial ones do not. In the social sciences we have only the superficial, observable regularities but no deep laws involving causal mechanisms, which are sufficiently well established to allow reliable predictions. A third argument against prediction is that things change radically at certain times and create "discontinuities" or "tipping points" where old trends become irrelevant.[5]

The defender of predictive IR theory has several possible responses to these arguments against predictiveness. One is to note that most of the negative arguments rely on a very narrow definition of "prediction." They write as if nothing could count as a prediction that is less precise and less deterministic than a Newtonian "point prediction"—for example, the prediction of how long it will take a ball to drop a specified distance. This is not an accurate definition of "prediction" in the context of evaluating merits and limits of IR theories, since it is not what policy makers mean by the term and, more importantly, it is not what they need in order to be able to make policy. Of course, for policy makers, the more precise and certain a prediction is the better. But, in fact, policy makers often benefit from a prediction that simply gives them a better basis for action than the basis they have without any predictive guidance. If the predictions are right most of the time, then that may be sufficient (though there are some cases where very high probabilities are needed).

This book often has noted that social science theories, and the regularities and laws they include, are probabilistic and not deterministic. We have to acknowledge either that our predictions will mostly be of unsurprising events (e.g., that Canada will not invade China in the next twenty years), or that we might have to restrict most of our predictions to a shorter time frame (e.g., that 150,000 U.S. and UK troops invading Iraq in March 2003 will be sufficient to defeat Saddam Hussein's military forces within six months time) because the longer chain of probabilistic statements when all are conjoined, the lower the probability.[6]

Reflectivist Theories and Prediction

We saw in Chapter 2 that prediction is necessary if theories are to have any practical use to policy makers. Let us suppose that a policy advisor for a fictional British political party writes the following letter to the foreign ministers of the four partners in the Six-Party Talks on North Korean nuclear program stating: "Even though we are quite sure North Korea is moving ahead with its nuclear weapons program today, and that it has been doing so for a number of years, there is no need to take any action because prediction is impossible; so, for all we know, it is just as likely as any other outcome that North Korea will end its nuclear weapons program tomorrow and dismantle what has been built." The states involved, particularly the United States, Japan, and South Korea, would reject that hypothesis and offer the following prediction: (P1) If North Korea is building nuclear weapons today, it will be building them next year unless some external forces intervene.

The prediction P1 is most likely true. It is highly improbable that North Korea will spontaneously stop its weapons program. The four states believe that North Korea is only likely to halt the program if its conditions change, either by other states offering a package of concessions or using military force. Only because a state believes that P1 is true will it be willing to pay the costs of using military force against North Korea or of making concessions to it. If we had absolutely no idea whether or not the prediction P1 is true, then there would be no reason for choosing any course of action, even if we were absolutely certain that North Korea plans to continue producing nuclear weapons. As Chapter 2 showed, policy makers base their decisions on beliefs about the future, including conditional and probabilistic beliefs like, "if we do A, they will probably do B." The strongest grounds we can have for believing a (conditional, probabilistic) prediction would be that it has been justified by our best methods for analyzing all of the available data. So, if theory is going to offer any help to policy makers, it must be able to provide a basis for predictions.

A reflectivist might tell us that social theories can give us moral guidance but no empirical predictions whatsoever; for example, they might add that we have a moral obligation to minimize nuclear weapons around the world—both the number of nuclear weapons that exist and the number of states that possess them. So far, so good. But upon hearing someone propose that the United States should send North Korea precision tools and centrifuges that are useful in building nuclear weapons, the hypothetical reflectivist theorist might say that is a perfectly good idea. We would, of course, expect the reflectivist theorist to oppose this suggestion. But if there is no basis for any prediction, then there is no reason to think that the shipments will lead to more North Korean nuclear weapons. So there must be some, even if limited, prediction if theories are to help guide action. Once the reflectivist theorist admits that some predictions are possible, even simple ones (like Canada will not invade China), then it is just a matter of drawing the line between what is predictable and what is not, which involves learning what theories and what types evidence are needed to make reliable predictions.

Most reflectivist theorists adamantly deny that prediction is possible in social interactions, including IR. They argue that in various ways, as Chapter 4 described, the social world is either too subjective or too unstable to allow reliable predictions. They do not qualify the statements and say "some predictions are possible." They reject prediction outright and state their opposition in emphatic terms. Among reflectivist theorists, Frankfurt School Critical Theorists are best able to defend some sort of social prediction the most.

As scholars we must always be intellectually honest. If careful reasoning based on the best available evidence leads us to a particular conclusion, then no matter how uncomfortable that conclusion is for us we have to accept it. We should continue to search for flaws in the reasoning or for better alternatives. But until we discover those flaws, we should admit that the most compelling conclusion is just that. How readily we should change our behavior when new conclusions appear to be true will differ from case to case and depend in part on the stakes. That is, higher standards of proof are to be demanded when more is at stake in giving up the old ways. This is not an inconsistency as long as we are consistent in applying the variable of "degree of importance" or "what is at stake."

Let us take a simple example. If someone wants to prove that the local trains are always on time, we should demand a certain level of proof of that person, such as a large enough sample of past cases at different times of day and different local rail lines. In contrast, let us consider the claim made by various ancient philosophers who invoked "Zeno's paradoxes" that all change, including motion, is illusion.[7] If their conclusion is right, then when we see a person standing on railroad tracks in front of (what appears to be) an onrushing train, the motion of the train is an illusion and her impending death is, too. Zeno's paradoxes are ingenious, but a lot more is at stake in accepting the argument that follows from them than from the argument about trains running on time. The variable "what is at stake" is crucial, since not much is at stake if we are wrong in accepting that trains are always on time. But a great deal is indeed at stake if we are wrong in accepting that the speeding train will not crush us as we stand on the track. In the first case, if we mistakenly expect our train to be on time and we thus arrive at a station too early, the result is that we will have to wait until the train arrives. The cost of being wrong is relatively low. In the second case, if we mistakenly expect that an apparently onrushing train will not produce any change because all change is illusory, the result is that we are crushed to death. Because the cost of being wrong is so high in the second case, it is reasonable to demand a much higher standard of proof there than in the first.

When we examine the debate over social science prediction, we should accept the negative conclusion if the arguments against prediction are solid and unassailable. If we are to accept an argument against prediction in IR, we have to give up the idea that studying IR can offer any real help to policy makers. And we have to abandon the hope that we can change the world in ways we want, even a little bit, by following the right policies. This is a great deal to give up. Because there is so much at stake if we are wrong, these arguments must be very compelling; that is, the standard of proof should be extremely high. Most reflectivists hold that we should give up prediction. Poststructuralists are very explicit in this, as are many interpretive constructivists. Some reflectivists simply avoid explicit discussions of "prediction." But those who do mention it firmly reject it. *Most reflectivist theories reject prediction in the study of IR, which entails that IR theory is of little use for policy-making purposes.*

Logic and Reasoning in IR

Naturalism, Interpretivism, and Hypothetico-deductive Reasoning

Theories tell us how the world works. They show us the causal and constitutive connections between kinds of events. In so doing, they refer to various sorts of entities. If the theory does what a good theory is supposed to do, then we might assume the entities exist (according to scientific realists), or assume the theory is the best and operate *as if* they exist (as instrumentalists argue).

Interpretivists are often so determined to reject older forms of naturalism, especially logical positivism, that they are inclined to reject almost anything associated with it, including hypothetico-deductive reasoning. However, without recognizing it, most interpretivists rely on it. When they examine many possible interpretations of a work of art, a passage in Scripture, or an historical event, they ask, which interpretation should be accepted? Or they ask, which interpretation, at least among those so far considered, is the best interpretation? While some poststructuralist theorists say that all interpretations are equal, most reflectivists believe that some are better than others and that there is a way to find out which is the best. How do they go about it?

The general sort of method for answering the question of which interpretation, for example about President Bush's behavior in concealing North Korea's nuclear announcement in 2002, is to ask, If he has that character, how would we expect him to act in other situations? They would then examine some of those other situations (those for which we have made observations) and determine, within the confines of the hermeneutic circle, which interpretation gives the best answer most of the time. As the other cases are reexamined, adjustments might be made to how we interpret them. But as we think through the process in both directions, we are looking at a body of beliefs, drawing out expectations regarding specific cases, and then looking to see if those expectations are met. That is, interpretivists use the hypothetico-deductive method as much as naturalists do in seeking the best available interpretation.[8]

Stronger Arguments Use Fewer Premises

We would like a theory of IR to be to able to solve the policy problems at hand as efficiently as possible. We will have to deal with some issues of metatheory to get our answers. But we might not have to deal with others. And if we find the answers we seek and can avoid certain sorts of difficult philosophical questions, then we should. This is a guiding principle for the development of strong arguments.

This book has looked at some philosophical issues raised by IR metatheorists that we cannot avoid. This book seeks to explore the metatheory debates and problems that are relevant to policy decisions, chiefly the naturalist arguments of Chapter 3 and the reflectivist criticisms of Chapter 4, and also to point out what metatheoretical and philosophical problems are not relevant for IR theorists. If certain philosophical issues must be tackled in order to develop a sound IR theory applicable to a particular problem at hand, then we must tackle them. But various IR theorists have raised difficult philosophical, ethical, and religious problems. And some of them are unnecessary for the purpose of developing a theory of IR. In general, in the course of advancing their positions, interpretivists tend to raise far more philosophical questions than naturalists do. This appears to be a strength of interpretivism. But if the philosophical principles it develops are either unnecessary or false, then, ultimately, it becomes more of a weakness than a strength. As we engage in IR metatheory debates, we must be careful to separate what is really essential from what is irrelevant. *We should only tackle questions that appear to be alien to IR if it can be shown that we need to do so.*

Criteria of Theory Choice and Reflectivist Theories

The reflectivist theories discussed in Chapter 4 reject scientific methods of theory choice. The scientific-style criteria of theory choice discussed in Chapter 3 were internal consistency, coherence, simplicity, range, falsifiability, concreteness, fecundity, and methodological conservatism. Among these criteria, reflectivist theorists would generally accept internal consistency, since they avoid explicit or overt contradictions in formulating their positions and thus they endorse the idea that an argument should be free of contradictions. They would also seem to agree on coherence, since they generally prefer a holistic view of the social world. With respect to simplicity, interpretive constructivists and possibly Critical Theorists would prefer a simple theory to an otherwise equivalent more complex theory. Similarly, interpretive constructivists reject complex and convoluted interpretations and prefer simpler ones. Poststructuralists, in contrast, show no particular preference for simplicity. Critical Theorists would place a much higher emphasis on human emancipation than on simplicity and seem to place relatively little value on the latter, as compared with natural scientists or naturalist social scientists. Range would appeal to interpretive constructivists, but there is no reason why either a poststructualist or a Critical Theorist would argue in favor of a theory that has a wider range than a rival theory that scores higher on other criteria.

Falsifiability is closely related to a scientific view of the world. One must believe that the empirical consequences of a theory are important to a theory, where all reflectivist theorists place much weight on the ability of a theory to level normative criticisms at existing theories as well as society. Such claims within a theory are not empirically falsifiable. Correctness, or accuracy, presumes that there is an independent reality of the social world that is being described and explained. Interpretive constructivists, and especially poststructuralists, vigorously reject this claim. Critical Theorists, in contrast to the other sorts of reflectivists, would place some positive weight on correctness, since they do believe that it has value, along with the necessary normative critique. Methodological conservatism, again, does not connect to the core of any of the reflectivist theories. The normative critiques that reflectivists endorse are usually radically different from those they seek to replace, namely, the dominant theories that are acceptable to the dominant or hegemonic discourse of the society. Reflectivists

Table 5.1 Reflectivist theories

Criteria	Interpretive constructivism	Poststructuralism	Critical theory
1. Internal consistency	Yes	Yes	Yes
2. Coherence	Yes	Yes	Yes
3. Simplicity	Yes	No	No
4. Range	Yes	No	No
5. Falsifiability	No	No	No
6. Concreteness	No	No	Yes
7. Fecundity	No	No	No
8. Methodological conservatism	No	No	No

generally agree that radical change is needed, at least in some cases, like the various societies in twenty-first century.

Interpretation and Policy Rationales

The investigation of reflectivism in Chapter 4 adds a good deal to the conclusions drawn about naturalism in Chapter 3. Reflectivist philosophers discussed in the previous chapter, like Charles Taylor (1985), believe that the natural sciences deal with many straightforward facts, and the social sciences deal with none. Naturalists believe that the social sciences are closer—at least somewhat closer—to the natural sciences than Taylor describes. Naturalists believe that there are straightforward facts in the social sciences, for example, that the British fought the Germans at the Somme in 1916. While there is no need for interpretation in this case, there are other factual-appearing claims that require degrees of interpretation. To cite one case, General Haig's leadership at the Somme was very flawed. That is not a fact like the occurrence of a battle, as it requires judgment as well as a framework for judgment or interpretation of the term "poor leadership," as explained in Chapter 4.

In Chapter 1 we looked at rationales and divided them into factual and theoretical. Now when we look at the cases of Iraq, North Korea, and China, we can see there are three different sorts of theoretical rationales. We will call them "causal," "interpretive," and "moral." Table 5.2 shows how these break down. We examine these briefly only in the case of the Iraq rationales. The same process can be carried out for the North Korea and China rationales.

We see that not only causal theories are needed, but some means of choosing ends or goals and some method for interpreting various judgment. Statements about Saddam's ability to be deterred or about the strengths or weaknesses of the system of the UN chain of command are interpretive judgments. They are not explicit cause-and-effect claims. Thus in the case of Iraq, rationales R4 and R5 are interpretive. If we carefully separate out the causal claims from the interpretive claims, then typically there are fewer interpretive claims that are essential to a

Table 5.2 Nature of Iraq war rationales

Rationale*	Factual	Casual	Interpretive	Moral
R1 Saddam Hussein supports terrorists through money and weapons.	X			
R2 U.S. demonstration of force shows foes they cannot win.	X			
R3 A democratic Iraq will be more peaceful to the West.		X		
R4 Saddam Hussein is a dictator who cannot be deterred.		X		
R5 UN chain of command has flaws and weaknesses.		X		
R6 Spreading war costs to many states helps the United States.	X			
R7 Iraq invasion is legal only if sanctioned by UN.				X
R8 Cooperation restraining Iraq aids cooperation in the war on terror.			X	
R9 Information on Iraq's arsenal increases effective policy.			X	
R10 War in Iraq requires a large portion of U.S. armed forces	X			
R11 War against Iraq is only a last resort.				X
R12 Avoid a return to Western imperialism.				X
R13 Iraq (2002/03) lacks capabilities to threaten the United States or the West.	X			
R14 Iraq does not aid anti-U.S. terrorist groups.	X			
R15 Killing Iraqi civilians is immoral and unjustifiable.				X

The column header spans: **Nature of Supporting Principles**, with **Factual** and **Theoretical** (the latter spanning Casual, Interpretive, Moral).

policy choice. But they are part of the process. Hermeneuticists argue that there is a circular process of interpreting a particular observation or fact and developing an interpretive framework. Naturalists might also argue for this sort of interpretation, especially by taking the position that there are rigorous methods for finding better and better interpretations of facts over time (a view poststructuralists strongly oppose). By holding that there are such methods for reaching or approximating the best available interpretation, naturalists and interpretivists who agree conclude that the hermeneutic circle in this sense is a circle, but is not a vicious circle. In this way, they need not accept the skepticism that poststructuralist analysis produces.

The previous chapter noted five of the major differences between naturalism and reflectivism. It began with the role of causation, observing at the outset that a major difference between naturalists and critical reflectivist theorists is the role they give to the appraisal of the role of "causation" in the social world. We noted that reflectivists are resistant to seeing the social word as having cause-and-effect connections. Similarly, most naturalists do not see the study of the social world as fundamentally involving interpretation; however, some do. That is, some naturalists continue to endorse a scientific understanding of the world, including objectivity of facts and the predictive capacity of theories, but acknowledge that interpretation is important. While they support scientific explanation, they also support "understanding." The most general system-level structural theorists acknowledge the need for interpretation less than theorists of the more specific or finely tuned accounts of individual-level behavior. When dealing with individuals like Saddam Hussein, Kim Jong-il, or Hu Jintao, it is important to understand the character of such leaders. So the nonfactual part of the study of IR will include a range of kinds of theoretical statements. We have thus far seen three.

When we face a decision about what to do in our cases, we must scrutinize and evaluate the rationales that support the possible policy choices. The class of theoretical statements, we now see, can be divided into different types. We have identified three clear categories of nonfactual statements: causal, interpretive, and moral/normative. With this more finely grained set of distinctions, let us briefly return to one of the cases in order to see how the distinction allows us to make better sense of the rationales.

One Solution: Conventionalism

As just noted, when we ask whether naturalists are right in claiming that IR can be descriptively objective, ethically neutral, and predictively potent, the strongest "yes" comes from logical positivism, and the strongest "no" comes from poststructuralism. As we have seen, logical positivism is generally regarded as untenable and poststructuralism requires that we give up any real hope that theory can help policy makers or might improve any aspect of the world we live in. Because both extremes have drawbacks, it is worth mentioning conventionalism as a promising alternative metatheory: conventionalism avoids both excessively optimistic views about comprehending the social world in a fully natural science-like way and the excessive subjectivism we find in poststructuralism, which leads to the rejection of social science prediction. Pierre Duhem championed conventionalism in physics a century ago, but it is relatively unknown within the social sciences.[9] This section summarizes a few ways in which conventionalism solves some of the problems raised in the preceding chapters.

Conventionalism and Physics

First, we note that the thorough objectivity that scientists like to think is possible, and that was part of logical positivism and older accounts of science, does not seem possible now in light of the criticisms that we have reviewed in this book. However, conventionalism does not claim for science that sort of objectivity, because it acknowledges that there will always be an element of conventional agreement among the scientists in their acceptance of a new theory. The process can be illustrated by looking at an example.

According to Newton's theory, developed in the seventeenth century, physical space conforms to Euclidean geometry, which entails that parallel lines in physical space satisfy the "parallel postulate." Any pair of parallel lines never meet and the shortest distance between them is always a contant distance. Physicists continued to accept Newton and the parallel postulate for physical space, even though mathematicians were demonstrating that there are systems of geometry where the parallel postulate does not hold. Newton's theory was unable to explain certain new observations about the movements of planets. And in the early twentieth century Einstein was able to explain the anomalies by means of a theory that depicted space as curved and non-Euclidean. Within a short time Einstein's theory was universally accepted.

If we desperately wanted to retain the idea that space is Euclidean, could we do so? The principle of underdetermination of theory by data, UD (see Chapter 3), associated with Duhem and Quine, tells us we could. In fact, there have been successful attempts to formulate a system of laws of physics that allows us to account for all observations and describes space as Euclidean (see Havas 1967, 140–41). But there are no physicists anywhere who claim that this Euclidean-based theory is true, in part because all physicists accept certain metatheoretical criteria of theory choice (as described in Chapter 3), including "simplicity." The Euclidean-based physical laws are so far from being simple that no one would seriously suggest Einstein is wrong about the shape of space.

The weight of scientific opinion is overwhelmingly on the side of Einstein's description of the geometry of our universe. Still the choice of which theory to accept is a matter of convention. There is nothing in the rules of pure logic that prevents someone from adopting the Euclidean physical theory. Scientists accept conventions about what criteria lead us to choose the best theory and, significantly, about how to *measure distance*. In particular, they all accept the "measure stipulation," which merely stipulates that the solid rod we use for measuring distance does not change own length when moved from one place to another. There is no way to prove this. It is an assumption that cannot be demonstrated by any experiment.[10] Yet all modern physicists accept this "measure-stipulation."

Some conventionalists like Henri Poincaré argue that the conventions about theory choice we all adopt are worthy of our acceptance *simply because* we all adopt them; hence they are arbitrary. Any other stipulation would work equally well, as long as it was universally accepted. In contrast, Duhem argued that the conventional elements are not purely arbitrary, while admitting that the conventions cannot be derived from pure logic. The conventions are chosen by means of philosophical debate over the various possible alternatives. And such debates are settled on rational grounds, which is why such widespread agreement among scientists is possible. The considerations that lead us to accept them are not drawn from pure logic, nevertheless, they are not arbitrary because they are drawn from proper reasoning.

It is interesting to note that in 1904–1905, Duhem published his view that non-Euclidean physics was possible, which was before Einstein challenged the Euclidean theory. Many physicists and philosophers (including Poincaré) believed, for various reasons, that physicists could never give up the view that space is Euclidean. Duhem was one of the very few thinkers to see the conventional nature of this belief.

Extending Conventionalism to IR: Prediction and Progress

The core priciples of conventionalism may be extended to IR and other social sciences. Among the observations about the history of IR theory that need explanation are that there has been very little progress, as realists, liberals and others have disputed many points with similar sorts of arguments for centuries; there are a few debates in IR where there seems to have been progress; and IR theorists have historically viewed the field as capable of generating assistance to policy makers, which requires that some parts of the field are predictive.

With respect to the first point, conventionalism holds that without agreement on key concepts, especially the equivalents of the measure-stipulation in physics, sciences would not be able to progress. This seems to accord with the history of the debates in IR where there has been much disagreement on stipulations followed by disagreement on theoretical conclusions. On the second point, we note that there have been areas of discernible success and progress, even if they have not been as impressive as the progress we see in physics. Agreement on some matters is not a sufficient condition of progress and does not constitute progress, but it is a necessary condition, in that progress cannot occur if there is no such agreement. In the areas where we see agreement on conclusions, we see also conventional agreement on "measure-stipulations."

Let us recall that the debates over policy options in the cases discussed (Iraq, North Korea, and China) depended in part on whether we accept democratic peace claims. In our discussion of the cases we noted that "democratic peace studies" have largely converged on two points. One is that we should reject as false the "monadic hypothesis," which claims that democracies fight fewer wars than non-democracies. The other is that we should accept as true the "dyadic hypothesis," which states that any two democracies are unlikely to fight one another (see Chapter 3). It has been argued that the conventional agreement on how to measure "democracy" and "war" (parallel to the "measure-stipulation" in physics) has been essential in allowing this theoretical progress in the IR literature, which exhibits a lot of agreement between realists and liberals who otherwise rarely agree.

Conventionalism explains progress by focusing on the conventions of measure-stipulation. There has been clear agreement in democratic peace studies about how to define "peace" and "war" (using the Correlates of War database definition) and "democracy" (using the definitions of the databases developed by Polity and Freedom House).[11] In many other areas, like the morality of great power intervention to halt ethnic conflict, there are no areas of agreement on the key measuring concepts. One result is that we have decade after decade of disagreement between liberals, realists, and others. So the agreement on the monadic and dyadic hypotheses in democratic peace studies is striking. Conventionalism as a metatheory of IR can explain the cases of successful and progress and the lack thereof.

In the case of democratic peace studies, we noted that the claims of the (falsified) monadic and (unfalsified) dyadic hypotheses are probabilistic. The states of a democratic dyad (that is, a pair of democratic states) will be less likely to go to war against one another than a dyad in which one or both states are nondemocratic. The prediction we can make is that any two democracies are less likely to go to war in the next twenty years than any two otherwise-similar nondemocratic states.

Democratic peace claims do not entirely rule out the chance that two democracies might go to war. The notion of a democratic dyad (or "mutual democracy") having a lower likelihood of war than other dyads is only one of many forces relating to war and peace. There are other forces that push states towards war or peace. If two states had all of the war-inducing forces operating on them and only "mutual democracy" as a peace-inducing force. It is conceivable that a democratic Iraq or a democratic Palestinian state might, at some time in the future, go to war against democratic Israel, since many of the other forces for peace or war are pushing them toward war. The probabilistic war-inducing forces could overwhelm the probabilistic peace-inducing influence of their being democracies.

With respect to the third point, conventionalism is a naturalist account, as it is adapted from a metatheory of physical science. It supports nomic generalizations and predictions in the social science. This excuses us from having to rethink the entire nature of the IR enterprise and its potential contributions to the real world. Conventionalism helps to explain not only the history of the natural sciences but also certain features of the debates in IR. Conventionalism allows for the possibility of theoretical progress and prediction and thus policy applications. Duhem, who was also an historian of science, argued that there was over time genuine progress in the history of science, and he believed that prediction was central to that progress. If Duhemian conventionalism can be adapted to IR metatheory, it will help explain how there can be progress and will provide a basis for prediction which, as we know, is required by the application of IR theory to policy making.

The advantages of conventionalism as a metatheory are significant:

1. Conventionalism does not require absolute objectivity, since it recognizes that theory choice always requires an element of conventional choice; thus it avoids the extremes of older forms of positivism.

2. The element of conventional choice, at least on Duhem's account, is not

arbitrary; it is founded on rational philosophical arguments about criteria of theory choice; thus it avoids the extreme subjectivity of many interpretivist approaches.

3. Conventionalism is consistent with the idea that systematic social sciences are possible, although the laws and predictions are probabilistic rather than deterministic.

4. Conventionalism fully supports prediction, which allows some IR theories to be of value to policy makers.

Conventionalism can, but need not, allow the addition of a theory of causality.[12] Thus, there are metatheories such as Duhemian conventionalism that provide solutions to most of the metatheory challenges raised in Chapters 3 and 4.

In Sum

We have examined the argument that intelligent and rational policy making will require an empirical understanding of the causal and constitutive connections in the empirical world, empirical evidence about conditions, and moral values. All are necessary to guide policy makers to choose the proper goals for the state or the international system, as well as to calculate which policy options are most likely to move them, with acceptable costs, closer to those goals. We have seen that some versions of naturalism aiming for all three are flawed. And we have seen that some versions of reflectivism deny that any but the last is possible.

Along the way we have seen that many methods that are often considered to be at odds with one another might, in fact, work together to provide a deeper and richer understanding of world politics. We should be pluralistic as we choose methods. The best methods and theories must fit the specific type of problem that we are setting out to solve. IR theorists ask many different sorts of questions and these different questions are best answered by employing those methods that are most appropriate to them. Anyone who wants to make sound foreign policy choices must work hard to uncover evidence in the most effective ways possible and must make honest choices about which empirical theories are most useful and appropriate (or true) to solve the policy problems at hand. Progress in developing theories, as well as progress in making the world a better place, will be possible only if we use carefully scrutinized criteria of theory choice and apply them in ways that avoid any preexisting ideological biases. This process will most effectively help us to make sincere and honest choices among metatheories, theories, and policies.

Notes

Introduction

1. This book follows the standard convention of capitalizing "International Relations" and the abbreviation "IR" to refer to the discipline or study of the field. The book uses the lower case terms "international relations" or "international politics" to refer to the interactions of states with one another.
2. Questions relating to IR may be very concrete, very abstract, or anywhere on the scale between them. Jørgensen (2001, 37) divides the range into four different levels of enquiry: (1) philosophy of science, including natural and social science; (2) metatheoretical and methodological; (3) theoretical, which includes substantive theories that offer principles that explain aspects of international politics; and (4) empirical, which includes data collection and research on specific systems, regions, and leaders. In this work we will treat the first two together in a single category, the second two together in another category, and add a third category of issues concerned with what policies should be adopted given a specific set of conditions.

Chapter 1

1. See *East Asian Strategic Review* 2001: 145; cited by Cha and Kang 2003: 79, note 14.
2. http://msnbc.com/news/754330.asp.
3. This case study ends with North Korea's nuclear test in 2006. In July 2007 it shut down its plutonium reactor and allowed UN inspectors back—but began to deny it had a uranium program and refused any schedule for disclosing its bomb arsenal or its plutonium stockpile (Sanger 2007).

Chapter 2

1. Some of the excellent textbooks on IR theory include Waltz 1959, Russett and Starr 2005, Sterling-Folker 2005, and Doughtery and Pfaltzgraff 2001. These works focus more on a detailed exposition in order to show their strengths and weaknesses. The present text describes the competing theories only to the extent needed to show how they link policy questions with metatheory debates.

2. Nixon and Kennedy had a vigorous disagreement in their televised presidential debate over how to deal with the islands of Quemoy and Matsu, which are near the mainland but were controlled by Taiwan. Both candidates agreed that Taiwan should be protected, but Kennedy said that the protection included only Taiwan while Nixon said that these islands should be included in the territory of Taiwan.

3. The leader must believe this or some other causal statement that serves the same function of justifying the action, such as "our loyal ally will be more secure if we attack B," or "our economy will revive if we attack B," or even "our political party is more likely to be retain electoral power if we attack B."

4. A more complete definition of "prediction" that captures the very broad way the term is ordinarily used is the following: a prediction in the natural or social sciences is a statement that refers to the future, is based on justifiable evidence beliefs, is based on evidence that may be imperfect and incomplete, and may be probabilistic or deterministic or conditional (Chernoff 2005, 8).

5. In June of 1950 the Soviet delegate, as a statement of protest, did not attend, failing to realize that the UN Security Council would authorize a war against its close ally, North Korea.

6. "However, it is possible to define 'rationality' in a less rigorous way, closer to the ordinary meaning of the term, and yet preserve a modest role for game models. One may define it, for example, as the choice of means (strategies) so as to maximize expected value across a given set of consistently ordered objectives, given the information actually available to the actor or which he could reasonably acquire in the time available for decision" (Snyder and Diesing 1977).

7. See Jackson 2004, who argues that both individuals and states are irreducible in that they have "emergent properties."

8. During George W. Bush's first term they were, respectively, Secretary of Defense; Deputy Secretary of Defense; Undersecretary of Defense for Policy; and Chairman of the quasi-governmental Defense Policy Advisory Board.

9. Mearsheimer 2005 notes how neoconservatives minimize the role nationalism in world politics.

10. Mearsheimer is generally regarded as a neorealist rather than a classical realist; but both agree on many points and disagree with democratic realism in similar ways.

11. Of course, it is always possible that a policy maker may choose a foreign policy option for reasons other than a sound IR theory. If the leader believes that the best policy will lead to reelection defeat, then the best policy may not be followed. This book shows only how an honest attempt to accomplish one's foreign policy goals will require identifying those goals, finding the facts of the matter, and choosing a theory. Chapters 3 and 4 deal with the metatheory questions surrounding how we should properly identify and choose a theory.

12. On realism and China see Christensen 1999, Kissinger 1994, Friedberg 1993, and Cha and Kang 2003. Friedberg's view contrasts sharply with David Kang's view that Asia has historically had hegemonic stability under the leadership of China.

13. For idealists the moral principle that the means can never justify the ends may be used as grounding for the rationale that it is immoral to negotiate with extreme abusers of human rights and violators of international norms. Overthrow of such leaders might then be justifiable or even obligatory. Idealism might justify either the military option or the option of isolating North Korea.

14. U.S.-China Business Council, cited in Friedberg 2005, 12n12.
15. U.S.-China Security Review Commission, cited in Friedberg 2005, 13n13.
16. On liberalism see Duffield 2003, Rosecrance 1986, Russett and Oneal 2001, and Stein 1993.
17. Zehfuss 2001 does a good job of distinguishing key features of Wendt's, Kratochwil's and Onuf's versions of constructivism in IR.
18. Henry R. Nau, who takes the constructivist approach seriously as he tries to combine it with power analysis, treats constructivism as predictive: "Constructivism tends to predict high levels of institutionalization among states if state identities are cooperative and not competitive" (Nau 2003, 215).
19. The idea of shared knowledge is important to liberal theorists (see Keohane 1984) and has been developed by constructivists (see, for example, Adler and Hass 1992). For a recent application to communities of diplomats see Cross 2007.
20. On constructivism see Berger 2003 and Johnston 2003. Johnston cites several top Clinton administration officials who expressed the idea of teaching China to behave like a normal state (2003, 110).

Chapter 3

1. See Nagel 1979; Dessler 2002; and Gunnell 1995.
2. John Vasquez endorses the Lakatosian view according to which the superior theory has excess empirical content, that is, can predict novel facts; explains unrefuted content of the older theory; and includes excess content, some of which is corroborated (1998, 28). He endorses the criteria of: accuracy, falsifiability, explanatory power, progressive research program, consistency with other fields of knowledge, and parsimony/elegance (Vasquez 1998, 230). In Kuhn's later statement on the subject, he endorses "accuracy, consistency, breadth of application, simplicity, and so on" (Kuhn 2000, 118).
3. As Bertrand Russell once put it, causality, like the British monarchy, is widely but mistakenly thought to be harmless (Russell 1918).
4. For powerful critiques of Kuhn see, for example, Donald Davidson 1984 and Norris 2004.
5. Max Weber was one of the most influential early advocates of the need to study the social world without infusing our moral values into our study, which is different from studying the moral values of societies or people. Weber stated forcefully that there must be an "unconditional separation of facts and the evaluation of those facts" (1949).
6. Another IR scholar summarizes critical realism in a recent paper as follows: (1) Causes exist as ontologically real forces in the world around us and causes are ubiquitous ("nothing comes from nothing"); (2) Many causes are unobservable and the empiricist observation based [sic] approach to causal analysis is problematic; (3) causes do not work in "when A, then B" manner and always exist in complex causal contexts where multiple causes interact and counteract; (4) social causes are of many kinds: from reasons and norms to discourses and social structures. Interpretation is central to causal analysis in social science (Kurki 2007, 363; Brown 2007, 414; and Wight 2006, 26–45).
7. There could be cases where the evidence is so striking that, because there is some overlap between the different philosophical accounts of science, all investigators,

regardless of which philosophical account they prefer, would choose the same among the rival theories. Newton's new theory, given available seventeenth-century evidence, is an example.

8. The claim that neorealism does not perform well on Lakatos's MSRP account of science is drawn from the extensive work of John Vasquez (1997, 2003). See also the application of Lakatos's account by James Lee Ray (2003). Some neorealists have defended themselves against Vasquez's argument that Lakatosian criteria discredit neorealism by switching to other philosophical criteria of theory choice (Walt 1997). James 2002 offers the best sustained defense on this point. We should note here that "predictive success" requires that a theory be able to generate predictions and that those predictions match observed outcomes. Thus a theory may be able to fail on predictive success criterion either by having trouble generating specific predictions or by failing to match observed outcomes. An inability to generate predictions at all would be a failure to satisfy the falsifiabilty criterion.

Chapter 4

1. **A Note on Terminology**: The term *constructivism* was used in Chapter 2 to refer to a substantive theory. That theory was considered alongside the "rationalist" theories, liberalism and realism. There is a wide variety of scholars who call themselves "constructivists." Some have focused on substantive principles about how the international system can and should operate, while others have focused on what scholars need to understand about the nature of social enquiry as a grounding for their substantive theories. The metatheory of constructivism considered in this chapter is especially important because constructivism, more than other approaches to IR, developed initially from investigations into metatheory and philosophy. These investigations focused on criticizing the principles that traditional IR theories implicitly accepted. Constructivists did not want these assumptions to be accepted without scrutiny and one of their chief purposes has been to draw attention to them. The substantive principles of constructivist IR theory regarding how states can and should interact have been derived in part from the interpretive constructivist metatheory.

Because constructivism has become so popular in the past twenty years (the term itself was only first applied in IR in 1989 by Onuf) and because it is still such a new term in the field, there is no clearly fixed meaning—even less than with other IR approaches. So the term "constructivism" has been applied by a wide variety of authors to their own work. The plural "constructivisms" is used by some who want to emphasize the differences between specific constructivists and, in particular, to emphasize the different sorts of substantive theories that could all share a constructivist methodological approach. This book separates conventional (American) constructivism from interpretive (European) constructivism and notes that the former has worked more to develop substantive principles, which are discussed in Chapter 2, while the latter has been somewhat more focused on metatheory, philosophy of science, and a critique of rationalism.

Critical Theory is a view developed by Frankfurt School thinkers and is capitalized. The theory was inspired by a desire to revise Marxism to bring it in line with post-Marx developments in philosophy and politics. For example, socialism had

Reflectivist terminology

Critical social theories	Postmodern	Not fully postmodern
Constructivists	Kratochwil	Wendt, Katzenstein
Critical Theorists	Linklater	Adorno, Habermas
Poststructuralists	Foucault, Lacan, Derrida	None

come about, but not in the places or in the way Marx predicted. It emphasizes the idea that social theory must not only describe but also critique society.

Reflectivism is a term Keohane and Martin uses to refer to all of the views discussed in this chapter. All are critical of previous traditional theories and methods for studying the social world and all of them see this theory as a tool inherently for critiquing society, as well. This group includes contemporary IR theories, such as constructivism, poststructuralism, Frankfurt School Critical Theory, feminism, and followers of Marx and Gramsci.

The term *critical theories*, which in its general form is expressed in the plural and lowercase, is used by Alexander Wendt to describe roughly the same range of theories as Keohane and Martin refer to with the term "reflectivism." Because this chapter focuses on Frankfurt School-inspired "Critical Theory," this book uses "reflectivist theories" to refer to the range of theories covered in this chapter.

Postpositivism is used as an equivalent for reflectivism and critical theories. This book has avoided the use of the term "positivism," except in connection with the formal name of "logical positivism," because it has created even more than usual confusion and it has been seen as "loaded." As one scholar (Der Derien 1997) has joked, IR theorists have to be prepared to don their intellectual flak jackets if they use the term "positivism." People who are considered positivists rarely use the term. So it has come to be used by critics as a way of expressing disapproval. The term "postpositivist" is equivalent to "antipositivist." But the preface "post" seems to add the connotation that positivism is old, discredited, and abandoned, thus implying that the battle between positivists and antipositivists is over and has been won by the "anti's." The term that has arisen for authors who believe in the empirical testing of hypotheses and theories that is used without utter contempt is *neopositivism*.

Poststructuralism is a view developed in France that rejects both French structuralism and Enlightenment-inspired rationalism. It is a more specific term than the broader and commonly used term, *postmodernism*, which is used in many different fields. It was initially applied to a movement in art. As with all of the other names for schools of thought or intellectual traditions, the terms are imprecise in that they have been applied to a range of authors who have relatively little in common other than they reject many of the dominant academic ideas. It is somewhat harder to pinpoint exactly what the principles are that they accept.

Even in the arts there is some disagreement over whether the movement took modernism in art to its most far-reaching conclusion, whether it was a way of turning modernism on its head or whether it indicated a way of moving beyond modernism. In the world of social science the term may be usefully understood as rejecting key elements of modern philosophy, such as objective knowledge, universal truth, and the belief that there are solutions to all intellectual and practical problems.

There is some disagreement about exactly which authors are postmodern. While the term "postmodern" is widely used, very few authors use it to refer to themselves. This is in contrast to "constructivism," which is widely used by authors to characterize their own work. Since this book is intended as a guide to understand the existing literature in IR and social science metatheory, this chapter will apply the term "postmodern" to authors who are generally so regarded. And the authors generally described as postmodern include primarily poststructural followers of Foucault. While some regard scholars in the tradition of the Frankfurt school of Critical Theory as postmodern, others regard them, especially Gadamer, as radical critics of modern theories that still make use of modern foundations. European or interpretive constructivists are generally postmodern. Some Critical Theorists are postmodern; some are not. All poststructuralists are postmodern.

2. Creating a coherent whole was a major part of this effort. Even if a passage looked like it had a particular meaning when it was examined on its own, it might turn out that that meaning is inconsistent with much of the rest of the text. So if there was an alternative interpretation available that might not fit the passage taken on its own as well as our first attempt, it might still be a better interpretation if the alternative helped the whole of the text/scriptures produce a more meaningful message.

3. Wendt says, "Realism is a self-fulfilling prophesy" (1999, 186–87).

4. See Jørgensen 2001; Barkin 2003; and Jackson and Nexon 2004. Ian Johnston (2003) argues that there is a constructed "strategic culture" and argues that China, as an offensive-oriented strategic culture, will create more of a realist world as it comes increasingly to dominate Asia.

5. Among constructivists, Checkel (2006) is particularly focused on the centrality of discovering causal mechanisms.

6. There are, though, some authors who say that it is really a modification, albeit a major one. See Laclau 1988.

7. Quoted by Culler 1986, 109.

8. The biggest break with Saussure's view was the revolutionary "transformational grammar" of the American linguist, Noam Chomsky, who argued that languages have a "deep structure," which is common across cultures.

9. See Foucault 1980a, 97. Foucault says, "We should try to grasp subjection in its material instance as a constitution of subjects" (Quoted by McHoul and Grace 1993, 22.

10. I thank Professor Al Yee for these two examples.

11. When President Reagan saw Iran as becoming too powerful after the fall of the Shah and Iran's surprisingly strong showing against Iraq in the Iran-Iraq war, Reagan worked to help Iraq in the war, especially by providing intelligence to Saddam Hussein on the movement of Iranian troops (see Crile 2003, 274–76). Despite the recent hostage crisis, Reagan was not ideologically aligned with either side, and so he was not in favor of either Iran or Iraq gaining too much power over the other. Indeed, he worked with Iran to finance the U.S.-sponsored insurgency war against the government of Nicaragua. For accounts of U.S. support for Iraq see Woodward 1987, 235–39.

12. See Linklater 1996b, 280; Cox 1987; and Hoffman 1987.

Chapter 5

1. A fuller answer to the naturalist-reflectivist debate is offered in Chernoff 2005 and Chernoff 2008a.
2. A hypothetical example would be an argument purporting to show that physical science is inadequate and not worth studying because (1) Aristotelian physical science is a version of physical science; and (2) there are many observations, especially about the movements of the planets, that are incompatible with Aristotelian theory. The argument concludes that physics is an inadequate discipline. Obviously today there are versions of physical theory far superior to Aristotle's.
3. That fallacy occurs when someone says that there are only two possible answers to a question, A and B, when in fact there are other possible answers (C, D, E, etc.); the person then shows that A is false and concludes that B must be true.
4. See Kelsen 1939 and Chernoff 2005.
5. Bohman (1993) argues against predictions based on open systems. Little (1991) discusses the problem posed by superficial versus deeper regularities in the social sciences. Discontinuities are discussed by Doran (1999) and Bernstein, et al. (2000). For a rare interpretivist endorsement of some predictions, see Hopf 2007.
6. For responses, see Chernoff 2005, chapter 5.
7. See Bakewell (1907), 22–28. Zeno's paradox of the racecourse, showing that motion is an illusion, is discussed by Aristotle, *Physics*, 239b, 11–13.
8. Pollins (2007) provides a very clear argument showing the overlap between naturalist and interpretivist use of hypothetico-deductive reasoning.
9. A detailed defense of this or any particular solution is impossible in a few pages. For a full discussion of conventionalism in physics, see Duhem 1954. For an application to IR, see Chernoff 2005.
10. If all objects grow by 10 percent, when moved from point A to point B and shrink back when returned to point A, it would be impossible to prove there is a change by measuring the difference, because the measuring instrument would be growing and shrinking similarly. See Duhem 1954.
11. See Freedom House 2006 and the Polity data archive, http://weber.ucsd.edu.
12. Conventionalism in the natural sciences is seen as noncausal. It is entirely consistent with a supplementary account of "causality."

References

Abu-Lughod, Ibrahim. 1970. *In The Arab-Israeli confrontation of June 1967: An Arab perspective*, ed. Ibrahim Abu-Lughod, with a forward by M. H. Kerr, 3–21. Evanston, IL: Northwestern University Press.

Adler, Emanuel Adler, and Peter M. Haas. 1992. Conclusion: Epistemic communities, world order, and the creation of a reflective research program. *International Organization* 46: 367–90.

Ashley, Rick, and R. B. J. Walker. 1990. Speaking the language of exile: Dissident thought in international studies. *International Studies Quarterly* 34:259–68.

Art, Robert J., et al. 2002. War with Iraq is *not* in America's national interest. *New York Times*, September 26, 2002.

Babst, Dean. 1964. Elective governments: A force for peace. *Wisconsin Sociologist* 3:9–14.

———. 1972. A force for peace. *Industrial Research* April:55–58.

Bakewell, Charles M. 1907. *Sourcebook in ancient philosophy*. New York: Charles Scribner's Sons.

Barkin, Samuel. 2003. Realist constructivism. *International Studies Review* 5: 325–42.

Bennett, Scott, and Allan C. Stam. 1998. The declining advantages of democracy: a combined model of war outcomes and duration. *Journal of Conflict Resolution* 42:259–77.

Berger, Thomas U. 2003. Power and purpose in Pacific East Asia. In *IR theory and the Asia-Pacific*, ed. John Ikenberry and Michael Mastunduno, 387–419. New York: Columbia University Press.

Bernstein, Richard, and Ross H. Munro. 1997. *The coming conflict with China*. New York: Alfred A. Knopf.

Bernstein, Steven, Richard Ned Lebow, Janice Gross Stein, and Steven Weber. 2000. God gave physics the easy problems: Adapting social science to an unpredictable world. *European Journal of International Relations* 6:43–76.

Bhaskar, Roy. 1997. *A realist theory of science*. 2nd ed. London: Verso

Bohman, James. 1993. *The new philosophy of social science: Problems of indeterminacy*. Cambridge, MA: MIT Press.

Brown, Chris. 2007. Situating critical realism. *Millennium: Journal of International Studies* 35:409–16.

Bush, George W. 2002. Transcript: Confronting the war on terror. *New York Times*, October 8, 2002, A1.

Carnap, Rudolf. 1937. *The logical syntax of language*. Trans. Amethe Smeaton (Countess von Zeppelin). New York: Harcourt Brace.

————. 1959. The elimination of metaphysics through the logical analysis of language. In *Logical positivism*, ed. A. J. Ayer, 60–81. New York: Free Press.

Cha, Victor D., and David C. Kang. 2003. *Nuclear North Korea: A debate on engagement strategies*. New York: Columbia University Press.

Checkel, Jeffrey T. 2006. Tracing causal mechanisms. *International Studies Review* 8:62–70.

Chernoff, Fred. 2004. The study of democratic peace and progress in international relations theory. *International Studies Review* 6:49–77.

————. 2005. *The power of international theory: Re-forging the link to policy-making through scientific enquiry*. London: Routledge.

————. 2007. Conventionalism as a meta-theory. *European Journal of International Relations* (Forthcoming).

————. 2008a: *The ontological fallacy: A rejoinder on the role of scientific realism in international relations*. Review of International Studies (forthcoming).

Christensen, Thomas J. 1999. China, the U.S.-Japan alliance, and the security dilemma in East Asia. *International Security* 23:49–80.

Copper, John F. 2006. *Playing with fire: The looming war with China over Taiwan*. Westport, CT: Praeger Security International.

Cox, Robert. 1987. *Power production, power and world order*. New York: Columbia University Press.

Crawford, Neta. 2002. *Argument and change in world politics: Ethics, decolonization, and humanitarian intervention*. Cambridge: Cambridge University Press.

Crile, George. 2003. *Charlie Wilson's war*. New York: Atlantic Monthly Press.

Cross, Mai'a Davis. 2007. *The European diplomatic corps: Diplomats and international cooperation from Westphalia to Maastricht*. Houndmills, Basingstoke: Palgrave-Macmillan.

Culler, Jonathan. 1986. *Ferdinand de Saussure*. Ithaca, NY: Cornell University Press.

Daalder, Ivo H., and James M. Lindsay. 2005. *America unbound: The Bush revolution in foreign policy*. Hoboken, NJ: Wiley.

Davidson, Donald. 1984. *Essays into truth and interpretation*. Oxford: Oxford University Press.

Der Derian, James. 2005. Imaging terror: Logos, Pathos, and Ethos. *Third World Quarterly* 1:5–22.

Dessler, David. 1989. What's at stake in the agent-structure debate. *International Organization* 43:441–73.

————. 2002. Explanation and scientific progress. In *Progress in international relations theory: Metrics and methods of scientific change*, ed. Colin Elman and Miriam Fendius Elman, 381–404. Cambridge, MA: MIT Press.

Dewey, John. 1948. *Reconstruction in philosophy*. Boston: Beacon Press.

Doran, Charles F. 1999. Why forecasts fail: The limits and potential of forecasting in international relations and economics. *International Studies Review* 1:11–41.

Doyle, Michael. 1983a. Kant, liberal legacies, and foreign affairs: Part 1. *Philosophy and Public Affairs* 12:205–35.

————. 1983b. Kant, liberal legacies, and foreign affairs: Part 2. *Philosophy and Public Affairs* 12:323–53.

Duffield, John R. 2003. Asia-Pacific security institutions in comparative perspective. In *IR theory and the Asia-Pacific*, ed. G. John Ikenberry and Michael Mastunduno, 243–70. New York: Columbia University Press.

Duhem, Pierre. 1954. *The aim and structure of physical theory*. Trans. Philip P. Wiener. Princeton, NJ: Princeton University Press.

Feyerabend, Paul K. 1962. *Explanation, reduction and empiricism*. Vol. 3 of *Minnesota studies in the philosophy of science*. Ed. H. Feigl and G. Maxwell. Minneapolis: University of Minnesota Press.

Fleck, Ludwig. 1986. *Cognition and fact : Materials on Ludwik Fleck* . Ed. Robert S. Cohen and Thomas Schnelle. Dordrecht, Boston, and Norwell, MA: D. Reidel.

Foucault, Michel. 1980. *Power/knowledge: Selected interviews and other writings, 1972–77*. London: Harvester.

Freedom House. 2006. Freedom in the world 2006. New York: Freedom House.

Friedberg, Aaron. 1994. Ripe for rivalry: Prospects for peace in multipolar Asia. *International Security* 18:5–33.

———. 2005. The future of U.S.-China relations: Is conflict inevitable? *International Security* 30:7–45.

Fukuyama, Francis. 2004. The neoconservative moment. *The National Interest* 76:57–68.

———. 2006. *America at the crossroads: Democracy, power, and the neoconservative legacy*. New Haven, CT: Yale University Press.

Gunnell, John G. 1995. Realizing theory: The philosophy of science revisited. *Journal of Politics* 57:923–40.

Haas, Peter M. 1992. Introduction: Epistemic communities and international policy coordination. *International Organization* 46.

Hacking, Ian. 1999. *The social construction of what?* Cambridge, MA: Harvard University Press.

Hanson, Norwood Russell. 1958. *Patterns of discovery*. London: Cambridge University Press.

Harrison, Selig S. 2005. Did North Korea cheat? *Foreign Affairs* 84 (January/February): 99–110.

Havas, Peter. 1967. Foundation problems in general relativity. In *Delaware seminar on the foundations of physics*, ed. Mario Bunge. New York: Springer-Verlag.

Hoffman, Mark. 1987. Critical theory and the inter-paradigm debate. *Millennium Journal of International Studies* 16:231–49.

Hopf, Ted. 2007. The limits of interpreting evidence. In *Theory and evidence*, ed. Richard Ned Lebow and Mark Lichbach, 55–84. New York: Palgrave Macmillan.

Hume, David. 1977. *Enquiry concerning human understanding*. Indianapolis: Hackett.

Jackson, Patrick Thaddeus. 2004. Hegel's house, or states are people, too. *Review of International Studies* 30:281–87.

Jackson, Patrick Thaddeus, and Daniel H. Nexon. 2004. Constructive realism or realist-constructivism? *International Studies Review* 6:337–41.

James, Patrick. 2002. *International relations and scientific progress: Structural realism reconsidered*. Columbus: Ohio State University Press.

Johnston, Alastair Iain. 2003. Socialization in international institutions: The ASEAN way and international relations theory. In *IR theory and the Asia-Pacific*, ed. G. John Ikenberry and Michael Mastunduno, 107–62. New York: Columbia University Press.

Jørgensen, Knud Erik. 2001. Four levels and a discipline. In *Constructing international relation: The next generation*, ed. Karin M. Fierke and Knud Erik Jørgensen Armonk, 36–53. New York: M. E. Sharpe.

Kang, David. 2003. Hierarchy and stability in Asian international relations. In *IR theory and the Asia-Pacific*, ed. G. John Ikenberry and Michael Mastunduno, 163–89. New York: Columbia University Press.

Kant, Immanuel. 1989. Perpetual peace. In *On history*, ed. Lewis Whitel Beck, 85–136. New York: Macmillan / Library of Liberal Arts.

Katzenstein, Peter J. 1996. Introduction: Alternative perspectives on national security. In *The culture of national security*, ed. Peter J. Katzenstein, 1–32. New York: Columbia University Press.

Kelsen, Hans. 1939. The emergence of the causal law from the principle of retribution. *Journal of Unified Science (Erkenntnis)* 8:169–230. Reprinted in Hans Kelsen, 1973. *Essays in legal and moral philosophy*. Trans. Peter Heath, 165–215. Boston: D. Reidel.

Keohane, Robert O. 1984. *After hegemony: Cooperation and discord in the world political economy*. Princeton, NJ: Princeton University Press.

Keohane, Robert O., and Lisa L. Martin. 1995. *The promise of institutionalist theory. International Security* 20: 39–51.

Keohane, Robert O., and Joseph Nye. 1977. *Power and interdependence: World politics in transition*. Boston: Little Brown.

Kessler, Glenn. 2005. America alters policy on N. Korea to allow discussions. *New York Times*, July 28, 2005, A8.

King, Gary, Robert O. Keohane, and Sidney Verba. 1994. *Designing social inquiry: Scientific inference in qualitative research*. Princeton, NJ: Princeton University Press.

Kissinger, Henry. 1994. *Diplomacy*. New York: Simon and Schuster.

Krasner, Steven D. 1982. Structural causes and regime consequences: Regimes as intervening variables. *International Organization* 36:185–205.

Kratochwil, Freidrich. 1989. *Rules, norms, and decisions on the conditions of practical and legal reasoning in international relations*. Cambridge: Cambridge University Press.

———. 2006. History, action and identity: Revisiting the "second" great debate and assessing its importance for social theory. European Journal of International Relations 12:5–29.

———. 2007. Evidence, inference, and truth as problems of theory-building in the social sciences. In *Theory and evidence*, ed. Ned Lebow and Mark I. Lichbach, 21–54. New York: Palgrave Macmillan.

Krauthammer, Charles. 2004. Democratic realism: An American foreign policy for a unipolar world. Washington, DC: American Enterprise Institute. http://www.aei.org/publications/pubID.19912,filter.all/pub_detail.asp (posted February 14, 2004).

Kuhn, Thomas S. 1962. *The structure of scientific revolutions*. Chicago: University of Chicago Press.

———. 2000. *The road since structure: Philosophical essays, 1970–1993*. Ed. James Conant and John Haugeland. Chicago: University of Chicago Press.

Kurki, Milja. 2007. Critical realism and causal analysis in international relations: Causes all the way down. *Millennium: Journal of International Studies* 35:361–78.

Laclau, Ernesto. 1988. Politics and the limits of modernity. In *Universal abandon? The politics of postmodernism*, ed. A. Ross, 63–82. Minneapolis: University of Minnesota Press; Edinburgh: University of Edinburgh Press.

Levi, Isaac. 1965. *Gambling with truth: An essay on induction and the aims of science*. Cambridge MA: MIT Press.

Levy, Jack. 1989. The causes of war: A review of theories and evidence. In *Behavior, society and nuclear war*, ed. Philip E. Tetlock, Jo L. Husbands, Robert Jervis, Paul S. Stern, and Paul Tilly. New York: Oxford University Press.

Linklater, Andrew. 1996. Citizenship and sovereignty in the post-westphalian state. *European Journal of International Relations* 2:77–103.

Little, Daniel. 1991. *Varieties of social explanation*. Boulder, CO: Westview.

McHoul, Alec W., and Wendy Grace. 1993. *A Foucault primer*. New York: New York University Press.

Mearsheimer, John J. 2001. *The tragedy of great power politics*. New York: Norton.

———. 2005. Realism is right. *The National Interest* 81:10.

Mearsheimer, John and Steven M. Walt. 2003. An unnecessary war. *Foreign Policy* 134:51–59.

Morgenthau, Hans J. 1967. To intervene or not to intervene. *Foreign Affairs* 45: 425–37.

Mosher, Steven W. 2000. *Hegemon: China's plan to dominate Asia and the world*. San Francisco: Encounter Books.

Nagel, Ernst. 1979. *The structure of science: Problems in the logic of scientific explanation*. Indianapolis: Hackett.

Nau, Henry R. 2003. Identity and the balance of power in Asia. In *IR theory and the Asia-Pacific*, ed. G. John Ikenberry and Michael Mastunduno, 213–41. New York: Columbia University Press.

Nickles, Thomas. 1987. Lakatosian heuristics and epistemic support. *British Journal for the Philosophy of Science* 35:181–205.

Onuf, Nicholas. 1989. *World of our making: Rules and rule in social theory and international relations*. Columbia: University of South Carolina Press.

———. 1998. *The Republican legacy in international thought*. New York: Cambridge University Press.

Pipes, Daniel. 2006. Survey of Muslims yields dismaying results. *Sun*, June 26.

Pollins, Brian. 2007. Beyond logical positivism: Reframing king, keohane and verba. In *Theory and evidence*, ed. Richard Ned Lebow and Mark Lichbach, 87–106. New York: Palgrave Macmillan.

Putnam, Hilary. 1975. *Philosophical papers*. New York: Cambridge University Press.

Quine, Willard van Ormand. 1953. Two dogmas of empiricism. In *From a logical point of view*, ed. W. V. O. Quine, 20–46. Cambridge, MA: Harvard University Press.

Ray, James Lee. 2003. A Lakatosian view of the Democratic peace research program. In *Progress in international relations theory: Appraising the field*, ed. Colin Elman and Miriam Fendius Elman, 205–44. Cambridge, MA: MIT Press.

Richardson, James L. 1994. Asia Pacific: The case for geopolitical optimism. *National Interest* 38:28–39.

Rorty, Richard. 1979. *Philosophy and the mirror of nature*. Princeton, NJ: Princeton University Press.

Rosecrance, Richard. 1986. *The rise of the trading state*. New York: Basic Books.

Russell, Bertrand. 1918. On the notion of cause. In *Mysticism and logic and other essays*, ed. Bertrand Russell. New York: Longmans.

Russett, Bruce. 1993. *Grasping the Democratic peace: Principles for a post-cold war world*. Princeton, NJ: Princeton University Press.

Russett, Bruce, and John R. Oneal. 2001. *Triangulating peace: Democracy, trade and international organization*. New York: W. W. Norton.

Russett, Bruce, Harvey Starr, and David Kinsella. 2000. *World politics: The menu for choice.* 6th ed. Boston and New York: Bedford-St. Martin's.

Sanger, David E. 2007. North Koreans say they've shut nuclear reactor. *New York Times,* July 14, p. 1.

Sellars, Wilfred S. 1963. Empiricism and the philosophy of mind. In *Science, perception and reality,* 127–96. London: Routledge & Kegan Paul.

Shapiro, Ian, and Alexander Wendt. 1992. The difference that realism makes. *Politics and Society* 20:197–223.

Small, Melvin, and J. David Singer. 1976. The war-proneness of democratic regimes. *Jerusalem Journal of International Relations* 1:50–69.

Siverson, Randolph. 1995. Democracies and war participation: In defense of the institutional constraints argument. *European Journal of International Relations* 1:481–89.

Snyder, Glenn, and Paul Diesing. 1977. *Conflict among nations.* Princeton, NJ: Princeton University Press.

Stein, Arthur R. 1993. Governments, economic interdependence and international cooperation. In *Behavior, society and international conflict,* ed. Philip E. Tetlock et al. New York: Oxford University Press.

Taylor, Charles. 1985. Interpretation and the science of man. Vol. II of *Philosophy and the human sciences: Philosophical papers.* Cambridge: Cambridge University Press.

Terrill, Ross. 2003. *The new Chinese Empire and what it means for the United States.* New York: Basic Books.

Thucydides. 1996. *The landmark Thucydides: A comprehensive guide to the Peloponnesian War.* Trans. Richard Crawley. Ed. Robert B. Strassler. New York: Free Press.

Tunç, Hakan. What was it all about after all: The causes of the Iraq War. *Contemporary Security Policy* 26:335–55.

Van Fraassen, Bas C. 1980. *The scientific image.* Princeton, NJ: Princeton University Press.

———. 2002. *The Empirical Stance.* New Haven, CT: Yale University Press.

Vasquez, John A. 1997. The realist paradigm and degenerative versus progressive research programs: An appraisal of neotraditional research on Waltz's balancing proposition. *American Political Science Review* 91:899–912.

———. 1998. *Power of power politics: From classical realism to neotraditionalism,* 2nd ed. Cambridge: Cambridge University Press.

Walker, R. B. J. 1988. *Inside/Outside: International relations as political theory.* Cambridge: Cambridge University Press.

———. 1988. *One world/many worlds: Struggles for just world peace.* Boulder, CO: Lynne Reinner.

———. 1989. *The Prince* and the pauper. In *International/intertextual relations: Postmodern readings of world politics,* ed. James Der Derian and Michael J. Shapiro, 25–48. Lexington: Lexington Books.

Walt, Stephen. 1997. The progressive power of realism. *American Political Science Review* 91:931–35.

Waltz, Kenneth N. 1979. *Theory of international politics.* New York: McGraw-Hill.

Weber, Max. 1949. The methodology of the social sciences. Trans. and ed. Edward A. Shils and Henry A. Finch. New York: Free Press.

Wendt, Alexander. 1995. Constructing international politics. *International Security* 20:71–81.

———. 1999. *Social theory of international politics.* Cambridge: Cambridge University Press.

Wight, Colin. 2006. *Agents, structures and international relations: Politics as ontology*. Cambridge: Cambridge University Press.

Wight, Colin. 2007. A manifesto for scientific realism: Assuming the can opener won't work! *Millennium: Journal of International Studies* 35:379–98.

Woodward, Bob. 1987. *Veil: The secret wars of the CIA, 1981–1987*. New York: Simon and Schuster.

———. 2006. *State of denial: Bush at war, part III*. New York: Simon and Schuster.

Yee, Albert S. Semantic ambiguity and joint deflections in the Hainan negotiations. *China: An International Journal* 2, no. 1 (March 2004): 53–82.

Zehfuss, Maja, Constructivisms in international relations, Wendt, Onuf and Kratochwil. In *Constructing international relation: The next generation*, ed. Karin M. Fierke and Knud Erik Jørgensen. Armonk, 54–75. New York: M. E. Sharpe.

Index

The letter n following a page number denotes a note.
The letter t following a age number denotes a note.

demarcation criterion, 96, 98. *See also*
Popper, Sir Karl
democratic domino theory, 10
democratic peace hypothesis, 52, 63, 90,
92, 195, 196
Democratic Peoples Republic of Korea
(DPRK). *See* North Korea
democratic realism, 52–54; and
nationalism, Mearsheimer on, 200
Derrida, Jacques, 132, 153, 177.
See also poststructuralism
Descartes, René, 154. *See also* rationalism
descriptive theory, 4, 13, 54, 107, 170
Dewey, John, 110, 116, 180. *See also*
instrumentalism; pragmatism
Dialectic of Enlightenment (Adorno and
Horkheimer), 172
Diesing, Paul, 200
Dilthey, Wilhelm, 132, 136, 156. *See also*
constructivism, interpretive
discourse: ethics, 174; theory, 160–61
distribution of capabilities, 50
domestic politics–international politics,
analogy, 44, 48–49, 51, 61, 69
dominant discourse, 156, 161–63,
165–67, 171, 173–74, 178.
See also poststructuralism
Dougherty, James E., 199
Duffield, John, 201
Duhem, Pierre, 100, 113, 193–97;
conventionalism and, 113, 193–97;
history of science and, 196; on
measure-stipulation, 194–95, 205;
on underdetermination, 100, 113,
194. *See also* conventionalism
Durkheim, Emile, 88
dyadic hypothesis, 92, 101, 195

East Asia Summit, 67
Edkins, Jenny, 166
Eisenhower, Dwight, 14, 25
emancipation as a goal of theory and
practice, 122, 171, 177
emergent properties, 200
empiricism: constructive, 183;
metaphysics, 109–17, 182–83;
metaphysics, and instrumentalism,
118; theory of knowledge, 82,
86–89, 124; theory of knowledge,
challenges to, 118–20; theory of
knowledge, criticisms of, 93–109;
theory of knowledge, David Hume

and, 124 (*see also* Carnap, Rudolf,
foundationalism; instrumentalism;
logical positivism; metatheory;
Russell, Bertrand; theory); theory of
knowledge, epistemology, 5, 79, 180.
See also theory of knowledge
epistemic communities, 199
epistemic fallacy, 121, 183
epistemic norms and values, 45, 109,
172, 178
epistemological relativism, 121
essentialism and anti-essentialism, 165.
See also identity of agents
ethical naturalism, 107.
See also naturalism
ethical theory, 5
Eurocentrism, 164
evaluation, criteria of, 175
explanation, in IR, 29, 81, 93, 104;
causal, 81–83, 92, 117, 122;
covering law model of, 85, 122;
deductive-nomological, 84, 85;
descriptive versus, 185; inductive-
statistical, 85; philosophical problems
and, 5; scientific realism and, 112,
118, 123, 149, 193; theory and
policy relationship, 37;
truth and, 111

facts, interpretation of, 132–33
factual and moral-value statements, 107
fact-value distinction, 87–88, 107,
108, 185
fallacies: epistemic, 121, 183; false
dichotomy, 180–81, 183–84;
ontological, 183; straw man, 180–81
falsifiability, 190
falsificationism, 97, 98, 115
fecundity, criterion of theory choice,
85–86, 129, 190–91
Feith, Douglas, 52.
See also democratic realism
Feyerabend, Paul, 105. *See also* paradigm
Fichte, Johann Gottlieb, 87
Fleck, Ludwig, 94, 103.
See also Kuhn, Thomas
Ford, Gerald, 25
foreign aid, conflicting perceptions of,
63–64
Foucault, Michel, 132, 153, 155;
archaeology and genealogy, social,
159–62, 163; dominant discourses